To my parents
and to George and Elizabeth Hope who, first,
last and always, gave me
Scotland on a plate.

The woodcuts at the chapter heads
and before the recipe sections
are the work of Alyson MacNeill, to whom
the author is much indebted for producing,
in a very limited space of time,
such delightful vignettes.

TABLE OF CONTENTS

INTRODUCTION

This book was written in response to the puzzlement I often felt as an incomer to Scotland many years ago, when I read or was told about the inhabitants and their diet. So much of what I had read or heard seemed conflicting or contradictory. The Scots used to live entirely on oatmeal, said someone; their cooking was a product of the Auld Alliance with France, said someone else. Their favourite dishes were all developed out of the extreme hardship caused by the infertility of the soil, I was told; others spoke of the lavish use of eggs, butter and cream, the great abundance of game, and the lushness of Lothian and the Carse of Gowrie. Reading books on agricultural history I was left with the impression that the lot of the farmer – any farmer – before about 1820 was consistently one of desperate poverty; reading Sir Walter Scott or books such as *The Scots Household in the 18th Century* by the late Miss Marion Lochhead, the impression was of a contented peasantry living frugally but not desperately, a prosperous middle class, and an aristocracy which lacked for nothing. Even statistics were puzzling: to take but one example, even today the total area of cultivated land in Scotland is barely more than 25% of the whole country, yet there is room to grow and export the largest quantity of raspberries produced by any one country within the European Economic Community.

The only way to find out more was to read more; the only way to make sense of it all was to write it down, and then to try to check, prove, or modify. Out of this endeavour grew the present book. It is an attempt to present a balanced and truthful picture of one aspect of a country which is nothing if not full of paradoxes. For so small an area, it is astonishing how much diversity there is, in soil, in climate, in agricultural produce, in language, religion, history, and social structure. This, of course, is one of the reasons it exerts such fascination over those who know it.

Since the book is so much the outcome of my personal interest in the topic, I hope that omissions and deficiencies will be forgiven.

At the end of the book there is a bibliography, so that anyone interested may pursue the subject for himself or herself.

The recipes are mostly traditional, from a variety of sources. All are for 4–6 people except where otherwise stated. In the matter of measurements, I have not been consistent in translating from Imperial to metric measures. If 1 lb is roughly 450 g, and ½ lb is 225 g, to translate ¼ lb as 112.5 g makes nonsense. The approximations I have used are not consistent because in some recipes a little more flour, or a little less liquid, are needed than in others. Each recipe stands by itself and I hope no cook will come to grief over the quantities.

My gratitude is due to the many people who encouraged me in the two years it took to write the book. In particular I owe a great debt to my husband, whose constant support, belief and patience kept me going, with what sometimes seemed an impossible task. Many people made useful suggestions or gave me valuable information. In particular I should like to thank Dr Alexander Fenton, of the National Museum of Antiquities of Scotland, Professor D. M. Henderson, Regius Professor of the Royal Botanic Garden, Edinburgh, Professor J. MacQueen of Edinburgh University's School of Scottish Studies, and members of the White Fish Authority at Sea Fisheries House, Edinburgh – all of whom were kind enough to find time to talk to me or write several letters in reply to my questions. I should also like to thank Mrs Jean Jones and Mr Ewan Maclean, who plied me with useful references, documents, and snippets of information. The librarians at the Scottish section of Edinburgh Public Library, the National Library of Scotland, the Mitchell and University Libraries in Glasgow, Edinburgh University Library, and the School of Scottish Studies Library were all most helpful and patient. Mrs Joan Broome, of Maryborough, Queensland, NSW, and Mrs Clare McAllister of Victoria, BC, responded most kindly to my appeal for information from people of Scots descent living abroad. Miss Elaine Bullard, VC Recorder for Orkney, and Mr Walter Scott, VC Recorder for Shetland, and Dr David Stewart gave me valuable information and references. The Canadian Consulate General in Glasgow and the officials of the New Zealand High Commission in London were also very helpful. I should also like to thank Dr Lindsay Errington of the

National Galleries of Scotland, Sotheby's and my good friend Joe Rock. Finally, my grateful thanks to Christian Curtis of Easter Weems farm, Bonchester Bridge, who used the milk from the farm's superb Jersey cows to test the recipe on page 177 without the aid of rennet.

Annette Hope
April 1987

1

FOOD FROM THE WILDERNESS

Does your heart still beat with the old excitement
As you wait where the Scotch expresses are?
Does it answer still to the old indictment
Of a fond delight in the sleeping-car?

Alfred Cochrane

As the quotation suggests, about a century ago the very word 'Scotland' evoked just one set of images in the mind of the average upper-class Englishman: a barbaric region populated by picturesque natives, but remarkable chiefly for an abundance of creatures offering excellent sport. Yet, although the Victorians were the first to pursue Highland game systematically, the history of hunting spans the whole country and starts with man's first arrival in it some 5000 years ago. It is a tale which moves from bows and arrows to sophisticated, fast-firing, lightweight rifles, with traps and snares as ever-present alternatives; it concerns changes in method, from the driving, the coursing, and the *tinchel* of the Middle Ages to the solitary or two-man stalk for deer of our own time; it includes the wildfowler and the angler, both of whom claim that nowhere in Europe – perhaps nowhere in the northern hemisphere – is their sport more satisfactorily pursued than in Scotland. Running parallel to all is an ecological theme: how man has altered the environment by deforestation, to such an extent that the feeding, the habits, the location, the very nature of his quarry, have also changed — to a point which would certainly baffle a 12th-century hunter were he to reappear among us.

This deforestation was extraordinary both in its scale and its effects. So significant is it, not only for hunting, but for almost every topic with which this book is concerned, that it may be as well to describe briefly the process as it occurred over thousands of years.

It is not too difficult to picture Scotland as it was 5000 years ago, 6000 years after the end of the last Ice Age. Most of the land was wooded, the lowlands with a mixture of deciduous trees — birch, alder, oak, and some beech — the hill slopes with pines and birches. Higher up, the forest thinned considerably to a sort of scrub of birch and hazel. Higher still the mountains, scraped by glaciers and whipped by constant wind, were as bare as they are today. To anyone with an acquaintance with Canada, Norway or indeed the Pyrenees, such a landscape is not unfamiliar.

Wildlife was far more extensive, both in species and quantity, than in any part of Europe today. Bears, elks, wild ox, reindeer, wolves, beavers, and the ancestors of what is now Britain's largest mammal, *cervus elaphus*, the red deer, flourished; badger, polecat, pine marten, and lynx were prominent among smaller mammals. Though man was not responsible for the fate of all these species, there is little doubt that by destroying permanently almost all the Scottish woodlands, he played a major part in the extinction or near extinction of many.

This is not to say that no natural causes contributed. Fluctuations in temperature, natural fires, increased or diminished rainfall over long periods, might all affect both the size and the composition of the woods. When nature was left to itself, nevertheless, regeneration was fairly constant, whereas the changes brought about by man allowed no renewal.

Initially, human impact must have been slight. The development of agriculture meant that some woods had to be cleared for fields. The presence of dangerous animals such as bears and wolves made desirable another patch of cleared ground round each village or cluster of huts. Timber itself was obviously one of man's chief needs, providing homes and heat, furnishings and tools, stockades and shelter.

Even so, only a tiny proportion of the woodland would have been affected by this type of exploitation. It was the discovery of iron which engendered an attack on the trees on a scale which became fatal: to smelt ore from which weapons and tools (some of which would be used to cut down yet more trees) were made, vast quantities of wood were required. Writers on natural history all agree that iron-smelting, which began in the mid-first millennium B.C. and continued right into the 20th century, is the single most potent factor in the destruction of the Scottish woodlands.

Yet other industries were also to take their toll over the centuries. In the 9th century A.D. Viking invaders and settlers brought with them their skill at boat-building and the development of first a fishing fleet and then warships made heavy demands on timber supplies. To give an example, the *Great Michael*, a warship constructed in the reign of James IV, was said to have used all the wood in Fife except for that at Falkland.

Destruction was further accelerated by the frequent outbreaks of war between Scotland and England, for on both sides of the border large areas were laid waste; time and again, not only the enemy's crops, but also his woods, were put to the fire. Even so, it seems that few people were alarmed by the implications. Froissart, writing in the 14th century of the Scots dislike of their French allies, notes that the Scots almost preferred to be at war with the English than have the help of the French.

They will very soon eat up and destroy all we have in this country, and will do us more harm, if we allow them to remain amongst us, than the English could in battle. If the English do burn our homes, what consequence is it to us? We can rebuild them cheap enough, for we only require three days to do so, provided we have five or six poles and boughs to cover them.

Quite clearly, it was taken for granted that there would always be trees which could be used for building.

Nonetheless, pressure on Scottish forests was increasing all the time. When at last there was peace between the two countries after the Union of the Crowns in 1603, and trade communications improved, Highland forests provided wood for English smelters, builders, shipwrights, and furniture-makers. No doubt the Scots

themselves were much to blame as the pace of depredation accelerated. After the rebellions of 1715 and 1745, many exiled lairds lived
off the revenue coming from their timber; many more, when they
returned, sold off what trees remained without attempting to
replace them. By the end of the 18th century the country was, as
most travellers observed, virtually denuded. Dr Johnson was not
alone in his perception of Scotland as a treeless waste, though he
made rather a drama of it. (When he lost his stout oak stick – an
old and valued friend – on Mull, he was convinced it had been
stolen. 'It is not to be expected,' he declared, 'that any man in Mull,
who has got it, will part with it. Consider, sir, the value of such a
piece of timber here!')

The consequences of such changes in the landscape were far more
serious than could have been foreseen and affected equally wildlife
and agriculture. The mean annual temperature was lowered, and
the pattern of rainfall altered. The land became vulnerable to
erosion from wind and water. Inevitably, small plants which had
depended on trees for shelter and drainage of the land, failed to
survive. Thus, a number of animals were deprived at once of shelter
and cover, and of food. There was a general movement into the
forests which still existed, but these could not support large
numbers of animals. Eventually, some species died out altogether.
Others diminished in number. Others again, by adapting to the
new circumstances, survived successfully.

Most prominent among the latter were the red deer, moving ever
higher into the hills, adapting to changing conditions by feeding on
heather rather than young tree shoots or grass, and by growing
thicker winter coats. The lower temperatures in the mountains also
forced them to convert food into energy rather than weight, which
explains the smaller size of Scottish deer when compared with their
English counterparts or with farmed deer, even at the peak of
condition.

At the earliest time from which useful references to hunting appear
in the records – about the 12th century – very few of the
consequences of deforestation were yet evident. The country was
still well wooded, and rich in all sorts of game. Dotted over the
whole area from the Borders to the far north were newly established

'forests', most belonging to the king, but some owned by the Church or the aristocracy. Many consisted of scrubland rather than being forests in the present sense of the word – *forestis* in medieval usage simply meant a protected hunting area. Within these, all game was preserved. Cattle belonging to tenant farmers might not graze there, and even pigs could only be taken in under permit to root for acorns or beech mast. The names of some of these royal forests sound strangely in our ears considering the landscape now: Selkirk and Traquair, Pentland and Moorfoot, Stirling and Clackmannan. Yet here were to be found deer, wolves, and boar, as well as lesser game like hares, badgers, foxes, and all manner of wildfowl. Meanwhile, in the far north, the Viking earls of Orkney thought little of sailing across the Pentland Firth to hunt reindeer in Sutherland.

Our hypothetical 12th-century hunter, had he been a commoner, would probably have had access to the lesser game, at least outside the protected preserves, and in this he was more fortunate than English or French peasants. In Scotland the principle of free hunting was not rejected till 1621, although in practice landowners exercised an embargo long before that date.

The point must here be made that, if the ability of deer and other creatures to adapt to a changed environment was crucial for their survival, it was not the only cause. A second, and important factor, was that they were hunted not only for food but also for pleasure. Such animals tend to be accorded 'rights' which in fact are thinly disguised human self-interest. For this reason alone kings and parliaments have passed laws protecting some species which, though recognized as *ferae naturae*, came to be considered an individual's property so long as they were on his land.

Two kinds of law concern hunting. One attaches itself to the preservation of species: the first in Scotland was passed under James II in 1447, when

anent the preservation of birds and wild fowl that are fit to eat for the sustentation of man, such as partridges, plovers, wild ducks, and such like fowls, it is ordained that no man destroy their nests nor their eggs, nor yet slay wild birds in moulting time when they may not fly; and that all men according to their power destroy nests, and young of birds of prey.

Other early laws of course protected the rights of landowners. For instance, at the Justice-Aire of Jedburgh in 1510 it was laid down that men be brought to trial

> If there be any that slay red-fish in forbidden time or their fry in mill-dams;
> If there by any slayers of deer, by stalking within other lords' parks;
> If any steal hawks or hounds;
> If there be any breakers of orchards or dovecots or gardens;
> If there be any destroyers of others' rabbit-warrens.

While thus giving rights to landowners, this second type of law was particularly hard on tenant farmers. None, without his baron's express command or permission, might kill deer, rabbits, hare, fish or birds for himself; and though in the Highland wilderness the law was often breached, early travellers like Daniel Defoe, who thought that 'a deer is every man's own that can kill it' and were amazed at the frequent appearance of game on the tables of their hosts, would have told a different tale had they sojourned among the poor.

Moreover, the law deprived not only the common people of a source of food which many considered ought to have been theirs by right, but it inflicted a more hurtful evil: farmers were prevented from defending their hard-won crops against predators, whether deer, rabbits or pigeons. Even an enlightened 18th-century farming pioneer, John Cockburn of Ormiston, is found writing to his gardener that he need not feed the pigeons in the 'doocot' after April, for the farmers will then have sown their seeds and the birds will have plenty of food. Small wonder that, when he and others wished to plant their estates with trees, the tenants objected strongly. In their eyes, the trees would but serve as more roosting-places for the birds they themselves would have liked to exterminate.

In effect there were two quite different approaches to hunting. At one level, it was a practical means of getting food, for oneself or more probably one's overlord – as late as the 18th century the guardian of the Lord Lovat of the day hoped publicly that his ward would not so far derogate from his position as to think of going into the forest to shoot deer for himself, for such a practice was neither dignified in a gentleman, nor customary.

(There may be a reference here to Cluny Macpherson – a prominent Jacobite in real life and the fictitious host of Alan Breck and David Balfour in Stevenson's *Kidnapped* – who is said to have been the first clan chief to have stalked his own game for pleasure.)

The second approach to hunting – as a social pastime – was until the 19th century the almost exclusive prerogative of the monarchy and the aristocracy. The noble status of the sport, associated as it was with warlike pursuits, courage and all the attributes of chivalry, was unquestioned.

All through the Middle Ages hunting on horseback was the most popular method in the Lowlands. Hawks or dogs were used to go after and secure the quarry but many kings were particularly fond of falconry, and owned several establishments, each with its own falconer, in different parts of the country. James IV was once painted with a hawk on the wrist; he was passionately fond of the marshes of East Lothian, and also enjoyed the sport at Falkland, Linlithgow, and on the outskirts of Edinburgh – where, no doubt, the Nor' Loch (today's Princes Street Gardens) provided a sufficiency of waterfowl.

Crossbows were at first the principal weapon, though catapults were also used. Later, firearms (with some misgivings as to the sportsmanship of the practice) were introduced. Nets and snares were left to those who hunted professionally.

Deer and other large animals such as wolves or boar were usually coursed or driven. Coursing involved the pursuit on horseback of a single animal with the help of greyhounds, which attacked the quarry and held it until the hunters galloped up. It was a method used by commoners and noblemen alike.

An altogether different and more formal affair was the drive, which required so many participants that it was more or less reserved to the monarchy and the richest of the aristocracy. The noble huntsmen, on horseback, took up prearranged positions outside a wood or at the entrance to a glen, waiting for beaters to move the game from the shelter of the trees to within range of their dogs, arrows, and spears. It could be a dangerous amusement, for once the hunters were out of sight of each other, they ran the risk of getting no help if attacked by an infuriated or terrified stag. (This is one of the points of the story of the founding of Holyrood Abbey: David I, who had, in contravention of his confessor's counsel, insisted on going to the chase on the Feast of the Exaltation of the Cross, suddenly found himself alone, far from 'the noys and dyn of bugilis', confronted by an enormous and angry white stag. In an extremity of fear he prayed for help, and found that, in place of the short sword which was his only weapon, he held a cross, at sight of which the stag turned and fled. David in penitence and gratitude founded the Abbey of the Holy Rood, whose emblem ever after remains a stag's head with a cross between the antlers.)

Such expeditions needed a massive effort of planning and co-ordination; besides arranging for beaters and planning the strategies of the hunt, the organizer had to provide accommodation and food for up to 400 people. Sometimes a hunt lasted several days, sometimes weeks. Usually the expense was met by local officials, who were later reimbursed by the Crown. If the king was a popular figure, gifts would come in from the country folk – butter, cheese and eggs; more esoteric delicacies were often supplied from the estate of the local landowner. There seems to have been no question of hunting parties commandeering by force all the food in the area, as frequently happened in France and Germany.

Neither coursing nor driving were possible in the Highlands, where the scale of the landscape, the steep rocky slopes and treacherous peat hags were quite unsuitable for horses moving at speed. Here, a different method was adopted. It was called the *tinchel* (the word is Gaelic) and continued to be practised, certainly into the 18th century. Sir Walter Scott introduces his readers to a tinchel in *Waverley*. Following his usual custom, he draws heavily on factual writers, and his account is a transposition of several earlier descriptions. Before looking at one of his sources (John Taylor the Thames bargee, who visited Scotland in 1618) it may be helpful if the three principal elements of the tinchel are outlined.

First, it required the building of strategically placed walls of stone or brushwood on either side of a glen, converging on an enclosure at the head.

Second, a large force of men, on foot and over a period of days (or weeks, according to one account), drove the deer from the hills into this confined space.

Third, all around the enclosure, but chiefly near the spot at which the deer entered it, hunters took up position, armed with bows and arrows, swords, spears, axes, even stones – and ready to face the panicking animals as they attempted to escape from the trap.

Like the drive, the tinchel was always a hazardous affair. The deer, prevented by the high walls of the enclosure from going forward or sideways, turned and bolted back the way they had come, their thudding hooves and heavy bodies throwing to the ground every object between them and flight. Not only courage, but agility and quick-wittedness were essential, and even spectators (the tinchel was a prestigious spectator sport) could be at risk.

Taylor's tinchel took place at what he calls the Braes of Mar. It was an occasion which impressed him deeply, lasting altogether twelve days; he was grateful for the kindness of the Earl of Mar's son, Lord John Erskine, who took charge of him and saw that he was properly lodged and fed. The accommodation was of the simplest – a hut built of turf – but the food was good, with

many kettles and pots boyling, and many spits turning and winding, with great variety of cheere; as venison bak't, sodden (boiled), rost, and steu'de beefe, mutton, goates, kid, hares, fresh salmon, pidgeons, hens, capons, chickens, partridge, moorecoots, heathcocks, caperkellies, and termagants; . . .

The difference between the status of hunting for sport and hunting for food is made perfectly clear in Taylor's next remark:

All these, and more than these wee had continually, in superfluous aboundance, caught by faulconers, fowlers, fishers and brought by my Lords tenants and purveyors to victuall our campe, which consisteth of foureteen or fifteene hundred men and horses.

If Scott is to be believed, post-medieval tinchels had sometimes more sinister aims than the mere slaughter of deer. He was often remarkably close to fact in his fictitious writing, and may, as a boy, have heard of some specific tinchel used as a cover for political or military activities before the '45. In any event, the break-up of the clans ended the requisite ready supply of manpower.

It would not be surprising if, as Taylor asserts, the men driving the deer for the tinchel sometimes, 'licked their own fingers'. In his day free hunting was no longer permitted, and ordinary people had no legitimate access to the game which was such a valuable addition to the daily diet of the rich, in an age when for many months of the year no other fresh meat was to be had.

The Scots aristocracy were great meat-eaters. Not only did every large house have its own 'doocot' (many still stand today), but on big estates professional trappers and fowlers were part of the permanent establishment, relied upon to keep the household supplied. And when lairds went visiting (especially if they had been invited to celebrate some great family occasion) game was a customary gift, much as today's guest brings his host a bottle of wine or a box of chocolates. At the funeral of the 4th Earl of Montrose, father of the great Marquis, the gifts were recorded in the factor's book: partridge and plovers from Lord Stormont, a blackcock, five moorfowls (grouse), 'the fourth of a hynd' from the Laird of Lawers, and 'a great hind' from Glenorchy. But the larder was already filled against the arrival of expected guests: venison, beef, mutton, lamb, veal and hams, 28 moorfowls, 12 ptarmigans, 5 blackcock, 2 capercailzies (later these birds were to become extinct in the Highlands, but they were successfully reintroduced in 1837), 20 pairs of plover, 3 partridge, 10 wild geese, 6 golden-eyes, and 3 woodcocks.

The House Book of Ochtertyre (1737–9) shows clearly how important a regular supply of game was in an everyday context. On this estate, wildfowl were eaten throughout the year, apparently snared or caught by the estate falconer rather than shot, for the accounts show payments to 'Joseph the fowler', and there are bills for 'meat for the hawks'. The bag was unpredictable and highly miscellaneous, quite a test, surely, for any cook: among the items listed are fieldfares, plover, snipe, curlew, ptarmigan, moorfowl, wild goose, solan goose (at the time a prized delicacy, though

Defoe declared it almost uneatable for its greasy, fishy taste), quails, partridge, teal, wild duck – even seagulls. Blackbirds are also mentioned, but these may have been blackcocks. Among mammals, rabbits appear only twice; perhaps there were no warrens on the estate. But hare, roasted or in soup – 'Dinner hare soop hares in it' is an early entry – was frequently on the menu. Venison was rarely mentioned, but on one occasion when a deer was sent from the forest, what to do with it seems to have been something of a problem. Half was sent 'in complyments' (i.e., to friends); the rest, in the form of 'soop', collops, roast meat, pies, and miscellaneous dishes for the servants, came twice a day to table for over a week.

If this was the rich man's legitimate diet, there were some among the poor who were undeterred by Acts of Parliament from taking what they felt was theirs by right. The Scots poacher is a familiar figure in fact and fiction from an early date, and despite stringent penalties – amputation of the right hand, transportation, even death – he stubbornly defended the validity of the Highland saying that taking salmon from the river, a tree from the forest, and a deer from the mountain are three actions no Gael was ever ashamed of.

It was not solely a need for food or money – though these were certainly factors – which drove most poachers to break the law. It was first of all the feeling that the law was unjust, that wild animals were no man's property, and should be available freely. Added to this was the lure of the sport itself, given extra piquancy by the threat of being discovered. For some, poaching was an addiction. Scott told his son-in-law and biographer, John Gibson Lockhart, of his very first appearance as a counsel in a criminal court at Jedburgh autumn assizes. He was called to defend a veteran poacher and sheepstealer, and, by chance or by skill, succeeded in his case. 'You're a lucky scoundrel,' he whispered to his client when the verdict was announced. 'I'm just of your mind,' came the reply, 'and I'll send you a maukin [hare] the morn, man.'

One of the difficulties about legislation was that post-medieval courts found it hard to decide to whom the game belonged when it was on unenclosed ground as opposed to parks. The old idea that all deer, and some lesser game, were Crown property had lost its immediacy with the removal of the monarch to London. When, as happened in many cases after the '45, estates fell into neglect, the rights of landowners seemed tenuous and remote, especially in the eyes of people who were often on the brink of starvation. An anonymous writer in the mid-19th century, speaking of this period, put the people's view clearly:

People liable to periodical famines, who had occasionally to resort to every possible means for procuring food to preserve their lives, thought it an unbearable hardship to be withheld from using the resources nature had put within their reach.

Another writer, W. McCombie Smith, expressed the dilemma in a book entitled *The Romance of Poaching*, published in 1904 but covering a period of roughly 100 years. Speaking of a stag born and bred on the Queen's estate at Balmoral which strayed into an adjoining forest, was shot at, and missed, by a sportsman, and was finished off by a poacher who happened to be passing, he asked.

to whom does this dead stag really and truly belong? Whether to the gracious lady who fed it, or to the gruff laird whose ground it fell on, or to the wealthy aristocrat who sent two bullets and a dog after it, or to the free forester who sent two bullets into it?

The Romance of Poaching well illustrates the hostile relationship between poacher and gamekeeper, and also the ambivalent attitude of many landowners. The story of Alexander Davidson (1792–1843) is an example. He is the prototype of the poacher as hero – a man, says McCombie Smith (who never met him), far removed and superior to the ordinary run of poacher. He stood at just under six feet (tall for a Highlander) and measured 18 inches round the calf. Reckoned to be one of the handsomest men of his time, he was a notable and prize-winning dancer, whose fine appearance in a Highland reel was much acclaimed even by the men whose game he might have poached the previous day. He was extremely hardy, dressing lightly even in winter and sleeping outside for much of the year, able to spend hours immersed up to the neck in some dark pool, waiting to spear a salmon. Morally, he was all that a poacher should be, respecting close seasons, giving away his booty to those who sheltered him or were in need, reading his Bible with devout enthusiasm, and expressing feelings of awe and piety when confronted with the terrible loneliness of the high tops, the fearful drama of a thunderstorm, or the Wrath of the Lamb. He never smoked, never ate pork, and subsisted chiefly on oatmeal saturated with whisky and rolled into sausage-shaped patties. He did have, one is glad to learn, a major failing:

It was such a strange fact that so keen a sportsman should take such bad care of rod and gun – but so it was. Rod, reel, line and hooks received the worst of usage, and badly executed repairs. When the rod was laid aside in June to take up the rifle, the latter would be found covered with rust inside and out, and in like state would the gun be found when the 12th of August came.

Davidson was respected and even liked by many of the landowners, if not by their gamekeepers. It was his habit to warn them if he intended to pass through their estates, and he was always scrupulous in not shooting any game that was out of his path, yet his view was that 'the fish out of the water, and the deer out of the forest, are mine as well as the rich man's'. Typically, when he died on the hills of Glenbucket near Ballater, alone save for his little brown dog, there was in his pocket an invitation to stay at Gordon Castle.

That *The Romance of Poaching* should have been written at all is significant of a change in attitudes; that it should end with an emotional account of the death of a poacher, shows how profound the change was. There were a number of reasons for this.

The virtual extinction of game animals from the easy terrain of the south, and the tendency even in the Highlands for them to choose the more remote and inaccessible areas, made the old methods of hunting impossible and brought the art of stalking into prominence for the first time. Another factor was the disbandment of the clans, greatly reducing the manpower available to chieftains wishing to hunt. Thirdly, improved firearms design was making shooting safer, more accurate, and pleasanter, and did away with the need for dogs. And fourth, the continuing financial difficulties of many returned Jacobites and their families, which originally led them to sell off their timber and put sheep to the hills, led the next generation to clear the sheep from the hills and remake deer forests to be let out for stalking.

The skilled stalker, then, whatever his social status, became a man to be respected, and in prosperous 19th-century Britain the only real threat posed by poachers was to the gamekeepers, who might, if their actions went unhindered, lose their jobs.

Yet the slow development of stalking as a sport meant that, in the latter half of the 18th century and the early part of the 19th, the number of deer diminished dramatically. Since there was little hunting there was also little or no attempt at conservation. In addition, the deer were threatened by the presence of the sheep, for their summer grazing grounds, and their cover, were much reduced. Grouse and deer can live happily together, but sheep and deer compete for the same amenities. By contrast to all this, game birds and fish, always protected by a close season, maintained their number during this period.

Ultimately it is perhaps to the accounts of travellers, like Dr Johnson and the Frenchman Barthélemy Faujas de Saint Fond, that the emergence of Scotland as a sportsman's paradise can be attributed. Their books were widely read, and the frequent mention of game (albeit inanimate on a dining-table rather than alive on a hill) seemed designed to whet the sporting appetite of Southerners.

One of the first was a wealthy eccentric, Colonel Thomas Thornton. Hunting and self-admiration were the pivots of this man's life (it is characteristic that he named his illegitimate daughter Thornvillia Diana, in an allusion to both passions) but his *Sporting Tour through the Northern Parts of England and Great Part of the Highlands of Scotland* displays an eye for natural beauty, warm appreciation of friends, and lively – if occasionally unsubtle – sense of humour. His writing has a very personal, readable quality. Of the spate of travellers' accounts written at that time, his was the only one to deal specifically with sport, and his enthusiasm stimulated much interest among the fraternity.

Thornton stayed at inns, or with friends; and he seems to have had little trouble getting permission to shoot wherever he wished. However, before the onset of the third decade of the century, a new idea was coming into prominence – that of landowners charging for the right to kill animals on their land.

Who initiated it, and how it began, is not clear. Already in 1812 a few shooting lets were being advertised in the national news-papers, at very small rents but offering few or no amenities: there was usually no accommodation, and often no roads. Despite this, the excitement of deerstalking in mountainous and often dangerous terrain under an uncertain sky, with no prospect of comfort at the end of the day, obviously appealed to some. To spend a day walking, running, crawling, lying flat with one's nose in a peat bog or a tuft of heather, or to inch one's way on one's stomach up an icy burn – but then to return with a fine twelve-pointer and the congratulations of stalker and ghillie: that was an experience both novel and delightful and one which could be relived many times in the pleasant glow of memory.

And so, once again, the forests were set up. The red deer's ability to profit from favourable circumstances made the operation easy. All one had to do was to move the sheep off the land, and keep it quiet for a couple of years, allowing the deer to take possession and increase at their natural rate. After that, the fun could begin. In 1811 there were six preserved deer forests, by 1825 there were 18, and by 1842 the number had reached 40. The craze was under way, carrying with it scores, even hundreds, of people who had never before taken up a gun.

With them came also the anglers and the wildfowlers, for they too were discovering what Scotland had to offer. These sportsmen created their own literature: books with titles like *Lays of the Deer Forest, Sporting Experiences in the Highlands of Scotland*, and *With Rod and Gun*. Most, on the 'I never shot better, nor killed so many' theme, are deservedly forgotten. Some few stand out, including two by William Scrope, of which the naturalist Frank Fraser Darling wrote in 1947 that they 'had an influence on the Highlands almost as great as the Rising of a hundred years before'.

Scrope was 50 when he first came to Scotland. Having persuaded Sir Walter Scott to recommend him, he visited the Duke of Atholl, from whom he rented the forest of Bruar; for ten years he pursued grouse and deer with equal skill and enthusiasm, supplying the Duke, the Duke's friends, and his own (including Scott) with game. He made friends with the local people, and learnt fast; so that when age forced him to take up less strenuous pursuits he had in memory a multitude of experiences and conclusions which he was able to set down in vivid language. His first book, *The Art of Deerstalking*, was published in 1838, and subsequently reprinted under an altered title, *Days of Deerstalking*. He could be coy, facetious, and obscurely pompous, but on occasion he wrote well, and like Thornton passionately loved his subject, at several levels. He could convey accurately and movingly a sense of place, as in the following passage about the high tops:

Here, everything bears the original impress of nature untouched by the hand of man since its creation. That vast moor spread out below you; and those peaks in the distance, faint almost as the sky itself, give the appearance of an extent boundless and sublime as the ocean ... you shall find no dwelling, nor sheep, nor cow, nor horse, nor anything that can remind you of domestic life; you shall hear no sound but the rushing of the torrent, or the notes of the wild animals, the natural inhabitants; you shall see only the moor-fowl, and the plover flying before you from hillock to hillock, or the eagle soaring aloft with his eye to the sun, or his wings wet with mist.

And again, musing on the qualities required of a good stalker:

Your consummate deer-stalker should not only be able to run like an antelope, and breathe like the trade-winds, but should also be enriched with various other undeniable qualifications. As, for instance, he should be able to run in a stooping position, at a greyhound pace, with his back parallel to the ground, and his face within an inch of it, for miles together. He should take a singular pleasure in threading the seams of a bog, or of gliding down a burn *ventre à terre*, like that insinuating animal, the eel; accomplished he should be in skilfully squeezing his clothes after this operation, to make all comfortable ...

He should rejoice in wading through torrents, and be able to stand firmly on water-worn stones, unconscious of the action of the current; or if, by fickle fortune, the waves should be too powerful for him when he loses his balance, and goes floating away upon his back (for if he has any tact, or sense of the picturesque, it is presumed that he will fall backwards), he should raise his rifle aloft in the air, Marmion fashion, lest his powder should get wet and his day's sport come to an end.

When no longer able to stalk to his own exacting standards, Scrope gave up his beloved Bruar and returned to an earlier passion – angling. He was, in fact, an angler for a much longer period than he was a deerstalker, renting various houses and large fisheries on

Tweedside for about 20 years, and remaining there sometimes all year round except in the close season. He knew every pool, every bend, every rock in the river. Although less useful as an angler's manual than others which appeared about the same time, Scrope's second book stands out because, like *Days of Deerstalking*, it appeals to the reader at many levels. In *Days and Nights of Salmon Fishing in the Tweed* (London, 1843) we have once more a mixture of practical advice, fanciful prose, and anecdote. But most of the pomposity has gone, and so, mercifully, has the coyness. From the story of his very first venture on the river ('I had been guilty of almost every error possible', he writes engagingly) to his account of the methods used by salmon poachers, he can hold our interest.

The two chief instruments of salmon poaching, according to Scrope, were a *pout-net* – a large semi-circular net with which a man could sweep the water – and a *leister*. The common type of leister was simply a large fork or trident, ideal for the capture of fish when they came into the river in great numbers to spawn. A second type, the throwing leister, was used chiefly in shallow water. It had five prongs of unequal but regularly graded length, with a rope, called the *lyams*, fastened to the top bar of the spear just above the shortest prong. The other end of the lyams, which measured about twelve yards in length, was fastened to the thrower's arm, so that after the fish had been speared, when the top of the shaft fell beyond the vertical point towards the opposite bank of the river, the catch could be pulled back to land by hauling in the lyams. The men who used the leister were often known as the black fishers because frequently they disguised themselves with masks made of black crape.

Night poaching from boats, using leisters, was called 'burning the water'. There were usually three men to a boat, each of which had a central upright pole, fixed to the top of which was a metal frame filled with fragments of tar-barrel and rags steeped in pitch. When the boats had silently taken up their positions, at a given signal lights were applied to the contents of the metal baskets which by their bright blaze attracted the fish to the surface of the water. Scrope's description of the scene could hardly have been bettered by Scott himself:

As the rude forms of the men rose up in their dark attire, wielding their long leisters, with the streaks of light that glared partially on them, and surrounded as they were by the shades of night, you might almost have fancied yourself in the realms below, with Pluto and his grim associates, embarked on the Stygian lake . . .

. . . He now stood upon a rock which hung over the river, and from that eminence, and with the assistance of the firebrand, examined the bottom of it carefully. His body was bent over the water, and his ready leister held almost vertically; as the light glared on his face you might see the keen glistening of his eye. In an instant he raised up his leister, and down he sprang from the rock right into the river, and with that wild bound nailed the salmon to the channel. There was a struggle with his arms for a few seconds; he then passed his hands down the pole of the weapon a little way, brought himself vertically over the fish, and lifted him aloft cheered by shouts of applause from his friends on the shore.

Scrope makes difficulty or discomfort, even danger, seem a worthwhile price to pay for wonderful experiences. Despite his failings as a writer, his books were deservedly popular with his contemporaries, and have become collectors' items in our own day.

Three other writers from the same epoch who played a part in bringing southerners to Scotland should have brief mention. Thomas Tod Stoddart, with *The Art of Angling as practised in Scotland* (Edinburgh 1836); *Angling Reminiscences* (1837), and *The Angler's Companion* (1847), wrote the first proper manuals on Scottish fish and fishing waters, in an (usually) elegant spare style. James Wilson, FRSE, collaborated with the pseudonymous writer 'Oakleigh' in an extraordinary but widely read volume entitled *The Rod and the Gun*. It contained some good practical advice, some attempts at humour even more embarrassing than Scrope's, and a good deal of misinformation; but Wilson's chapter on grouse-shooting is still evocative and readable. The third writer was Charles St John, one of the earliest of those Victorian naturalists whose ambivalent attitude to wildlife is so difficult for us to understand. He seems to have hunted for the pleasure of killing, or at least of gaining possession, rather than for the sport. He certainly admired the creatures he killed; his notes are filled with expressions of sadness, even penitence, when he had shot an eagle, an osprey, or a pair of peregrines, yet he seemed unwilling to stop. He was, as

Duff Hart Davis says in his book *Monarchs of the Glen*, a fascinating specimen of that odd breed, the shooting naturalist. In his books and articles (the first, *Natural History and Sport in Moray* (1846), very quickly became a classic) he made a notable contribution to the literature which was attracting people to the Highlands.

It can hardly have been coincidence that this decade of 1835–45, during which so many sporting books on Scotland appeared, saw what amounted to an explosion in the number of Englishmen coming north. Whatever its causes, the new fashion soon received the highest social endorsement, for the Royal Family, having tested the water rather gingerly in 1842 ('Albert says many of the people look like Germans', wrote the Queen delightedly), rapidly succumbed to the simple pleasures of the rich. They were not to revisit the country for another five years but when they did they were persuaded that nothing could be more agreeable than to lease an estate themselves. Balmoral was recommended; it 'reminded them much of Thüringen', and without further discussion they took over the lease from the Earl of Aberdeen. Within a few years they had bought it outright together with adjoining estates. Now the Prince could shoot and fish to his heart's content, while his wife walked, sketched, admired his skill when he was successful, and commiserated when he was not.

For most Victorians, this was an age of prosperity. The Industrial Revolution was bringing in enormous profits to manufacturers. Abroad, the Empire was at its furthest-flung and fortunes were being made in trade. The only problem with money was how to spend it. Travel to foreign lands, except in the cause of duty, was not a habit of Britons. But here, on the doorstep, was an untried playground, offering a new sport which could be indulged in at many levels of competence and which had peripheral pleasures. It was the very thing to amuse and distract those tired of London society, or unable to enter it. Provided a man had money and knew, or was willing to learn, how to behave – for a strict though unwritten etiquette rapidly developed – he was accepted in the oddly egalitarian little world of forest, river, and moor. Frock-coats (to borrow a phrase from Fraser Darling) were left at home: Lord Tomnoddy donned the tweeds of the country and was happy to crawl in a burn or through the glaur of peat hags in the acute discomfort which the Highland weather of September and October can impose.

For the local people, the years between 1880 and 1914 were prosperous to a degree which their grandparents would have found hard to credit. Free at last from financial embarrassment, the lairds built comfortable houses for themselves and grand new shooting-lodges for their guests or tenants; for the lower classes, there was almost full employment, whether in making roads and building or manning the railways, or running the local Post Office and cooking or cleaning at the Big House. On the hills where formerly shepherds herded the Blackface sheep, deer grazed, and the shepherds had new titles – gamekeeper, stalker, ghillie.

An influx of people, all determined to shoot at something, was naturally not without effect on local wildlife. Previously the Forest Laws, backed up by the inadequacy of early firearms and the fact that those with hunting rights were a very small minority of a sparse population, had been sufficiently protective. Now, with perhaps five times as many hunters out each season, all armed with light, fast, accurate rifles, the danger of extinction of species came very close. Almost anyone could learn to shoot, and if a man aimed to go after deer or grouse or duck, what better way was there to get his eye in than by potting at any wild creature which came within his sights? Boys of ten or twelve were given guns and encouraged to practise, and their victims were indiscriminately chosen. Osgood Mackenzie tells how, as a small boy of nine, he was promised a gun of his own as soon as he had learnt to swim. This he did very quickly, and at once

a little single-barrelled muzzle-loader weighing only three pounds was ordered from a gun-maker in London. Some wise folk thought my mother was making a great mistake by letting me start shooting so early, one of the chief reasons brought forward being that I should soon become quite blasé and should not enjoy sport when I grew up to manhood. But all these prophecies were completely falsified, as I was the keenest of sportsmen all my life, until I gave up the gun when I was over seventy.

The birds-nesting craze was another menace. Even the protected varieties were endangered: as we read in the following extracts from Mackenzie's *A Hundred Years in the Highlands*:

What a big pile it would make if all the black game I shot there between 1855 and 1900 were gathered into one heap. Now, alas! there are none, and why, who can tell?

And again:

My total in the year (1868) was 1314 grouse, 33 black game, 49 partridges, 110 golden plover, 35 wild ducks, 53 snipe, 91 blue rock-pigeons, 184 hares, without mentioning geese, teal, ptarmigan and roe, etc., a total of 1900 head. In other seasons I got sometimes as many as 96 partridges, 106 snipe, and 95 woodcock. Now so many of these good beasts and birds are either quite extinct or on the very verge of becoming so.

From the sportsman's point of view the life was indeed a fine one, and one which scarcely changed over a period of 60 or so years. The world outside altered considerably: there were wars in the United States, in the Crimea, in the Sudan, in South Africa. Urban daily life at home was changing too as new inventions came tumbling one after the other. But there remained through it all the unvarying routine of August and September: the train from King's Cross, packed with good fellows, their rods, their guns, their manservants; the dog-cart waiting at the little station; the long days in the heather or fishing some brown, peaty burn; the hot baths and hearty meals; the yarns round the smoking-room fire. The trains got faster by degrees, the dog-cart was replaced on some progressive estates by a car, and the plumbing was brought up to date – but even the First World War made little impact, initially, on the shooting- and fishing-lodges and their inhabitants. In fact, once the war ended, the therapeutic value of a Highland holiday came to be widely recognized, as two verses from a poem first published in *Punch* by Alfred Cochrane testify:

> Does your heart beat with the old excitement
> As you wait where the Scotch expresses are?
> Does it answer still to the old indictment
> Of a fond delight in the sleeping-car,
> As it did when the rush through the autumn night meant
> The Gate of Desire ajar?
> . . .
> See! from the tops the mist is stealing,

Out with the stalking-glass for a spy;
Round Craig an Eran an eagle's wheeling
Black in the blue September sky.
A fig for the years! Why, youth and healing
At the end of your journey lie.

No one has more brilliantly described the atmosphere of the lodges than John Buchan, himself a keen sportsman. Stalking is a secondary theme in many of his novels, and where the quarry is human, as in the *Thirty-nine Steps*, the analogy of the deer forest is never far away. In the superbly dramatic climax of *The Three Hostages*, hero and villain actually stalk each other in the desperate wilderness of a Highland corrie, with the deer for once spectators rather than participants. Fishing, infrequently referred to in the novels, is yet a topic given some prominence elsewhere in his writing, notably in the essays, 'May-Fly Fishing', and 'Night on the Heather', in the collection entitled *Scholar Gipsies*. There is also a striking and sinister short story, *The Black Fishers*, but that is less concerned with poaching than with human greed.

However, Buchan writes most vividly about sport in the novel *John Macnab*. The action takes place in the early 1920s. Three eminently respectable men of romantic soul (a paradox he loved) issue a challenge to the owners or lessees of adjoining estates in a remote part of the Highlands: 'John Macnab' (a collective *nom de guerre*) will, within a specified period and without being apprehended, poach from each estate, the game later to be returned to the owner.

It is interesting to note that Buchan took care to make his protagonists absolutely typical of the kind of people to be encountered in the Highlands at that time: on one side, a laird of ancient lineage, an American millionaire, an industrialist from the Midlands; on the other, a peer from the Borders, a well-known lawyer of Scots descent practising at the English bar, a distinguished banker in London.

It is perhaps Buchan's finest novel, for it works constantly on several levels, and contains many of his favourite preoccupations. Loyalty is a theme, so is that type of sportsmanship which makes opponents fight fair – though (untypically for the author) unsportsmanlike behaviour is here indulged in on both sides. But there are no villains, and the real heroes are the land and the weather. The contest of wits and physical abilities is both credible and immensely exciting. Descriptions of the actual stalking and fishing are economical without losing a single brush-stroke from the picture. Over all is the author's sense of place, his capacity to make the reader see and feel the landscape he is writing about.

That was in 1925, and one cannot help wondering what Buchan would make of the scene today, when Americans and Midlands industrialists have been replaced by Japanese manufacturers and Arab oil sheiks.

What would certainly puzzle him is the agitation which has arisen since his time over the extent of the deer forests. If it is true that 7 per cent of Scotland's population owns 84 per cent of the land, the issue need not for all that be political. Fraser Darling, and other naturalists, opined that 90 per cent of forest consists of land unsuited for any other use, so poor and bare is it, and in particular so short of winter grazing. Perhaps the deer do now roam over land which once supported a croft with a cow and a few sheep, but given the present trend of British agriculture such a croft would today be unworkable and uneconomical. The dream of self-sufficiency, in an age of mass-production and cheap food, requires not only hard work but a fertile soil, a moderate climate, and the ability to sell one's produce (for even the most self-sufficient need money) cheaply.

Another change would sadden, not only Buchan, but also the author of *The Romance of Poaching*. Poaching in the 1980s, particularly of deer and fish, has become big business, with the catch going not only to hotels all over the country, but also abroad. The advent of the landrover has made the process much easier than in McCombie Smith's day; and though fines are heavy, the profits are great when a large number of animals can be killed by a gang on a single day, and transported out of the area immediately. As the cost of manpower rises, fewer gamekeepers are available to protect the forests, and skilful thieves are rarely caught except by accident, as happened recently when three men became trapped on the hill by a snowstorm which lasted several days. It would have delighted McCombie Smith that, like his heroes, they roasted venison over an open fire to keep themselves alive, but one wonders how he would have reacted to the discovery of eight dead deer in their car.

It is not only the scale of the thefts which threatens the deer. Almost worse is the fact that many modern poachers have little hillcraft and no scruples about the animals they hunt. Failure to use the correct firearms or to follow up a wounded animal is commonplace, nor are they averse to shooting a hind accompanied by her calf.

Commercial demand for venison is increasing, especially from the Continent, which at present takes 93 per cent of Scotland's annual output. It may be that ultimately deer farming provides the best hope for survival of the species. Farming brings down the price of the meat, and makes pursuit of wild deer, retreating ever further into inaccessible corries, a less attractive proposition to men who are only doing it for money. At present few deer farms exist (it is an enterprise requiring a good deal of time and capital outlay) but the notion itself has been proved viable. Deer remain the most efficient animals on our hills when it comes to converting poor grazing into good meat, and as beef and lamb become more expensive the British may return to venison.

Salmon are similarly seriously endangered by illegal trapping. Even Scrope, who complained bitterly about some methods used by poachers, did not foresee the use of dynamite and gill nets. The latter, used for coastal fishing, are spread over a large area – as much as two miles – outside the legal nets. They are made of very thin nylon monofilament which, as their name suggests, traps the fish by the gills. At one time legal gear, they were banned when it was realized that every fish caught died painfully in the net, with much marking and bruising. Because they trap any size and type of fish indiscriminately, they do great damage to breeding stock, and their use is a matter for serious concern by the Department of Agriculture and Fisheries for Scotland.

Here again, the answer may lie in fish farming, which unlike deer farming is a boom industry – indeed Scotland's fastest growing agriculture industry. There are now more than 100 companies in business at 210 sites, both freshwater and saltwater. Many fish farms are small family businesses which conform to high standards in order to qualify for aid from the Highlands and Islands Development Board. All attempt to reproduce as far as possible conditions in nature; as a result farmed fish differs very little – connoisseurs say it is a hardly detectable matter of texture – from the wild variety. In 1986 about 10,000 tons of salmon worth around £42 million was produced, and the figure is expected to increase. Trout farming, after initial difficulties caused by disease and fluctuating freshwater supplies, is also developing rapidly. Competition from other countries could be a problem, but the unpolluted waters in which Scottish fish are brought to maturity are an important factor of their high quality, and ensure demand at the top end of the market. The steady year-round supply of farmed fish keeps prices at a reasonable level (though there are of course seasonal fluctuations) and it is to be hoped that it will discourage the kind of wholesale commercial poaching which causes such enormous damage to wild fish stock.

With grouse, too, an alarming situation has developed over the last five years, although poaching is apparently not the cause of a decline in stocks which landowners describe as catastrophic. Such is the general concern, particularly among proprietors in the Borders, that an association has been formed to fund scientists in a study of the habits, movement, food and diseases of grouse.

Scotland's game resources have always been recognized as being of unmatched excellence. There is acknowledgement, now, of the need for careful conservation and development. If the mistakes of the past can be avoided, it may be that the peat-bogs and heather of the hills, so long considered unproductive, will eventually be seen as a notable asset.

— **RECIPES** —

All game has a stronger flavour than domestic meat. Venison, even when farmed, is stronger than beef, grouse than domestic poultry, river salmon than farmed fish. The flavour of deer and birds depends also on what they have eaten and how long they have hung. Modern preference is for a short hanging time: 10–12 days for venison, less for birds. Our forebears would think us eccentric; they liked their meat 'gamey', that is, almost high. Even 25 years ago this was the prevailing taste, and my butcher, a man of great experience, once told me that some of his customers judged the 'ripeness' of grouse by laying their ear to the bird. If they could hear maggots moving in it, it was declared fit to eat.

Game, like ordinary farmed meat, does need to be hung for a period to develop both flavour and tenderness. It is, however, entirely a matter of personal preference. If you are buying from a butcher, you need nevertheless have no fear that he will give you meat which has hung too long. He will study your taste, you need not accommodate to his.

VENISON

In 1930 a very small book was published, called *A Highland Cookery Book*. Its author was Margaret Fraser, born on a Highland estate into a family of stalkers and keepers. She left home when quite young, to train as a cook, and later married the Head Stalker to the Duke of Northampton. His Grace must have appreciated her skills, for his introduction to her recipes is enthusiastic. Ninety per cent of them or 66 in all are for venison, using every part of the beast from its brains to its feet, not forgetting heart and stomach bag. The following two recipes call up the atmosphere of the kitchen of a shooting-lodge, with its large black-leaded range and open fireplace glowing with peats or logs of pine. As 'upstairs' relaxed after a day on the hills, soaking aching muscles in a hip-bath of hot water, the 'bag' was being brought into the outhouses. Who did the butchering? Mrs Fraser doesn't say.

Roast Haunch of Venison

Trim a haunch of venison and flour it well, taking special care that the parts which were cut are well coated.

Place in a roasting-tin with plenty of beef dripping, and let it have a very hot oven to start it – or hang before a very bright fire and roast in the usual way for four hours, basting frequently. Season and dish on a hotplate with plenty of good brown gravy and redcurrant jelly.

Method of Salting Venison

Take the venison to be salted after it has hung in the larder for two days. Cut it into pieces the required size. See that it is clean and free from fly, *but on no account wash it with water*. Take 2 lb (1 kg) kitchen salt, ¼ lb (125 g) demerara sugar, 1 teaspoon black pepper, ½ teaspoon nitre. Mix these well together. Rub pieces of venison on every side with this mixture for 2–3 days in succession. Then place them in a wooden tub, or earthenware jar, and press them well together. After 10 days the venison is ready for use. Venison treated in this way, if pressed into a jar and the air excluded, should keep for months, and a haunch which has been well salted in this manner for about three weeks can be hung up to dry as a ham.

In *Kidnapped* Alan Breck and David Balfour were entertained for a few days by Cluny Macpherson, who, as a Jacobite clan chief on the run, did in fact spend several months hiding from his pursuers in a kind of hut of trees, earth and wattle, half suspended from, half supported by, the mountain against which it was placed. This contraption was known as 'Cluny's Cage'. Stevenson tells us that Macpherson staved off boredom by developing an interest in cooking. The messenger sent to fetch the exhausted fugitives encourages them with talk of hot collops and, sure enough, Cluny,

even while he was greeting us in, kept an eye to the collops. 'They,' said he, meaning the collops, 'are such as I gave his Royal Highness in this very house.'

Alas for David! Fatigue had made him too ill to enjoy the delicacy.

Since Cluny's supporters kept him well supplied with little luxuries, the recipe for Venison Collops which follows probably approximates closely to what he offered Bonnie Prince Charlie. It comes from Meg Dods's* *The Cook and Housewife's Manual.*

* 'Meg Dods', who took her name from the landlady in St Ronan's Well was in reality Isobel Johnston, the wife of an Edinburgh publisher and a friend of Scott. The latter almost certainly had a hand in the recipe book entitled *The Cook and Housewife's Manual, by Mistress Margaret Dods* (Edinburgh 1826), which with its sensible approach and easy, relaxed, and amusing style, caused a stir when it first appeared and is still worth reading.

Venison Collops

4 venison cutlets
venison bones and trimmings, for gravy
1 teaspoon lemon or orange juice
1 glass red wine
pepper, salt, a pinch of cayenne, a little
    freshly grated nutmeg

Prepare gravy by simmering bones and trimmings in water for at least an hour. Then remove the bones and reduce the liquid by about half. Make a roux with butter and flour, gradually stir in the liquid, allow to boil for a few minutes, then strain.

Fry the cutlets in butter over a moderate heat. Put the gravy in a small pan, and add the fruit juice, claret, and seasonings to taste. Pour this sauce over the collops before serving.

Venison Stew

1 lb (450 g) venison
2 lambs' or ½ pig's kidney
3 tablespoons vegetable or olive oil
4 oz (125 g) small mushrooms
8 small onions (pickling size) or shallots
1 tablespoon flour
1 generous tablespoon apple jelly
1 tablespoon chopped parsley

Marinade

2½ glasses inexpensive Italian red wine
2 glasses fresh (or packaged) orange juice
1 garlic clove, finely diced
2 more garlic cloves, cut in half

salt and freshly ground pepper
about 10 leaves fresh lovage *or*
  2 tablespoons chopped celery leaves
1 medium onion, finely sliced.

Marinade venison and kidney for 24 hours. Turn the meat occasionally and, if it is frozen, separate the pieces as they begin to thaw out.

Next day, drain off and reserve the liquid. Cut the meat into cubes, carefully removing any fat or gristle. Heat the oil in a large deep frying pan, and brown the meat lightly over a good heat. Then put in the mushrooms and onions, and cook a few minutes longer. Remove meat and vegetables and put them in a heavy pot, earthenware if possible. To the oil remaining in the frying pan, add the flour, stir, then gradually add the jelly, the marinade and the parsley. Let the mixture boil and thicken, then add to the cooking-pot. Add some boiling water if you think there won't be enough liquid, and cook in a pre-heated oven at 350° F (180°C) gas 4 for 2 hours, checking once or twice that there is still enough liquid. Check the seasoning before bringing to the table, with potatoes steamed in their jackets.

Deerstalker's Stew Pot

If you do not have an opportunity to marinade your venison, or if you do not care for kidney, this recipe is ideal. It makes a deliciously warming dish on a cold day.

  1 lb (450g) stewing venison
  6 oz (175g) bacon, cut into ½-in (1-cm) cubes
  1 lb (450g) potatoes, peeled and cut into 1-in (2-cm) cubes
  6 oz (175g) carrots, cut into fingers
  8 small onions
  ¼pt (150ml) red wine
  ½pt (300ml) beefstock
  salt and pepper

> 2–3 tablespoons redcurrant jelly
> 1 dessertspoonful cornflour
> 3 tablespoons vegetable oil

Heat the oil in a pan and quickly brown the venison and bacon on all sides. Add potatoes, carrots, onions, wine, stock, and seasoning. Bring to the boil, then simmer gently for 2 hours. Add the jelly and allow it to dissolve. Take a little of the liquid, and add it to the cornflour which has been mixed with 2 tablespoons cold water. Mix well, then pour back into the pan. Stir and bring back to the boil, then check the seasoning and serve.

PHEASANT

'Unless kept to the proper point,' wrote an English cookery writer, Eliza Acton, in 1845, 'a pheasant is one of the most tough, dry, and flavourless birds that is sent to table'. A young pheasant, however, can be delicious – the moral seems to be that the bird must be chosen with care, and constantly basted while cooking. A brace, cock and hen, will feed 6–8 people.

Roast Pheasant

> 2 pheasants (a brace or two hens)
> 6 slices streaky bacon
> stuffing (see below)

For the gravy:

> ½ glass port wine
> 1 tablespoon grated orange rind

Cover each bird with strips of bacon. Set the oven fairly hot, at 375° F (190° C) gas 5. Stuff the birds with the chosen stuffing. Put in a roasting tin in the oven and, while they cook, baste them with the juices, or pour on melted butter if they look dry. Turn the birds after a quarter of an hour, and again after a further 15 minutes. Three-quarters of an hour should suffice, but they will benefit by being set to rest for 10 minutes in a warm place before serving, even more than would other meats. To make the gravy, add the rind and the port to the juice in the pan and stir well over a high heat for two minutes.

Stuffings for Roast Pheasant

1. A rich and good stuffing

1 roast pheasant
1 small roast chicken
2 turkey livers
1 cup fresh breadcrumbs
1 cup orange juice

Take the meat from the birds and mince it with the raw livers. Mix in the breadcrumbs and fruit juice to make a moist but not runny paste. Add salt and pepper if necessary, and stuff the birds.

2. A simple stuffing

¼lb (125g) (approx) butter
juice of 1 lemon
1 cup fresh breadcrumbs

Mix all the ingredients, season with salt and pepper, and stuff the birds.

The following method for pheasant avoids almost all risk of producing a 'dry, flavourless bird'. It is an excellent dinner party dish – easy, glamorous, delicious.

Pheasants with chestnuts casseroled in red wine
(for 7–8 people)

1 brace pheasants
1½oz (40g) butter
2 tablespoons olive oil
½lb (250g) dried chestnuts, soaked for at least 24 hours
¾lb (375g) button onions

2 tablespoons flour
¾pt (450ml) chicken stock
grated rind and juice of 1 orange
1 tablespoon redcurrant jelly
2 good glasses red wine (a Portuguese Dao is good)
a bunch of herbs – parsley, bay leaf, thyme, and
 lovage *or* 1 stick of celery
salt and pepper

Heat oil and butter gently in a large frying pan. Brown the birds in this, slowly, then put them in a large casserole. Put the onions and the chestnuts into the frying pan and cook briskly for a few minutes, shaking the pan, until they change colour. Lift them into the casserole with a slotted spoon. To the butter mixture remaining, add the flour (and more butter if it is very dry), stir well, and cook for 2–3 minutes. Then pour in, gradually, the stock, orange juice and rind, jelly and wine, stirring constantly until smooth. Add salt, pepper and herbs, and pour over the birds. Cover the casserole, and put in a moderate oven, 325–350° F (170–180° C) gas 3–4, for 1½–2 hours.

Turn off the heat ten minutes before serving. Dish birds on a large ashet with the onions and chestnuts; keep warm while you reduce the liquid by a third, by boiling it rapidly. Pour a little over the pheasants, hand the remainder separately.

GROUSE

One must acquire a taste for this bird – I myself have not quite managed it. It has a strong flavour and, like the pheasant, can be dry if not carefully dealt with. Marian McNeill's recipe for Roast Grouse is the best.

Roast Grouse

Pluck the birds carefully so as to avoid breaking the delicate skin, do not wash them, but draw and wipe inside and out with a damp cloth. Put an ounce or two of butter, into which you have worked a little lemon juice, pepper and salt, into each bird, but not in the crop. Some cooks stuff the birds with red whortleberries or cranberries, which brings out the flavour well and keeps them as moist as butter does. It is essential to avoid dryness. Wrap the birds well with fat bacon and enclose this with greaseproof paper till 10 minutes before serving; then remove the wrappings, flour the birds, and brown, or the bacon and the greaseproof paper may be omitted, and the birds basted frequently and freely with butter. The time allotted is 20–30 minutes, according to the size and age of the birds. (Pheasant and partridge must be well done, wild duck, solan geese, underdone; but grouse must be removed in the nick of time – neither over nor actually underdone.)

Boil the livers for 10 minutes, pound them in a mortar with a little butter, salt, and cayenne, and spread this on pieces of toast large enough to hold a bird. Place this toast under each bird during the last few minutes of roasting, but do not put it into the fat in the pan to get sodden. Serve with fried breadcrumbs, but without gravy in the dish.

The usual accompaniments are chip potatoes, watercress, French beans, mushrooms, and clear gravy. Bread, nut, or fruit sauce, and melted butter are also occasionally served. Cranberry or rowan jelly goes very well with grouse, and so do pickled peaches.

FISH

Fresh-caught trout cooked over a camp fire is a delicacy known to many countries and hardly needs a recipe. T. T. Stoddart, however, had his own way of doing it:

Simple recipe for cooking a Whitling or good Trout by the Riverside

Kindle a fire of dry wood. Then take your fish when just out of the water. Fill his mouth with salt: roll him up in two or three folds of an old newspaper, twisting the ends well together. Immerse all in the water, until the paper has become thoroughly saturated. Then lay the fish among the embers of your fire. When the paper presents a well charred appearance, the trout is properly done, and will prove a savoury and acceptable morsel.

The fish, I may observe, must *not* be cut open and cleaned. During the firing process, the intestines and other impurities will draw together, and not in the slightest degree injure the flavour of the trout.

Here is Margaret Fraser's way with small brown trout:

Cold dish of brown small Trout

About 12 small trout and one rather large one
2–3 oz (75g) melted butter
salt and pepper
tomatoes, vinegar, or anchovy sauce (all optional)

Clean the small trout, skin them, and split them open and remove the bone. Take a pie-dish (preferably greased) and in it lay the trout flat one above the other with a teaspoon of melted butter and a sprinkling of pepper and salt between each. When the dish is full lay on top the larger trout, cleaned and from which the bone, but *not the skin*, has been removed. The head on this one should also be left, and it should be placed above the others, skin uppermost, to form a cover. Spread a piece of grease paper on top and bake for fully ½ an hour. Put away to cool and serve for breakfast or lunch. This can be varied with the addition of tomatoes, vinegar, or anchovy sauce.

Scotch salmon has a texture and flavour superior to most. At one time it was so plentiful that it is said that servants complained when given it too often for meals.

Certainly, Defoe commented on its abundance and cheapness, particularly in the north. But disease and over-fishing took their toll, and by the early 1900s it was already food for the rich. It is a very versatile fish, equally good hot or cold, poached, grilled or baked.

Poaching should be very gently done, the fish put into cold water which is slowly brought to boil, the heat then immediately reduced so that the water merely simmers for about one minute. The heat is then turned off and the fish left in the water, covered, until quite cold.

Tweed Kettle

Once a very popular dish, this used to be sold in Edinburgh cookshops – an early 'takeaway'. Most 19th-century versions use white wine, mushrooms, shallots, and herbs, in which mixture the fish is gently simmered or poached. But Stoddart thought so highly of his own method that he gave the recipe at the end of his *Angler's Companion*, asserting that 'by one who has enjoyed in perfection what is termed a fisherman's kettle, the Metropolitan mode of dressing the king of fishes stands a chance of being resolutely decried in future'.

Here is the Stoddart method. It breaks all the rules by using a large quantity of water and boiling the fish hard – but one must bear in mind that the quantity of salt would lower the boiling point. To crimp (a word which occurs frequently in Victorian cook books), by the way, is to slash so that the fish's flesh contracts slightly.

Boiling of Salmon

It is essential that a salmon intended for boiling should have been newly caught; the fresher it can be procured the better, and a fish transferred from the net or gaff-hook to the pan or kettle, is always sure to give the most satisfaction. The way of treating a salmon, under one or other of these circumstances, is as follows:

Crimp the fish immediately on its being killed, by the water-side, making the cuts slantwise, and at a distance of two inches from each other; separate also the gills, and holding it by the tail, immerse its body in the stream for the space of three or four minutes, moving it backwards and forwards, so as to expedite the flowing off of the blood. In the meantime, give orders, if you have not previously done so, to have the fire briskened and the pot or cauldron filled, or nearly so, with spring water, set on to boil. The fish, after being crimped and bled, as I have directed, must now be conveyed to a table or kitchen-dresser, and there thoroughly cleaned inside. This done, divide it through the backbone into cuts or slices, of the thickness already indicated in the crimping, throwing these into a large handbasin as you proceed. I shall presume, by this time, that the water is at the boiling point. If so, convey to it a large bowlful of kitchen salt; do not scrimp the material or you ruin the fish. Allow the water, thus checked, again to bubble up and then pop in the cuts of salmon, head and all. Several minutes will elapse before the liquid contents of the pot once more arrive at the boiling point; when they do so, begin to note the time, and see, as you measure it, that the fire is a brave one. For all fish under nine pounds weight, allow ten minutes' brisk boiling, and when exceeding nine pounds, grant an extra minute to every additional pound. When ready, serve hot, along with the brine in which the fish was cooked. This is salmon to perfection, and constitutes the veritable kettle of Tweedside, such as frothed and foamed in the days of the merry monks of Kelso . . .

A fresh salmon thus cooked is remarkable for its curd and consistency, and very unlike the soft oily mass generally presented under that designation. Even when it has been kept a day or two, this method of boiling will be found to bring out equally the true flavour of the fish, than if it had been placed entire, with a mere sprinkling of salt, in the frypan.

Baked Salmon Steaks

4 good-sized salmon steaks
½ cup thick cream
2 drops Tabasco sauce
2 tablespoons flour
4 fillets of anchovies
2 tablespoons dry sherry
1 tablespoon chopped parsley
salt and pepper

Grease four pieces of aluminium foil, each large enough to wrap a steak completely but loosely. Coat each steak with flour seasoned with salt and pepper, then lay each in the centre of its piece of foil, on a baking tray. Wash the anchovy fillets in cold water, cut each in half lengthwise, then put two halves across each steak. Mix together the cream, the sherry, and the Tabasco, and pour carefully over the steaks turning up the edges of the foil to prevent the liquid escaping. Fold over the foil.

Heat the oven to moderate, 350° F (180°C) gas 4. Bake the fish for about 30 minutes. Sprinkle with the chopped parsley before bringing to the table.

Christopher North's Sauce for Game

Christopher North was the pen-name of John Wilson, Professor of Moral Philosophy at Edinburgh University in the early part of the 19th century. He is chiefly remembered today for his *Noctes Ambrosianae*, which were published in *Blackwood's Magazine* and purported to relate conversations between Wilson, James Hogg (the Ettrick Shepherd), and Thomas de Quincey (the Opium Eater). The conversations took place in Ambrose's Tavern, much frequented by the literati of the day.

North was a wild character, whose satirical wit first brought Blackwood's into prominence. He was very fond of food, as was Hogg, and both liked earthy dishes, strongly flavoured. The astonishing amount of cayenne pepper in his celebrated Sauce for Game may reflect this, or it may simply be intended to distract from the gamey flavour of the meat. With less cayenne, it is very good.

> 1 heaped saltspoon of good cayenne pepper
> ½ saltspoon of salt
> 1 small dessertspoon of castor sugar
> 1 tablespoon lemon juice
> 2 tablespoons Harvey's sauce
> 1 tablespoon mushroom ketchup
> 3 tablespoons port wine

Heat the sauce by placing the ingredients in a basin in a saucepan of boiling water. Serve it directly it is warm with geese, ducks, roast pork, venison, or any grilled meat. 'The proportion of cayenne,' says North, 'may be doubled when a very pungent sauce is desired.'

GUARDIAN OF THE FISHPONDS

Oh weel may the boatie row
That fills a heavy creel,
And cleads us a' frae head to feet,
And buys our parritch meal.

Traditional song

The sea has been kind to Scotland. One after the other, it has offered her some of its most valuable resources – fish, gas, oil.

'Piscinata Scotia' (Scotland the guardian of fish-ponds) is how the Spaniard Pedro de Ayala described the country at the end of the 15th century; yet it cannot be said that the very first inhabitants took much advantage of the bounty. They were not great fish-eaters, nor indeed did they exhibit any marked seafaring tendency. That favourite archaeological repository of knowledge, the midden, has shown that while mussels, whelks, and limpets were a prime component of daily diet, the tedium might be relieved, only occasionally, by the appearance on the beach of a stranded whale or a seal. Later, the construction of small coracle-type boats permitted additions to the menu when the weather was favourable: ling, cod, wrasse, sea-bream, conger eel, ray. But this small North British population could draw for its food on sources other than the sea, and although forced by the extent of the deep forest to settle wherever a sheltered coastline was relatively level and rock-free, it was still to the land that they chiefly turned for food. And once some knowledge of agriculture had been brought by settlers from the Continent, a landward-looking society developed, clearing woodland, planting crops, and grazing stock. Boats were vital in the establishment of trade along the coast and between islands, but people were not compelled, as for instance in Norway, to look for their chief sustenance to the sea. It was in fact the arrival of the Vikings in their large sea-going boats, in the 8th century, which first brought the concept of a fishing economy to the north and west of Scotland.

Initially the Norsemen came as pirates and marauders. Very quickly, however, lured by the attractions of a relatively fertile and sparsely populated country, they returned to settle, making their main bases in the Orkneys, Shetland and the Outer Hebrides. Another motive for their move may have been directly connected with fishing, for herring – an important element in the Norse diet – sometimes abandon their traditional waters for a space of several years. It has been suggested that the raiders, observing shoals of herring off the Scottish coastline when their own was deserted, migrated where the food was. Archaeological evidence marks the settlements as predominantly agricultural, but fishing was obviously a well-organized and highly developed activity. The Vikings were, literally, sea-men, as much at home at the helm as behind a plough, exploiting the sea just as they cultivated the land. Part of their confidence stemmed from the design of their boats, which were far in advance of any built elsewhere in Europe at the time: clinker-built (i.e., with overlapping planks), strong, light, fast and easily manoeuvrable. Their seaworthiness must have been a revelation, as must have been the fearlessness of the sailors. It is hardly too much to assert that it was Viking influence which made of the Scots a sea-going nation, and well into the 19th century Shetlanders were still building their 'sixareens' to the old Scandinavian design.

Another major 8th-century event influenced 'piscanata Scotia': the emergence of Roman Catholicism. Celtic Christianity had tolerated pagan beliefs in the divinity of the sea and its inhabitants, but the Romans, their roots still firmly in the cultural soil of Mediterranean lands, had no such sympathy. To them the sea was a source of food endorsed by Christ himself, and fish the chief permitted protein during Lent and other periods of abstinence.

More than half the days in the Roman Church calendar were officially meatless, and almost every monastery had its specially built fishpond; not surprisingly, commercial fishing soon became both necessary and profitable.

One big problem faced medieval fishermen, whether line-fishing off shore for saithe, codling, or haddock; or netting salmon, or going into deeper waters for ling, cod, mackerel, and herring: whatever the catch, it was highly perishable. Various short-term solutions had been devised, such as smoking or pickling. (Salmon, whose abundance early marked it as a natural resource for export, was treated in both these ways; salmon-curing was an important industry as early as the 13th century, continuing even during the worst years of aggression between Scotland and England.)

For certain kinds of fish, such as cod, whiting and haddock, a longer-term solution had been discovered: drying them in wind or sun. In this form they were a useful substitute for bread, in areas where the cereal crop was inadequate, for example in Shetland. But oily fish like mackerel and herring could not be treated thus. A further difficulty lay in the primitive condition of transport and roads. Clearly, if the fish were to reach any kind of market, it had somehow to be turned from a perishable commodity into a non-perishable one. It was largely this problem which for so long restricted the industry to the status of a localized, seasonal fragmented enterprise.

The man who, in the 14th century, is reputed to have discovered a solution was not a Scot, but a Dutchman, William Beukelsz (though some claim he stole the idea from the small Scots village of Crail). He hit on three vital points in the preservation of fish. First, absolute freshness; second, the fish should be packed to exclude as much air as possible; third, no liquid should be added. The moment the nets were hauled aboard the fish were gutted and rinsed. Then they were layered in barrels, bellies downwards, at an angle of about 45°. Between and around each layer was placed a large quantity of coarse salt.

It was not long before the implications of the discovery became apparent. The Dutch parliament, with that mixture of prudence and far-sightedness so characteristic of the nation, began passing laws regulating every aspect of the herring-fishing – the areas, the dates between which it might take place, the size of mesh in the nets, the quantity and quality of salt used, the method of packing and draining the barrels. The way for a Dutch monopoly of the herring trade lay clear ahead, and merchants and skippers hastened to follow the signs. By the time other countries awoke to the fortunes being made, they were chagrined to find themselves too late to do more than pick up the small change.

Nevertheless, Scotland, like France and England, made desperate attempts to establish her right to the fish in the waters at her doorstep. As early as 1493 James IV, bitterly conscious of 'ye greit innumerable ryches' swimming into Dutch nets, passed an Act designed to increase the size of the fishing fleet. All towns and burghs were to build busses (i.e., two-masted ships of Dutch design, specially suited to fishing for herring) of at least 20 tons, and to supply them with mariners, nets and equipment 'for ye taking of greit fische and small'. Officials of the burghs were to make 'all ye stark idill men within their bounds to pass within the said Schippes for their wages', under threat of banishment from the burgh. (Obviously James intended to kill two birds with one stone, nor was he the last to try to deal with unemployment in this manner. Queen Anne's parliament of 1705 also saw in the fishing industry 'not only a natural and certain fund to advance trade but also a true and ready way to breed seamen and set many poor and idle people to work'.)

But although anxious to procure some of the silver harvest for his own country, James seems not to have felt unduly threatened by the Dutch. The provinces were still a small dependent part of the great Spanish Empire; moreover, foreigners fishing in Scots waters were only permitted to do so under licences which were themselves a source of revenue. In 1494, therefore, the king granted permits to Dutch fishermen allowing them to fish *outside* a line 28 miles distant from the shore of the Isle of Lewis. Within that line lay a particularly lucrative area, a fact of which the Dutch were conscious – so much so that in order to gain a footing they offered to buy one of the smaller islands. James's refusal appears not to have damped their ambition; they simply trespassed, disregarding the terms of their licences and encroaching so much upon the rights of the locals that the latter eventually complained to the king.

There was, it seemed, little to be done. The Dutch had taken to protecting themselves with men-of-war, and short of open battle it was almost impossible to keep them out of Scottish waters. After James's death at Flodden they did not even trouble to pay for licences. By the 1540s, extreme hostility existed between the two fleets; the Scots could expect no protection from a government preoccupied with the serious problems of internal policy, succession to the throne, and continual English harassment. Thereafter, with impunity the Dutch fished in their waters, cut their nets, offered violence to their persons, and – crowning insult – boarded their ships and made off with whatever barrels of herring they *had* managed to amass.

Then, early in the 1580s, after long negotiation, James VI and the Dutch commissioners signed what was to be the first of many treaties. The Dutch promised that if their fishermen worked in Scottish waters, they would not fish 'within sight of the shoar, nor into any of the loughs nor in the seas betwixt the islands'.

James was well aware, like his great-grandfather, of the importance of a strong fishing industry, and was determined to control the territorial rights of the nation. Accordingly when he succeeded to the English throne in 1603, he lost little time in announcing to all foreigners that if they wished to fish in Scottish waters, they must apply in Edinburgh for the appropriate licence; those who wanted to work off the English coast must seek a permit in London. Predictably the Dutch alternately advanced good reasons why they need not pay the tax, or simply refused to do so, and during the major part of James's reign a state of armed truce existed as before between the two fleets.

A pamphlet by an Englishman, Tobias Gentleman, entitled, 'England's Way to Win Wealth', put the British point of view. Published in 1614, it begins by describing the composition and behaviour of the Dutch fleet when it fished in Scottish waters. There were more than 600 'great Busses', the biggest manned by twenty-four sailors, the small ones having sixteen to a crew. Gentleman estimated the total number of men at over 20,000, and said that as many as 40 men-of-war had been seen guarding the fleet.

Generally the fishing for herring began on St John's day, June 24th, off Shetland, but it was the custom for the ships to arrive early and put into Bressay Sound, whence the crews went ashore.

There they frolic it on land, until that they have sucked out all the marrow of the malt and good Scotch ale, which is the best liquor that the island doth afford.

But the moment the season opened, the junketing ended. The Dutch had obviously developed an early version of the factory ship, for the busses never left the area while work was in progress. Special ships brought supplies as needed – of men, food, barrels, salt and nets – and took away the cured herring for export to the countries of the Baltic and France.

Besides the herring fishing, there was also an all-year contingent of Dutch boats looking in Scottish waters for cod and ling. The former were to be dried, the latter split and salted, when, Gentleman tells us, they sold for four or five pounds per hundred – adding bitterly that they were called Holland lings, 'but they are taken out of His Majesty's seas, and were Shetland lings before they took them there.'

But there was ambivalence in Shetland on the whole subject of the Dutch. If they monopolized the sea, they undoubtedly also brought in revenue during their holiday periods, buying quantities of food and hand-knitted stockings. Yet the 'frolicking' had its less advantageous aspects. A list of grievances drawn up in 1618 makes many complaints: the fishermen chased and killed sheep, cut down timber for firewood, and 'spoiled pasturage by cutting their initials in it'; they enticed and sometimes forced the ablest men in the community to their service, broke down the seats in the Kirk, and injured the little Shetland ponies by trying to mount several stalwart Dutchmen at a time on each one.

It was all extremely unsatisfactory. In the opinion of many of James's advisers, what was needed for the entire British industry was a body representing all the fishermen, capable of organizing the fleets as the Dutch were organized, exerting judicial, fiscal, and financial power over its members, and responsible for a coordinated scheme of fishing, processing, and exporting. James himself was not in favour; to enter into open economic competition with Holland would, he thought, lead inevitably to confrontation and war. It was left to the Scots parliament and a convention of the fishing burghs to draw up a series of regulations for the control of standards in curing and packing, for ensuring discipline on the ships, and for restricting facilities to foreigners. Unfortunately what these bodies could not do, was to inject capital into the industry; nor could they establish a judiciary to deal with interburgh conflicts.

The first attempt at establishing a national body came from James's son, Charles I, who in 1630 sent a letter to the Scots Privy Council informing it of his decision to set up an Association for the Fishing, common to England, Scotland and Ireland. Since the base of the association was likely to be on the island of Lewis, and since the Scots wanted sole rights to the lucrative fishing in that area, a lukewarm response from the burghs was guaranteed. Predictably, they declared that association with England would be 'very inconvenient' and that they themselves were perfectly able to control all fishing within 28 miles of the coastline. They also pointed out that by law the English might not fish in Scottish lochs, nor sell their catch in Scottish burghs. But Charles remained unmoved and in September 1632 the Council approved his Charter. On Lewis, land was bought, buildings were erected, curing stations set up.

That Charles had the Association's welfare very much at heart can be seen by the measures he took on its behalf. He reintroduced Lenten observance, for instance, to increase the consumption of fish. He prohibited all importation of fish caught from foreign ships. He even undertook to buy food and stores for the Royal Navy from the Association.

Yet, in spite of all effort, by 1639 the Association was over £4000 in debt and had shown itself to be both corrupt and impotent. Charles's own troubles after that year, and the subsequent civil wars, effectively killed what remained of the venture. The naval war between Britain and Holland kept both fishing fleets in harbour for over two years, but when they once more put to sea it was clear that nothing had changed. By the time of the Restoration in 1660, British fishing generally was in a very poor state.

The efforts of Charles II to revive the Association in England failed due to lack of money; and the Royal Company for the Fishery of Scotland, established in 1670, also collapsed, partly because of the old hostility to government control but also because of the renewal of the Dutch wars. It was dissolved by an Act of Parliament in 1690.

In many ways the 17th century had been a particularly bad one for Scotland, with civil war and religious disturbances adding to the chaos and distress brought about by bad harvests, plague and repeated famines. Economically, it was one of the worst periods in the country's history. There was no money and, what was worse, a total loss of confidence prevailed. No longer was there any question of making the Scottish fishing fleet economically competitive with the Dutch, or indeed with any other. No capital existed to build and equip the large boats which would have been needed, nor to establish curing stations, nor even to import the right quality of salt for curing. (The salt question was in fact a very vexed one, for Scots salt was unsuitable; but imported salt was heavily taxed. Although the duty was lifted on salt for curing fish for export, the exemption was so hedged about with regulations and expensive permits, that any theoretical benefit evaporated in the process of claiming the exemption.)

Ironically, meanwhile, the quantity of fish in the sea appeared almost inexhaustible. There was already a saying that Amsterdam was built on a foundation of Scots herring-bones, yet the herring continued in their millions to throng Scottish waters. Daniel Defoe, who toured the country in 1705, was an amazed witness of the bounty that could be reaped from these northern seas. At Queensferry, on the Firth of Forth, he saw a fleet of between 700 and 800 Dutch busses come in, laden with herring – but Scots boats too, he was told, were making good hauls all the way up the coast as far as Aberdeen. Yet still 'the water of the Firth was so full of fish, that . . . in a little Norway yawl, or boat, row'd by two boys, the boys toss'd the fish out of the water into the boat with their naked hands only'. At Aberdeen, the herring-fishing 'is like the Indies at their door'. Off the Pentland Firth, 'you would have ventured to say of

the sea ... that it was one third water and two thirds fish; the
operation of taking them could hardly be call'd fishing, for they
did little more than dip for them into the water and take them up.'
In Glasgow, he thought they cured the herring superbly, so expertly
that a Glasgow herring was reckoned to be as good as a Dutch one,
and superior to anything produced in England.

Only in Kirkcudbright was Defoe's report less enthusiastic, and
it is worth quoting because it depicts so clearly the native poverty
which has always hampered the Scots:

Here is a pleasant situation, and yet nothing pleasant to be seen. Here is
a harbour without ships, a port without trade, a fishery without nets, a
people without business; ... though here is an extraordinary salmon
fishing, the salmon come and offer themselves, and go again, and cannot
obtain the privilege of being made useful to mankind; for they take very
few of them. They have also white fish, but cure none; and herrings,
but pickle none ... the reason ... is poverty; no money to build vessels,
hire seamen, buy nets and materials for fishing, to cure the fish when it
is catch'd or to carry it to the market when it is cur'd.

Kirkcudbright lies far to the south of the main west coast fishing
regions, but Defoe's observation encapsulates pretty well the condition of much of the west coast area, and highlights the differences
between west and east.

It would be a mistake to think of the Scottish fishing industry at
any time before our own day as forming a single unit. For reasons
of geography, social pressures, and marine biology, it has always
been fragmented into several small industries, each with its distinctive characteristics. Roughly speaking, at the beginning of the 18th
century the east coast villages constituted one unit, the north and
north-west down to the Mull of Kintyre another, Shetland and the
northern isles a third, the Firth of Clyde and associated lochs a
fourth, and the south-west, including Kirkcudbright, a fifth.

The villages of the east, some dating back to the 13th and 14th
centuries, stretched like a string of beads along the open, smoothly
curving coastline, whose configuration imposed its own limitations,
offering scant shelter and very few natural harbours. Here, most of
the fishing was offshore by line, from small boats which could,

more or less conveniently, be dragged high up the beaches to escape the lashing waves of a frequently violent sea. Haddock, whiting, codling, and turbot constituted the bulk of the catch, much of it sold fresh (especially in the south where Edinburgh provided an eager market); but some was also cured to local taste, for example Findon haddocks, which even at that early date were becoming well known.

Some east coast burghs had also a herring fleet. The most important was at Crail on the coast of Fife, from which until the mid-18th century hundreds of boats went out each year, the cost of the gear being often met by local landsmen in return for a proportion of the catch. But the activities of the Dutch fleet, and perhaps also a certain amount of over-fishing, caused a gradual falling-off of the industry; by the end of the century it had a negligible economic value, most of the fishermen being forced back to the traditional offshore grounds for white fish.

Fishing communities on the east coast differed from the others. Their chief characteristic was the peculiar isolation in which they functioned, communicating only at commercial level with the dwellers in the hinterland. It was a trait so marked as to give rise to many stories of the fishermen being descended from foreigners – Vikings, perhaps, or Dutchmen – stories which probably have little truth.

The real root of this isolation lay in the extremely close-knit structure of the families as a result of professional needs. The men, naturally, did the fishing, going out in their cobles whenever the weather allowed throughout the year, but returning home each evening. Their wives had many tasks, of which the chief was selling the catch. In many cases this meant walking with a heavy creel on their backs twelve or fifteen miles to the nearest town and back again. The women also set the price of the fish, and generally managed family finances. In addition, they baited the lines each day (a matter of from 500 to 3000 hooks), carried them to and from the boats, and hung out those not in use to dry. They also cured fish, knitted the family's stockings and jerseys and, in many villages, helped launch and bring in the boats and carried their husbands out to them pick-a-back – not a subservient action but a very practical one where men faced hours of work in open boats in often icy weather.

Children played their part too. Even seven-year-olds could collect bait and prepare it for the hooks. Older children took on much of the responsibility of feeding and caring for the family, and four- and five-year-olds had the task of watching over the very little ones.

At fourteen, boys accompanied their fathers to sea. By the age of eighteen or so they were fully trained fishermen, but earning a smaller share of the profits than the other members of the crew, for without a wife to bait his hooks and sell his catch a man could not take the same weight of responsibility in the coble as the others. Thus, the pressure was there to marry early, and to choose a girl already familiar with the work expected of her. Almost invariably, therefore, boys chose wives from their own or a neighbouring village.

Not surprisingly under these circumstances east coast fishermen felt themselves very much apart from farmers and peasants. Even in towns they lived in exclusive, ghetto-like enclaves, with their own customs, traditions, even, to some extent, their own language.

The rocky, indented coastline of Caithness, Sutherland, and the north-west provided very different conditions. Here, there were widely scattered, sparsely populated settlements huddling wherever an open beach backed onto a little arable land, for every family tried to live from farming as well as fishing. Poverty was the norm – poverty of the sour, rocky soil which responded so passively to a man's best efforts, poverty of the people who could only afford the smallest and frailest of boats and the most primitive gear. Not for them the work of the busses, trawling in the Minches or the open sea, nor the regular if meagre living of the east coasters. Single ownership of even a small boat was beyond anyone's means, so families combined to pay for boat and gear, hoping to recoup by a proportionate division of the catch or profit therefrom.

The insecurity did not end there. The only fish of commercial value within their reach was the herring, yet, dependent though these people were on the arrival of herring in their own particular loch, they had no means of preparing for a good year. In some years the lochs remained barren, denying them any chance of a catch at all, at other times they were almost solid silver as the fish shoaled for days or weeks on end; but without the requisite barrels, salt, and means of transport, the fishermen were helpless. Furthermore, their landlords customarily claimed a share of any catch or profit, often enough without contributing to the purchase of gear or curing materials. It was a desperate position, and one which through the years was aggravated as the shift from crofting to sheep in the Highlands forced more people onto the narrow coastal strips of arable land.

In Shetland, the industry was different again. Here, as in other areas of Viking settlement, there was a combination of farming and fishing, but the emphasis was definitely on the latter. The difference is illustrated in the old remark about Orkney and Shetland, that whereas Orcadians were farmers with boats, Shetlanders were fishermen with a bit of land. Eighteenth-century Orcadians fished almost exclusively for domestic purposes, while Shetlanders maintained the traditions of a much earlier period, and engaged in intensive commercial, if seasonal, fishing, locally for saithe, cod and haddock, further afield for larger cod and ling. Some of the catch was dried and, as we have noted, formed part of the staple winter and spring diet of the region. There was also, even then, a substantial demand for fish-liver oil. But the most important industry was the 'haaf' – deep-sea fishing for cod and ling, but especially the latter.

It was for the haaf that the famous Norse-design fishing boats were used. There were two types, differing only in size: open boats with a small sail, but designed to move mostly by the power of oars. A crew of six was needed for the 'sixareen', in which – incredibly – journeys of 30 or 40 miles were undertaken, west of the islands out into the open sea. The 'fourareen', with only four oarsmen, was used for shorter trips to the east of Shetland.

Haaf fishing was carried on during the summer months, from May to August, and to read today of the endurance of the crews calls up all one's sense of awe. Not only did they row for eight or ten hours at a stretch to reach the fishing-grounds but, once there, they baited their lines, then shot them, hauling them in again after two or three hours, and immediately removing the catch, cleaning and beheading it. Then the whole process was repeated once or twice more, each cycle lasting six to eight hours. Finally came the long row back to the curing station, the boat now heavily laden. The stations, by deliberate policy, were often some distance away from the men's own villages, for the whole operation was controlled and organized, not by the fishermen themselves, but by the landlords or tacksmen of the estate on which they were tenants. Stone huts served as temporary accommodation for both fishers and curing staff (another group of tenants).

Curing was by a combination of pickling in salt and drying in the sun, a lengthy process but a highly profitable one, for dried ling became, during the late 18th century, a major export, especially to Germany and Spain. Here again the landlords took charge of the marketing, for they alone had capital to pay for vessels and agents. At the end of the season, each crew's total catch was computed, and the men returned home with their share of the profit.

If profits from fishing were everywhere problematic and sometimes non-existent, perhaps it was in the Firth of Clyde region that the most prosperous fishermen of the 18th century were to be found, for the area's special fortune was in having both fish and market on the doorstep. Loch Fyne, the most westerly of the lochs sheltered by the Mull of Kintyre, was also the most productive of herring on the whole of the west coast, and only rarely did the fish fail. Glasgow and the surrounding towns provided an excellent local market, but there was also a brisk movement of fish down the west coast of England to Manchester, and also to London.

As elsewhere enterprises were almost always co-operative, but the rewards were less certain and could involve far less outside capital. It was here that there seemed to be, to those most concerned for the future prosperity of the country, real potential for independent development.

The fifth region comprised the southern part of Dumfries and the extensive Galloway coastline, on the shore of the Solway Firth. At Stranraer, not only was there a local herring fishery but also many boats went north to join in the Loch Fyne season. Elsewhere, however, commercial activity was more spasmodic and localized than might have been expected. As Defoe suggests, poverty was partly to blame, but also the muddy estuaries of the larger rivers, and the notoriously treacherous conditions present in the North

Channel, discouraged fishing in a region where the land was fertile and cattle were the main interest. The major exception was salmon fishing, and though Defoe had seen the salmon begging to 'obtain the privilege of being made useful to mankind', by the end of the 18th century Kirkcudbright had three salmon fisheries, each let for about £400 per annum. The haaf net at the river mouth was the principal method used – as it is today – and with waiting markets at Manchester, Liverpool, Whitehaven and London it could not fail to be lucrative; though, as Scott reminds us in *Redgauntlet*, leister fishers were often in fierce and embattled competition with the haaf-netters.

Further east, along the stretch of shore from the mouth of the Nith to Gretna, the fishing off shore was again reasonably good, and of great variety. Salmon trout, flounders, sturgeon, skate (the people of Edinburgh had a passion for skate), cod and herring all contributed a minor but still significant share to the county's economy.

Defoe's mission had been to examine and report on the economic condition of Scotland, before the passing of the Act of Union in 1707. It has been praised and criticized with equal vigour; but whatever one's opinion it did, undeniably, have dramatic consequences for Scotland, though these showed themselves but slowly.

It is tempting to telescope all subsequent events of the 18th century, to see them as a series of rapid developments – Improvement and Enlightenment sweeping across the country like any wind of change; but wind is always strongest on the mountain, and the movements which gusted and eddied round the prominent people of the day took a long time to reach the still, deep valleys where the populace lived. Before that could happen, there had to be a change of climate, and it was this which, affecting all aspects from agriculture to education, from fisheries to philosophy, is the most truly significant event of the 18th century.

The first action of the new Parliament to concern fishing directly was not particularly promising. The year 1727 saw yet another governmental attempt to inject economic life into the fisheries, with the inauguration of the Commissioners and Trustees for Improveing Fisherys and Manufactures in Scotland. Naturally, the Board of Trustees, as it became known, was unable to solve the multiple problems with which it was immediately confronted. But as an advisory body (though with some financial power) rather than a group of shareholders, it was able to maintain some momentum, though it was frustrated in its attempts to revitalize fishing. Within twenty years, both the effort and money expended on that part of its charge had been drastically reduced but it was eventually to be given new life in 1807 when it became the Fisheries Board for Scotland.

More influential, though short-lived, was the Society of the Free British Fishery, founded in 1749. By 1750 it had bought two large vessels, equipped them with Dutch nets, enticed a number of Dutchmen on board to join the crews, and sent them to Scotland, where a promising beginning soon petered out in the usual conclusion of inefficiency, debts, and bankruptcy. Like its predecessors, the Society had underestimated the amount of on-the-spot organization and ready capital needed, and like them it foundered. But traces of the Act which had sponsored it survived, notably in the implementation of a bounty system which, by its very inadequacies and shortcomings, succeeded in arousing interest in the herring fishing as never before.

The system was aimed specifically at the white herring trade, that is, the part of the industry which caught and pickled herrings for export; it was closely based on the Dutch model though the Dutch awarded no bounties. To qualify, boats had to be over 20 tons, and had to fish for herring, and only herring, within designated dates. They might only set out from, and return to, certain ports. In fact, for people with small boats and no capital behind them, these rules were impossibly demanding. Almost none of the boats in the north-west and north were eligible because they were too small. The designated ports were far from the fishing grounds and from the fishermen's homes, involving them in additional expense they could not afford. To add insult to injury, since the busses which were eligible for the bounty were too large to fish in the lochs, they took to dropping anchor at the entrances and lowering small boats to do the actual fishing, the crews driving the locals from the best parts of the water, destroying their nets, and even maltreating them. Furthermore, the embargo on line-fishing during the herring season put great strain on crews whose very survival depended on being able to catch whatever was in the water when they went out.

Arguably, the general effect of the scheme was deleterious. It encouraged the investment of capital, but promoted also the exploitation of the poorest in the trade. More and more, entrepreneurs among landlords, tacksmen and merchants saw the possibility of enriching themselves through the dependence of the fishermen on their capital for boats, gear, pickling materials, and transport to the markets. In addition, reliance on the bounty prevented the growth of an independent, self-financing industry.

On the positive side, whereas before there had often been little or no market for good catches in the more remote lochs, now the fish could usually be sold; if only a minority benefited immediately, the industry itself was developing in readiness to supplement and eventually supplant the activities of the Dutch.

The controversy aroused by the bounty scheme was symptomatic of the prevalent concern and interest in the fishing industry, at a time when Scots were beginning to see their country in a wider context, and to realize how far behind other European nations it now was economically. With fishery as with agriculture, pamphlet after pamphlet and book after book streamed from the presses, advising, exhorting, condemning, encouraging. Some were materially Gentleman's work brought up to date; the title of one, *An exact and authentic Account of the greatest White-Herring Fishery in Scotland, carried on early in the Island of Zetland, by the Dutch only*, says it all. Or almost all: amid so much repetition of the complaints against the Dutch, it is pleasing to see that the Shetlanders had in the interval between the two pamphlets learnt to defend by attacking, at least in the matter of the Shetland ponies.

There is no Horse-hire demanded here, unless it be in the Summer, when the *Dutch* are upon the Coast; during that Time, some of the Country People bring in their Horses for the *Dutchmen* to ride, and I must own, that if they were not better Sailors than Riders, I would not chuse to venture my Life so far as *Gravesend* in one of their best Bottoms. There is a Spot of Ground above the Town, about a Quarter of a Mile in Length, and pretty even Ground, which is very rare in *Zetland*; here the Countryman comes with his Horse, enquiring, in *Dutch*, who will ride; immediately comes a clumsy *Dutchman*, gives him a Dublekee [that is

Twopence] then up he mounts; the Owner of the Horse immediately falls a beating the Creature, and pricks its Tail with the Point of his Stick; then, behold! in an Instant, down comes the *Dutchman*; up he gets again, and mounts afresh, but before he gets on a second Time, there must be a second Dublekee, and he is scarce up before he is down again; so that the Fellow often makes a Shilling of the *Dutchman* before he comes to the End of the Place . . .

Improbably, it was a London bookseller with the unlikely name of John Knox who in the next generation was to set things in motion for real reform. Knox travelled quite extensively in the Highlands from the 1760s and was horrified by the poverty, deprivation and apathy he saw there. His first book, *A view of the British Empire, more especially Scotland*, came out in 1784, and immediately ran into three editions. He had an exceptionally clear and common-sense approach to what had by now become a most serious social problem, for the effect of the Clearances on the west coast population was all too evident. The American War of Independence had aggravated the situation by causing a rise in the prices of materials used in shipping, and reducing the number of able-bodied men free to join the fishing fleet.

Knox saw that the most urgent task was the construction of fishing villages and towns with good harbours and curing stations, on the west and north coasts. Furthermore, he revived the idea of two canals, one cutting 85 miles from the journey from the Clyde to the Sound of Jura, the other creating a waterway right across Scotland at its narrowest point, eliminating a 400-mile tour round the north of the country and the hazards of the Pentland Firth. James Watt had already surveyed what was to become the Caledonian Canal, but Knox's suggestions, coupled with the practicality of his other proposals, stressed the urgency of the matter.

By 1785, the year following publication of his book, a Parliamentary Committee had been set up. It acted quickly and efficiently, hearing evidence from Knox and others, and making immediate recommendations, so that in 1786 two Acts concerning the fisheries were passed. The first provided for the incorporation of still another Society, the British Society for extending the Fisheries and Improving the Sea Coasts of this Kingdom; the second attempted to improve the bounty scheme by giving more emphasis to the quantity of fish caught, and also by rewarding the catches of boats previously ineligible.

Narrowly indeed did the new Fisheries Society escape the fate of all its predecessors. That it did, was due in very large part to a stroke of good fortune: the Napoleonic Wars virtually wiped out the Dutch fleet, taking from Holland for ever the monopoly of East European trade. But credit must be given, also, to the concrete and practical proposals in the Society's charter, which adopted Knox's views on the building of 'free towns, villages, harbours, quays, piers, and fishing stations'. (The towns of Ullapool and Tobermory owe their foundation to the Society, and although ultimately only Ullapool was to survive as a fishing community, a number of small villages, promoted by local landowners caught up in the new crusade of social reform, did become viable.) Finally, by what has to be described as an Act of God, concurrent with the new enthusiasm and determination to spend money on the industry, came a succession of good herring seasons off the east coast. Where the Dutch, in former years, would have swept the sea clean, the Scots were in a position to respond.

Nevertheless, by no principle of Divine Succession was it certain that Scots wares would sell, in countries educated over generations into a taste for the Dutch product. The existing markets for Scottish herring, the West Indies (where planters bought them for their slaves), Ireland, and at home, were in each case looking for a cheap, nourishing food. In the Baltic countries, by contrast, Dutch herring was a delicacy, selling to the rich and self-indulgent; only fish cured to the very highest standards would be accepted as a substitute.

Realizing this, Parliament reanimated the Board of Trustees, giving it the new title of the Fisheries Board, in 1807, and immediately an attempt was made to establish a system of controls, identifying three crucial areas: the condition of the fish when caught, the speed and efficiency with which it was gutted, graded, and packed, and the rapidity with which the barrels could be shipped to their destination. The first two matters were dealt with by appointing Fishery Officers with power to inspect at random and to put the Board's own brand on those barrels fulfilling its stringent requirements.

The third involved the whole question of harbours and ports, and progress was slow, spanning the whole of the 19th century. Trying to disperse its money equitably, the Board was for a long time reluctant to invest large funds in any one new scheme, apart from the construction of Ullapool, Tobermory, and Lochbay on Skye. Consequently a great many small villages received inadequate assistance and the bulk of the grant was channelled to improve existing and already active harbours, such as Wick, Peterhead, Fraserburgh and Aberdeen. Sporadic developments, particularly along the east coast, did however occur, some sponsored by the Board and the rest by private individuals. Off the Moray Firth, Burghhead, Lossiemouth, Buckie and Macduff became significant though minor centres for the herring fleet; from Fraserburgh to Arbroath a number of harbours were built, at villages including Stonehaven, Montrose, and Arbroath itself; on the coast of Fife working harbours clustered closely together – Crail, Anstruther, Pittenweem, St Monance, Buckhaven – some of ancient foundation but now given new impetus. South of Edinburgh, North Berwick, Dunbar, St Abbs, and Eyemouth had all acquired artificial harbours by the 1870s. Ironically, by this time there was no longer a summer herring fishery in the area.

All through the century European demand for Scots white herring remained high, boosted by the establishment of railway networks in Germany, Russia, and the other countries of the Baltic. Norway was a serious competitor, but only at the cheaper end of the market. The Dutch, when they rebuilt their fleet, were never able to regain their monopoly. Their prices were now too high for all but the most exclusive trade, and the Scots were able to increase continental exports year by year, until by the 1880s almost all their barrelled fish went to the Baltic.

On the west coast, entrepreneurial enterprise continued to dominate. It could not be otherwise, given the long history of dependence by fishermen on the capital of a few individuals. The author J. MacDougall Hay has given us, in his novel *Gillespie*, set in the 1860s, a vivid and astonishingly accurate picture of conditions, where whole communities could be trapped into virtual slavery by unscrupulous men. The book's eponymous central character (hero he is not) is consumed by rare and single-minded greed. If in real life few people are so villainously grasping, Gillespie is credible because he is so powerfully drawn – and if no single person actually committed so many acts of atrocious callousness, many individual cases of such ruthlessness are certainly recorded.

The story begins at the time when west coast herring were caught by drift-nets – ring-nets (trawl-nets) being illegal. But Gillespie foresees a change, and his ultimate ambition is described early in the book:

Gillespie had scrutinized the fishermen. Chance crews were already secretly 'trawling'; he saw that the revolution of today was the convention of tomorrow: foresaw the fishing fleet of a hundred boats engaged, within the next few years, at their legitimate business in the seas of 'trawling'. At present these crews of some five hundred men were supplied with gear and provisions from impecunious small traders. His plan was to kill off those piffling merchants; build a large curing shed; a shed for 'smoking' herring; another for storing salt in great quantities; a store for housing fishing gear – nets, oil, ropes, varnish, tar and the like; a barking house; and especially to open a big shop in the square that would supply the whole fleet . . .

Three things prevented the immediate operation of Gillespie's plan: the present illegality of trawling; the want of suitable premises in the Square of Brieston; and especially the lack of capital.

Gillespie eventually acquires his shop. By calculated acts of generosity he attracts the custom of the fishermen and their wives. He allows them credit, and they are grateful. Then he begins to set the trap:

From time immemorial they had used the drift-net: but while he was in Muirhead Gillespie saw that the day of the trawl-net was coming. It was the transition period. Government declared trawling to be illegal, and sent a cruiser to patrol the Loch. The Brieston men were the chief culprits. Drift-net work was tedious. They had to hang by the drift-net all night and 'shot it' on the chance of getting herring. With the trawl-net it was different. They watched for signs of fish. The single 'plout' of a herring would sometimes reveal a whole school of fish, and at once the trawl was out between two 'company' boats, and in again within two hours with sufficient fish in the bag of the net to fill half-a-dozen boats . . .

. . . anything up to two hundred boxes at a pound sterling a box might be had within a couple of hours. Not infrequently the Fishery Cruiser caught them in the act . . . Was Gillespie not a benefactor? He supplied the trawls. It was only in reason, as the men were bound to recognize, that he raised the price of trawl-nets gradually – £35, £40, £45, £50. Look at the risk he was taking. He was liable to fine and imprisonment like themselves at Ardmarkie.

Nowhere, perhaps, are the hazards for both fishermen and buyers described more tellingly than in the next few pages:

Especially he watched the methods of the herring buyers. These were two. Either out on the Loch in smacks which, when a full cargo was taken aboard, set sail for Glasgow. If there was no prospect of wind they offered a low price for the herring because of the risk of transport. On Saturday mornings the smacksmen refused to buy at all. Other buyers waited on the quays to which those fishermen came who found no markets among the smacks. On the days of a 'big fishing' the fishermen had sometimes to throw whole skiff-loads into the Harbour for want of a market . . .

He studied the flow and ebb of the Glasgow Fish Market, and keenly watched the Baltic ports as a haven for salt herring. He discovered that Manchester and Liverpool would take unlimited supplies of fresh herring packed in ice. And he waited patiently. No one knew that he had leased from the Laird the long row of stores and curing-sheds stretching along the shore road from the Quay. On a June morning of perfect calm, when ducks were swimming about in the Harbour, a skiff was seen coming in at the Perch, deep to the gunwales. The men on the beams were sitting on herring as they rowed. She was followed by a second, a third, a fourth, and a fifth, under clouds of gulls. The smacksmen had refused to buy. The half-dozen buyers on the Quay were in a flutter; running about like hens, sharing their empty stock. They bought some seventy boxes between them. There yet remained four and a half boats of herring. The fishermen were now offering these at any price – instead of being offered at five shillings a box, four shillings, three, two, one. Standing on the Quay and looking down upon these fishermen in their loaded boats, one caught a look of pathos upon their rugged faces, tawny with sweat threshed out of them in a fifteen-mile pull in the teeth of the tide. Their tired eyes were grey like the sea, their blue shirts with short oilskin sleeves were laced with herring scales; and herring scales smeared the big fishing boots which come up over the knee . . . The dotard buyers shook their heads . . . One of them, in slippers, with a narrow face and rheumy eyes, gave a doleful shake of his head. 'No use, boys. It's the big market for them.' The 'big market' was the sea.

This, of course, is Gillespie's moment. He buys all the fish at a shilling a box, producing the boxes acquired over the years of patient waiting and kept in store. The men, awed and grateful for his miraculous intervention are only too willing to help in the next move: a huge tarpaulin is spread out in the Square, and the boxes of fish brought up.

Cran basket after cran basket was carried up the stone steps and poured out on the tarpaulin. Gillespie and Sandy the Fox stood, each at one end of the growing pile, with a shallow tin plate in his left hand, with which he scooped up salt from a barrel, drew his right hand across the salt, and hailed it down on the fresh fish, as a sower sows seeds.

When all is done, there remains the question of transport. Naturally, Gillespie has the answer. He charters the 'puffer' which has just discharged a cargo of coal – becoming the first man in the town to use steam for transporting fish – and sends two telegrams, one to a Manchester firm advising the dispatch of 330 barrels herrings in salt, the other to a merchant in Glasgow: 'Sending 645 boxes large herrings by special steamer; arrive night.' His fish, he knows, will be first in the market next day.

From this moment the fishermen are in Gillespie's pocket; he commands all their catch, not only the chancy herring but also the much steadier supplies of white fish – cod, ling, eel, skate, whiting. Thus, when trawling is legitimized, he is the man from whom they buy their nets. When bad seasons come, they turn to him for help. But now, of course, he moves in for the kill. He can give them no credit, he says; he would gladly help them, but he cannot. He will only consent to advance food and supplies – against a mortgage of boats and gear. And so it goes on.

This theme of the fishery is only the most powerful among several in this very fine novel, which perhaps has not received the attention it has deserved since it was first published in 1914. Quite apart from its literary merit, it should be read by anyone who wants to know the ins and outs of the west coast herring fishery in the 19th century.

If advances were most spectacular in the herring industry, substantial progress was also made in other branches of the trade. Britain's maritime successes at the beginning of the century consolidated the markets of the West Indies, where dried white fish took over from herring. Dried fish was also being sold in increasing quantities to Spain and Portugal and, with much of Africa joining the British empire, a huge market opened up for cod and ling.

At home, the effect of better roads, and eventually of railways, was to create increasing demand for fish, especially in the fast-growing towns. Oysters (so plentiful and so cheap in the 18th century that they were consumed by the hundreds at oyster-and-porter parties in the taverns of Edinburgh and Glasgow, and were lavishly used in cooking) could now be sent, packed in ice, all over Britain. Crabs, lobsters, mussels, scallops – plentiful and of superb quality – were as popular as whiting, haddock, and cod among the ever-increasing middle class in London, Liverpool and Leicester. Side by side with the growing sophistication of packing and transport, the fishwives continued their local trade: Scott's Maggie Mucklebackit, haggling over haddocks and whitings, bannock-flukes (turbot) and cock-padles (lump fish), with Jonathan Oldbuck (*The Antiquary*) may stand for all the genre.

For all types of fishing the 1850s to the 1880s were boom years, but most of all for herring, large catches of which were regular and frequent, as well as of good quality. But in 1884 the 'silver darlings', as if to maintain their reputation for unreliability, failed the fishermen. It was not that there were none – they were simply of inferior quality, and proved unsaleable. Curers, merchants, and exporters who had taken out bank loans to invest in more and better gear found themselves in difficulties, aggravated in the following two or three seasons when large catches kept prices low. By 1887, many involved in the trade – shipwrights and coopers as well as fishermen – had been forced out of business.

It was a much smaller fleet which met the return of the top-quality fish in the early 1890s. Again a boom period followed, and this time it lasted right up to the First World War.

The war gave the herring industry a bitter blow from which it never really recovered. Not only was the lucrative German market destroyed, but the revolution in Russia caused a major hold-up in trade as the British Government tried to decide whether or not to recognize the new Bolshevik State. The Norwegians (who had no such qualms) stepped in while the politicians swithered and, until Russia developed her own fisheries, dominated that area of trade.

(Oddly, a slight benefit to the British fishermen was that émigrés took their partiality for pickled herring with them, creating demand in the United States and even, ultimately, in Israel.)

The effects of the Depression which followed chaos after the war hit fishermen particularly hard. Thus must the Dutch have felt a century earlier. There were few ships, no money for investment, and even the markets had changed, with demand disappearing in some parts of the world and other countries competing for what demand survived. There was still plenty of fish, and at home it was still popular, but home consumption had never brought prosperity. In *In Search of Scotland* (1929), H. V. Morton presented a glowing image of abundance at Aberdeen's famous market:

Imagine the Strand from Temple Bar to Charing Cross carpeted with haddock, plaice, soles, whiting, hake, cod, skate, ling, and lobsters, and you have a hazy idea of the thing that happens in Aberdeen every morning of the year.

But from the fishermen's point of view the picture was very different. A new Board – the Herring Industry Board – came into existence. But before it could be effective, it was overtaken by a second world war. Once again the country was left in poverty and chaos and once again the fishermen suffered badly.

Even at home, it almost seemed as if the glorious Scottish privilege of a constant, fresh and varied fish supply had disappeared. In the 1950s and for years thereafter, the whole stock of an average fishmonger in a medium-sized town, drawing on the catches of ten or twenty boats, consisted only of cod, herring (at that time the cheapest and least regarded fish on sale, haddock and whiting, with, in summer, perhaps a little sole or plaice.

And exports? In 1951 dried white fish were still being sent to the West Indies and Africa, but half the herring catch was now being eaten by the population at home – only about five million people.

From this particular gloom the industry seems once again to have emerged. A long period of relative world peace, the increasing cost of other protein foods, and the introduction of new technology have altered its whole aspect. Demand for fish is again world-wide; but deep-sea fishing by British vessels is virtually ended, nearly all countries having established a 200-mile territorial limit within which foreign ships may not work without special permission. The trade in dried white fish has thus been effectively eliminated, since the principal fish involved, cod, is found in greatest number and best condition chiefly in the deep cold waters off Iceland and Greenland. In fact cod, once so common, is now rarely to be seen on the Scottish fishmonger's slab; although Britain consumes 300,000 tons, more than half that amount is imported, and the bulk goes to the frozen food processors and the fish-and-chip shops.

Membership of the European Economic Community has had enormously important consequences. The European Fisheries Convention, adopted in 1964 before Britain's entry, allowed for a six-mile exclusive fishery limit, plus an 'outer belt' within which vessels from other Community countries, like Holland, could claim rights by reason of historic precedent. As may be imagined, Britain was particularly hard hit by this clause, because 60% of the Community's allowable catch comes from British waters (75% of it fished by Scottish boats). On 25th January 1983 a new agreement was reached: most of the 'historic' rights were reduced or eliminated, and in addition quotas were allocated to each country in respect of each of the seven main edible species of fish.

But overfishing remains a problem. Sonar equipment, trawl-nets, and purse seine-nets can work too well and, in the case of herring, their known seasonal migration routes and well-documented diurnal habits have made them too predictable a quarry. Moreover, many skippers from countries whose interest in fish is agricultural, as fertilizer, rather than as food, are consistently unscrupulous, ignoring regulations about size, type and condition of catch. In 1977 the North Sea herring fishery had to be closed, and in 1978 a ban was also imposed on the west coast grounds. Nothing could more convincingly illustrate the precarious nature of the industry than the effect these bans, and delays in reaching agreement on quotas, have had on the market: the fishing grounds are open again, and herring are plentiful once more, but demand in Europe has shrunk so much that were it not for sales to Eastern European factory ships all the fleets would be experiencing heavy losses.

Now Spain has joined the Community. With the largest fishing fleet in Europe, its share of the quota must be substantial and the long-term effect is concerning all involved.

A further major change in the industry has been the advance of freezing technology, which has reached standards unthought of even ten years ago. If fish is caught at its peak condition, and properly frozen immediately, it maintains its high quality to a remarkable degree, and can be, for the consumer, an infinitely better product than the 'fresh' fish she or he used to buy ten or fifteen years ago.

In other ways too, consumers are undoubtedly better off. Traditional species may be harder to find, but some hitherto rejected fish are beginning to change our eating habits, and the variety offered is greater than ever before. The once-despised mackerel supplements the catches of herring, and shoppers can buy John Dory and ling, monkfish and shark, hake and halibut, skate and squid (for many years either thrown back into the sea or exported), mullet, conger eel, sea trout and dogfish. Crabs and mussels are once more almost commonplace, and even scallops and oysters – usually from fish farms – have a respectable presence at the top end of the market. Demand for the latter still exceeds what the farms can produce and it remains to be seen if eagerness on the part of fishermen to cash in on one of the profitable branches of the industry will prematurely exhaust the most accessible wild sources.

Perhaps the most interesting success story as regards change of public attitudes is that of the nephrops, Norway lobster, or langoustine. Until the 1960s, these crustaceans, like the squid, were regarded simply as a nuisance by Scottish fishermen. Then the growing number of British tourists abroad discovered that in Spain and Italy they are considered a delicacy. Demand began at home and now scampi, the status symbol of the gastronomic sophisticate, are on menus good and bad in restaurants all over the country.

Best news of all for the housewife is that fish remains astonishingly cheap. Scotland has always had access to some of the world's best (for it is generally recognized that fish from colder waters have on the whole better flavour and firmer flesh than those from warmer seas). Fish is one of the few remaining foods not fed with fertilizers or hormones, and is still relatively unaffected by pollution, at least in British waters. It is expensive to catch and often difficult to find, yet here it remains within reach of almost everyone's purse. Prices are based on markets in the south of

England, where there is still a certain resistance to fresh fish. It is a situation which is bound to change as people wake up to the excellence of this undervalued food.

There is a sense, of course, in which consumers can never pay for the product at its true value. As Maggie Mucklebackit put it: 'It's no' fish ye're buying: it's men's lives'. This stays true regardless of technological advance; there is no way to guarantee the safety of men who venture on the North Sea or the Atlantic Ocean. Boats are more expensive than ever before, yet they become 'old' after only ten years. Regardless of their age, accidents can happen. They may spring a leak or be driven onto rocks, engines may fail or radio sets go out of action, men may fall overboard or be washed or blown into the sea, or injured by the machinery for hauling in the nets. The risks are probably greatest after a spell of stormy weather, when the men, made impatient by days or weeks at home, go out before the tempest has properly blown itself out. But disaster can come without warning at any time. A hundred years ago, on October 14th 1881, 129 men were lost in a gale – a tragedy which became known as the Eyemouth disaster, and left 73 widows and 263 fatherless children.

In our own decade, during the winter season of 1979–80 the village of Buckie lost sixteen fishermen in eight months, and a further six vanished with their boat in March 1981 – the weather on that occasion being described as ferocious. The early part of 1983 was again a particularly bad period, and newspaper files make dramatic and often tragic reading:

12/1/83. A deckhand was knocked overboard as he tried to unload a net into the hold, and another man collapsed and died after attempting to rescue him.

1/4/83. The crew of the Banff-registered boat *Aquarian*, which sank in heavy seas, was rescued a short time later by the Stornoway fishing boat *Coral Strand*.

18/6/83. The port of Lossiemouth was yesterday mourning the loss of the five men from the *Arcadia* in a wrecking which mirrored in many ways the loss of another local vessel, the *Sapphire*, six years ago. The most cruel parallel was that one woman, who lost her first husband on the *Sapphire*, and who remarried only last year, has been widowed again . . . the boats were wrecked within a few hundred yards of each other

. . . conditions generally at this time of year were better than in winter
. . . it was impossible to say what might have happened.
27/6/83. A lobster fisherman was lost at sea and his boat found washed
ashore north of Arbroath.
27/6/83. Three Stornoway fishermen were winched to safety by an RAF
Sea King helicopter after spending more than an hour clinging to a hatch
cover off the coast of Lewis. Their boat had sprung a leak and sunk.

(All quotations by kind permission of the *Scotsman*)

That was a peculiarly tragic season, but it is well to remember,
when we visit our fishmonger, that no other food costs so little to
buy and so much to harvest.

— RECIPES —

Of all the fish used in traditional Scottish cookery, the herring is
undisputed king. Small and neat, plump yet streamlined, its silver
belly and sides shading to a blue-grey which becomes almost black
along the dorsal fin, on the fishmonger's slab it appears to glow
with life. The flesh, compact and gently fibrous rather than flaky,
is of a delicate creamy-pink which turns creamy-white when
cooked.

When Dorothy Wordsworth and her brother toured Scotland in
1803, they were offered herrings for breakfast at Cairndow, near
Glen Kinglas. They enjoyed them, slightly to their own surprise:

Tuesday, August 30th: Breakfasted before our departure, and ate a
herring fresh from the water, at our landlord's earnest recommendation
– much superior to the herrings we get in the north of England.

Lucky Wordsworths! They were being treated to the best herrings
Scotland can offer, caught in Loch Fyne, still famous today, and so
plump and succulent that they are nicknamed 'Glasgow Magistrates'. Probably they were fried in oatmeal, for the Scots early
discovered the affinity between these two foods which has created
one of the world's great traditional simple dishes. Needless to say
the fish should be fresh-caught, the oatmeal fresh also. Good
quality dripping is traditional, but vegetable oil does perfectly well.
Butter would be an affectation and a waste.

Fried Herring in Oatmeal

> 1 herring per person
> ½ cup (approx.) coarse-ground pinhead oatmeal
> 2 tablespoons dripping or oil

The method is simplicity itself. Having gutted and washed the fish, you can either remove the head and backbone (by pressing gently but firmly all along the spine on the outside) or leave the fish whole. The former saves trouble when eating and gives you double the oatmeal, since the fish will be coated inside and out. On the other hand, leaving bones and head makes for a superlative flavour.

Either way, season with salt and pepper and press all the surfaces gently into a plate of the oatmeal until they are nicely coated. Heat the dripping or oil in a frying pan and cook the fish gently until they are nicely brown on both sides and a knife goes easily through the flesh. Allow about 10 minutes for whole fish and about half that time for fillets.

Steamed potatoes with butter are the usual accompaniment, but home-made brown bread is very good.

Meg Dods gives a delightful variant of this dish:

Fried Herrings as dressed at Inveraray, and the Highland Sea Lochs

The best herrings are obtained in these localities almost alive. Cut off the heads, fins, and tails, scale, gut and wash them. Split and bone them or not, dust the inside with pepper and fine salt. Place two herrings flat together, the backs outmost, and dip in toasted oatmeal and fry them for 7 minutes. Serve hot. They are delicious, and, in the summer, add much to the breakfasts in the steamers on the Clyde, and round all the north-east and west coasts of Scotland.

Herrings, whole or filleted, are excellent baked or grilled. The two recipes which follow both make good supper dishes.

Herrings stuffed with Oatmeal and Anchovies

Anchovies were often used, especially in Victorian times, as stuffing for other fish. When cooked, they melt and almost disappear, leaving only their delectable flavour.

> 4 herrings, cleaned and boned
> 4 fillets of anchovies
> ½ oz (about 1 tablespoon) grated suet
> 3 oz (90–100g) coarse oatmeal
> 2 tablespoons chopped parsley
> a little milk

Mix together the oatmeal, suet and parsley with a little milk. Wash the anchovy fillets to remove excess salt. Lay each fish skin side down, and divide the stuffing equally between them. Put an anchovy on each, then roll up the fish from the head and fasten with cocktail sticks. Put them in a well-fitting buttered ovenproof dish, sprinkle with a little more oatmeal and lay a thin slice of butter on each, then bake in a moderate oven 350° F (180° C) gas 4 for 20 minutes.

Grilled Herrings with mustard

> 4 herrings
> 2 tablespoons finely chopped onion
> 1 tablespoon dry mustard
> ½ tablespoon (approx.) vinegar
> salt and pepper

Clean the fish but leave them whole. Mix the onion and mustard well, and use a little vinegar to bind them. Make deep slits in the sides of the fish, about 3 to each side, and put in as much of the onion mixture as each will hold – any left over can be put inside the fish. Sprinkle the herring with salt and pepper, and lay them on a piece of aluminium foil in the grid of a grill-pan, at least 3 in (8 cm) from the heat. When the skin is brown and bubbling, turn the fish. Allow about 5 minutes for each side. Serve with buttery mashed potatoes.

Staying at the inn at Tarbet, near Arrochar (not to be confused with Tarbert on Loch Fyne), the Wordsworths were troubled by the smell of herrings, which were hung to dry over the kitchen fire. These were not kippers, for kippers were not invented until some 40 years later, by an Englishman, John Woodger, at Seahouses in Northumberland.

Kippers are fine fat herring which are split, cleaned, and thrown into vats of highly concentrated brine, where they lie for a few minutes before being smoke-cured over wood-chips. The Scots, with their usual gift for knowing a good thing when they taste one, must quickly have adopted the idea, and few people now realize its Sassenach origins.

Kippers are now prepared in many places, but the best come from Loch Fyne, from Tarbert, in fact, which was the village taken by John MacDougall Hay as his model for Brieston in *Gillespie*. (But Gillespie was just a little too early to know about them.) They should be a subtle silvery-brown, rather than red, which is a sign of artificial colouring.

They are best cooked by grilling under a fairly strong heat until the backbone begins to lift. They should then be moist and succulent, hardly needing the touch of butter and lemon juice you will add if you are a true epicure.

Kipper pâté is a popular 20th-century dish, and kipper sand-wiches (add a touch of grated onion) make a delightfully substantial snack for hungry folk.

Kipper Pâté

It is difficult to give quantities for this recipe, which is largely a matter of taste and personal judgement.

> 2 kippers
> about 4 oz (125g) melted butter (unsalted)
> salt and black pepper
> lemon juice
> brandy (optional)

Cook the kippers by plunging them into a jar of boiling water and letting them stand for about 10 minutes. Cool them, then remove skin and bones and weigh the flesh. Add an equal quantity of unsalted butter and pound to a paste; or put through the food processor (this makes a very smooth pâté which to my mind slightly lacks interest). Season with ground black pepper and lemon juice to taste, and brandy.

The most popular fish in Scotland today is undoubtedly the haddock – not without reason because haddock from the North Sea is of superlative quality. The Scots have made it peculiarly their own, with many recipes and different methods of preserving it.

At that splendid, now almost defunct institution, 'high tea', haddock was a common main dish, particularly in the genteel teashops of the larger towns. It was always fried in breadcrumbs, and arranged on the plate with symmetrical lettuce leaves, a slice of lemon, and two well-behaved pieces of tomato.

There were, in former days, more exciting things to be done with the fish. Mrs Fraser's *Practice of Cookery, Pastry, Pickling and Preserving* (Edinburgh 1791) has an interesting recipe which can be adapted to modern taste.

To crimp Haddock with a white sauce

Gut and clean 4 large haddocks, stuff them with force-meat, rub them over with the yolk of an egg, and season with a little pepper and salt; strew grated bread and minced parsley over them, and stick pieces of butter on the top. Bake them in an oven, and baste them with their gravy.

For the sauce, set on a pan with 3 mutchkins of water, a pound of veal, two onions, and some parsley. Strain and thicken it with a little butter and flour, adding a glass of white wine, the squeeze of a lemon, and a quarter of a hundred of pickled oysters with a little of their liquor. When the fish are ready and crisp, dish them carefully, pour the sauce about them, and put in browned force-meat balls. Garnish with samphire and sliced lemon. Force-meat: boil a few haddocks, and clear them of the skin and bone, chop them very small, and season with salt and mixed spices; work this up well with a piece of butter, breadcrumbs, minced parsley, and a beaten egg to bind it; or after preparing the fish as before, take the crumbs of a penny loaf, a few anchovies boned, and pickled oysters seasoned with white pepper, salt and minced parsley, wrought up with butter and the yolk of an egg.

Here are the quantities and ingredients for adaption.

4 haddocks, cleaned but with the heads on
1 egg
pepper and salt
½ oz (15g) fresh breadcrumbs
1 oz (30g) parsley

Forcemeat

1 fillet of haddock, minced or chopped
salt and pepper
1 oz (30g) butter
1 oz (30g) breadcrumbs
½ oz (15g) chopped parsley
1 small egg, beaten
2 fillets of anchovies, chopped small

Sauce

1 oz (30g) butter
1 oz (30g) flour
1 onion, finely chopped
1 pt (500 ml) fish or chicken stock
4 oz (25g) potted shrimps (optional – replace the oysters)

A more anciently traditional dish of stuffed haddock probably originated in Shetland. A friend whose childhood holidays were spent on the Isle of Lewis remembers how she enjoyed her grandmother's version of Crappit Heids (the Crappin, or Krappin, is the stuffing).

Crappit Heids

4 haddocks, with heads and livers
1 oz (30g) oatmeal
pepper and salt
1 tablespoon milk

Chop the fish livers and mix them with the oatmeal and seasoning, adding milk to make a softish stuffing. Fill the heads with
this mixture, and boil them gently in milk with the fish. To serve,
remove the stuffing and flesh from the heads and put with the
haddocks on a plate.

Where the Scots excelled with white fish was in its preservation.
There were reisted (smoke-dried) haddocks, rizzar'd (sun-dried)
and tiled (also sun-dried) haddocks, blawn fish (wind-dried), and
speldings (split fish left to dry on the rocks by the sea), and of
course the famous Finnans and Arbroath smokies.

In *St Ives*, Stevenson's hero, invited to dine with a group of high-
spirited young men calling themselves the University of Cramond,
finds himself confronted by a typically Scots menu, to which,
Frenchman that he is, he is glad to do justice, telling us that after
grace

the Senatus Academicus sat down to rough plenty in the shape of
rizzar'd haddocks and mustard, a sheep's head, a haggis, and other
delicacies of Scotland.

Sir Walter Scott, on a youthful expedition to view the site of the
battle of Prestonpans, 'dined at Prestonpans on tiled haddocks very
sumptuously'.

Finnan, or Findon, haddocks are treated very much as herring in
the preparation of kippers. After being split and cleaned they are
immersed in brine, then drained. Where kippers are hot-smoked,
Finnans are cold-smoked, until they turn the palest of pale gold.
The colour deepens slightly after they are removed from the
smoke-house.

It is now time to speak of the admirable Lady Clark of Tillypronie, whose cookery book (a collector's item) epitomizes the

gastronomic life of late Victorian aristocracy. Even before her marriage Lady Clark had travelled much with her family, in France and Italy; there she developed an interest in good food which, unlike that of many contemporaries, was based much less on greed and a predilection for ostentation than on a delicate appreciation of quality. At her death, she left some thousands of manuscript recipes, notes and observations from which *The Cookery Book of Lady Clark of Tillypronie* was edited and published in 1909. These personal jottings – sometimes no more than aides-mémoire – unconsciously convey the world of the late Victorian hostess in London, abroad, and at home in Tillypronie. Because the provenance of most recipes is noted, her pages are peopled with shadowy figures, some of whose names we recognize, others quite unknown, but all united in the confraternity of what James Boswell called the 'Cooking Animal'. Here is what Lady Clark has to say about Finnans:

Findon Haddies

Soak them if necessary for half hour in cold water. Take out and wipe dry, skin them carefully. Rub them lightly over with olive oil. Cook them before a clear bright fire five or six minutes, in a double gridiron, turning often. Thickest part, the back, to be put to the fire in the first instance.

Hot dish. Hot napkin.

Another way is to toast them on a fork before the fire. Mr Davidson recommends their being cooked in the oven with a little milk only, nothing else.

Lizzie Emslie cooks them in cream till all but dry.

We have had to soak our Findon haddies in cold water all night, as the crofter said they were too strong in taste.

Sir Bartle Frere recommends buttermilk instead of plain water to soak them in.

One hesitates to add to such advice, but my own favourite method is to simmer them gently in milk with a bayleaf and a few peppercorns, and when they are tender to keep them warm in a dish, while I use the strained milk to make a thin bechamel. Slices of buttered toast are good with this.

Finnans also make good kedgeree; but their greatest contribution to earthly delight is probably that glorious soup, or stew, or soup-stew, Cullen Skink. Cullen is a fishing village on the Moray Firth; the word *skink* has been variously attributed, to Gaelic, from a word meaning 'essence', or to Low German *schenken*, liquor.

Cullen Skink

1 medium Finnan haddock
1 onion, sliced or chopped
4 peppercorns
1 pt (500 ml) milk
1 lb (450g) approx. potatoes
butter: ½–2 oz (15–60g) according to taste
salt and pepper

Put the fish, onion and peppercorns into a shallow pan with water to cover. Put on a lid, bring to the boil, and simmer until the fish is opaque. This only takes a few minutes. Remove the fish, and skin it as soon as it is cool enough to handle. Break the flesh into flakes and remove the bones. This is tedious but vital. Return skin and bones to the pan in which the water remains, cover again, and simmer for a further hour. Meantime boil and mash the potatoes, smoothly if you want an elegant soup, leaving some lumps if you prefer a hearty version.

Strain the fish stock into a clean large pan. Add the milk and bring to the boil, then put in the haddock and as much potato as is needed to give a thick soup, or more if you wish it to be a kind of sloppy stew. Just before serving, put in the butter cut in little pieces, but do not stir them in, as it is pleasant to find them melting, golden, through the creamy liquid.

Parsley may be used as a garnish.

Unprepossessing in appearance, but no less excellent than the Finnan, are Arbroath Smokies. To prepare these the haddock are not split, merely gutted, cleaned, and salted before smoking. The process originated at the tiny village of Auchmuthie, but with the growth of Arbroath as a fishing port, the Auchmuthians abandoned their homes and took their skills along the coast. Smokies are always prepared in pairs. The best way I have found of cooking them is to heat them under the grill for a few minutes each side (use a very low heat), then to open them a little, grind in fresh pepper, put in a generous ounce (30g) of good quality butter, and wrap them loosely in foil. They can then be put under the grill again, but will do better in a moderate oven for about 10 minutes.

Yet another version of the smoked haddock is the Aberdeen Fillet, a single fillet with the skin on, smoked for only a short while. This is the fish to use for Omelette Arnold Bennett, for which the author should have been awarded the Order of the Thistle, or at the very least made an honorary Scot.

Omelette Arnold Bennett

½ lb (225g) smoked filleted haddock
1 oz (30g) grated cheese
6 eggs
salt and pepper
1 oz (30g) butter
a little double cream

Cook the fish in water or under the grill, flake it, and add the cheese, salt and pepper. Melt a little butter in an omelette pan, pour in some very lightly beaten egg and stir gently for a few minutes. Put some of the fish mixture on top of the omelette and pour on a little cream. Put the pan under a hot grill for about 1 minute. Serve without folding.

Cod, salt or fresh, has been eaten throughout Britain for centuries. Again, Scots have had their own ideas about it. Captain Edward Topham, who visited Scotland in 1774 and wrote a vivid account of Edinburgh life, greatly enjoyed a dish called Cabbie-Claw, which he described as 'cod-fish salted for a short time and not dried in the manner of common salt fish, and baked with parsley and horse-radish. They eat it with egg-sauce, and it is extremely luscious and palatable.' This is interesting, for one of the French names for cod is *cabillaud*; the *Larousse Gastronomique* gives a recipe for *Morue à l'Anglaise* (salt cod in the English fashion) which closely resembles Topham's, going so far as to call the egg sauce with which it is served, Scotch sauce. Did the name Cabbie-Claw derive from *cabillaud*? Was it a mistake? Or was it deliberately used, to indicate that the cod was only lightly salted? (*Cabillaud* being habitually used to designate fresh fish; *morue* is the word for salt cod.) Whatever the answer, the Larousse recipe is probably as near as we can get to the original, and can be used for fresh or salted cod. If you use the latter, remember that it should first be washed, then soaked in fresh water for 24–36 hours before cooking.

Salt Cod in the English fashion

1 lb (450g) cod fillet, fresh or salted
½ oz (15g) fresh chopped parsley

For the sauce:

1 oz (30g) butter
1 oz (30g) flour
½ pt (500 ml) milk
2 large eggs, hard-boiled

For the garnish:

1 lb (450g) parsnips
1 oz (30g) butter
juice of half a lemon
2 large eggs, hard-boiled

Poach the cod in water until tender. Drain carefully. Lay it on a napkin, in a warm dish, and set aside to keep hot. Peel or scrub the parsnips and boil them gently in salted water until tender. Make a bechamel with the butter, flour, and milk and, when it is smooth and well-cooked, stir in 2 of the eggs, chopped.

Garnish the fish with parsley and the parsnips round it, and the halved eggs on top. Hand round the sauce and, separately, the melted butter mixed with lemon juice.

In the remote islands of Orkney and Shetland, a number of unusual recipes evolved. The reason lies in the early history of haaf fishing, before the introduction of shipboard freezing facilities. It was not possible to get fresh cod from Shetland to the mainland of Scotland – it all had to be salted and dried; and the fishermen began the process at sea by removing heads, roes, livers, and other internal organs before the catches reached the curing stations. These items were not discarded; they were the perquisite of the sailors, and ways to cook them form an important part of Orkney and Shetland culinary tradition.

The livers of white fish, thought to be most nutritious, were especially popular. *Liver-bannock* was a sort of sandwich made by baking bannocks with livers between them – a refined version, it may be supposed, of the raw livers placed between two slices of bread, wrapped in paper, and sat upon by the ship's skipper in the wheelhouse, described in one of Lilian Beckwith's delightful books about the Highlands. Another favourite was a potato, scooped out, filled with fish-livers, covered with strips of dough, and baked in the ashes on the hearth. *Liver-muggie*, or *crappin-muggie* was the stomach of a cod stuffed with a mixture of liver, flour and spices, and baked. *Liver-piltocks* were coal-fish roasted on the fire with the livers left in.

Most of the above dishes now exist only in the memories of old people, but two more, Stap and Slott, are sometimes eaten.

Stap
(recipe from *North Atlantic Seafood*, by Alan Davidson)

½ lb (250g) haddock per person
¼ lb (125g) fish livers
salt and pepper

Poach the haddock together with the livers, picked over and rid of any worms. Flake the cooked fish and mash it up with the livers. Sprinkle with salt and white pepper.

Slott

soft fish roes: 1 lb (500g) is ample for 4–6 people,
   as the roes are rich
seasoned flour
butter

'Fish roe was beat with a spoon till it was like cream, a little flour with salt was added, and the slott, roughly shaped into balls, was dropped into boiling water and boiled a short time. When it cooled it was sliced, fried in butter, and eaten hot.'

Jessie M. Saxby, *Food of the Shetlanders Langsyne*

Skate was a fish which varied greatly in popularity according to region. Scott, visiting the Northern Isles in 1814, wrote in his diary that Shetlanders 'would not touch skate, and said dog-fish "is only food for Orkney men".' Yet Jessie Saxby, herself a Shetlander, writing a hundred years later, claims that skate was habitually salted and dried for winter use.

Meg Dods also speaks of the popularity of skate in certain parts of Scotland. With her usual acerbic humour she remarks:

We have seen a small kind of skate which is caught along the northeast coast of Scotland, of a leaden blue colour – called by fishermen the Dane skate, which is more delicate than any other kind we have met. In places where this fish is a great part of the food of the common people, it is best relished when it is hung to dry, by which time it has acquired so strong a smell of ammonia as to be intolerable to the uninitiated. This fish in those primitive days when as yet mock turtle was not, was wont to be esteemed, when eaten *cold* with mustard and vinegar, a grand regale by the sober citizens of Edinburgh, who repaired on holidays to the fishing hamlets around the city. It is thought to eat like lobster – by those of lively imagination.

For the more convivial among Edinburgh's inhabitants, oysters were the grand regale. Robert Fergusson, the poet who died at the age of 24 and whom Burns so admired, once wrote a little carol to bring in the season:

      Auld Reekie's sons blythe faces wear,
      September's merry month is near,
      That brings in Neptune's caller cheer,

New oysters fresh;
The halesomest and nicest gear
O' fish or flesh.

Auld Reekie's sons were still at it 50 years on; another poet, James Hogg (the Ettrick Shepherd) was so fond of oysters that his friend John Wilson set down Hogg's remarks just before an oyster supper at Ambrose's Tavern:

'Hoo many hunder eisters are there on the brod, Mr Awmrose? – Oh! ho! Three brods! – One for each o' us! – A month without an R has nae richt being in the year. Noo, gentlemen, let naebody speak to me for the neist half-hour. Mr Awmrose, we'll ring when we want the rizzers – and the tosted cheese – and the deevil'd turkey – Hae the kettle on the boil, and put back the lang haun' o' the clock, for I fear this is Saturday nicht, and nane o' us are folk to break in on the Sabbath. Help Mr North to butter and bread – and there, sir – there's the vinnegar cruet. Pepper awa', gents.'

So fashionable did the taste for the delicious bivalve become, that it was perfectly proper at one time for women of quality to make up oyster-parties in a select room at a tavern, and even to invite men to join them. Only oysters and port were served in the early stages of the party, but when all had feasted and enjoyed the conversation, brandy punch would appear. This was often the signal for the women to leave, and ladies of the town might then join the men for music and dancing.

In the kitchen, oysters were a great deal used, sometimes alone, sometimes as a stuffing or sauce for fish or meat. An early 18th-century manuscript book now in Glasgow's Mitchell Library consists of recipes collected by Lady Castlehill. The one for mutton with oysters is all delicious simplicity:

To stuff a shoulder of Mutton with Oysters

Spit your Mutton, and cut it slanting, and put in the Oysters, and baste it with Claret Wine, Onyion, and some salt. When it is Rosted, take the Gravie that comes from it, with the Liquor of the Oysters, with some more Oysters, some Capers and Samphire, with a Lemon cut small, and boile them together. Then poure the sauce all over it, and serve it.

Lady Clark of Tillypronie also combined oysters with meat. She took small pieces of beef and wrapped an oyster in each, and covered the whole with pastry. 'It gives an excellent flavour,' she wrote, 'and the oysters themselves cook most agreeably in their beef blankets.' She calls it a Cornish dish, but a very similar recipe had been devised at the fishing village of Musselburgh near Edinburgh. It uses – naturally – mussels, but is clearly brother to the Cornish version.

Musselburgh Pie
Pre-heat the oven to 350° F (180° C) gas 4

1½ lb (675g) rump steak, beaten and cut
   into pieces about 2 × 4 in (5 × 4 cm)
2 medium onions, finely chopped
2 tablespoons oil
½ pt (500 ml) water
salt and pepper
2 tablespoons parsley, chopped
1 tablespoon seasoned flour
3 lb (1.35 kg) fresh mussels
1½ oz (45g) beef suet
½ lb (250g) puff or rough-puff pastry

Scrub the mussels well and remove the 'beards'. Put them in a pan with a very little water, bring to the boil, and cover the pan. After about 3 minutes they should have opened. Cool them, and remove them from the shells. Heat the oil and fry the onions until just golden. Lay out the meat, and put 2–3 mussels and a small piece of suet on each portion, season, and roll up. Dip in seasoned flour and place in a pie dish. The rolls should fit snugly. Sprinkle well with chopped parsley. Add the onions, pour in the water, and cover the dish with foil or a well-fitting lid. Cook for 1½–2 hours, then leave to cool a little. Roll out the pastry to fit the dish, remove the foil and replace it with the pastry, putting a pie funnel in the middle to keep it from collapsing. Trim, decorate, and brush with beaten egg, then put into a hot oven, 425° F (220°C) gas 7, for about 30 minutes.

When transport from the fishing villages to the towns was slow and costly, shellfish were only available to those who lived near the coast. Scallops, crabs, prawns, and lobsters were plentiful. Mostly, they were simply boiled and served with a little butter or cream – a method hard to beat when the fish is really fresh. Where the people were so poor that they did not even have boats in which to go fishing, they ate what they found on the sea-shore – cockles, whelks, winkles, limpets, even seaweed. This became especially true in the years of the Clearances when whole families, evicted from their homes, camped by the coast and lived off whatever they could collect. It was not always a healthy diet even if it stayed their hunger. Whelks, at certain times of the year, absorb the toxins of the bivalves they themselves eat. Limpets too can be dangerous; a description of the Western Isles published in 1703 mentions the risks of 'jaundice' from eating too many limpets in June. Stevenson, who like Scott was a past master at picking up odd scraps of information and turning them to advantage in his writing, must have heard something of the dangers of shellfish from his father, who was an Inspector of Lighthouses; for it will be remembered that poor David Balfour, marooned on a tidal islet, suffered horribly after eating raw winkles and limpets.

Better to leave to history even the limpet stovies for which some exiles are said to hanker. Instead, let us end with praise of a soup which (despite its Gaelic name) is known and loved all over Scotland. It is a dish to which there might well be written a poem, a song, even an anthem. This version is Lady Clark's recipe, half quantities:

Partan Bree

1 cooked crab
2–3 oz (30–40g) rice
1 pt (520 ml) milk
1 pt (520 ml) chicken stock (do not be tempted to

   substitute water or other stock)
salt and pepper
2 anchovy fillets, mashed, or a few drops anchovy essence
¼ pt (200 ml) single cream

Pick all the meat from the crab and set aside that from the large claws. Boil the rice in milk until soft and pass it with the crab-meat (but not that from the claws) through a tammy or in a liquidizer. Stir it with a wooden spoon till perfectly smooth and add to it, very gradually, sufficient white unseasoned stock for six to seven people. Do not make it as thick as a purée. Season with salt, white pepper, and anchovy. Put it all into a pan and stir it over the fire until quite hot, but do not let it boil. Add pieces of meat from the claws, and, just before serving, stir in the cream.

— 3 —

NOT NATURALLY BARREN

We began also to see that Scotland was not so naturally barren as some people represent it, but . . . might be made to equal, not England only, but even the richest, most fruitful, most pleasant, and best improv'd part of England . . . if they had the same methods of improvement, and the Scots were as good husbandmen as the English.

Daniel Defoe
Tour through the whole Island of Great Britain, London 1724—6.

The story of modern farming in Scotland begins in the 18th century, when landowners and politicians gradually became aware that their country though desperately poor, and backward by a hundred years in its agriculture, *could* become productive, if old ways were abandoned and replaced with more modern ones.

Yet Defoe's assessment was a little unsympathetic. When he was writing improvements in his own country were comparatively recent and some parts of rural England were still as undeveloped as anywhere in Scotland. Moreover, the Scottish system had worked effectively enough for many hundreds of years, keeping a small population adequately, if plainly, fed. It was events in the two previous centuries – a rise in the population, an increase in the pace of deforestation, internal strife, wars, and a succession of crop failures, famines, and plagues – which led to the barrenness and poverty which so appalled visitors at the end of the 17th century. Poverty is a viciously cyclical condition: although it is unwise to take money out of the bank without putting any in, the poorer you are, the more you need to draw upon your account. Despite Defoe's favourable view, in its natural state three-quarters of the land was unproductive and unworkable; if Scots peasants were apathetic and hostile to new ideas, it was not only because they were ignorant, but also because they were worn out by back-breaking toil and a century of economic hardship. Poor and uneducated, without the benefit of trees to conserve the soil and temper the climate, with no knowledge of drainage and only the most rudimentary conception of soil enrichment, they cannot be blamed for doing no more than their fathers had done, and dumbly enduring increasing deprivation.

At the end of the 17th century rural Scotland was still in the grip of feudalism. Rarely, farms were privately owned, by men who had managed to convert their rent into mere feu-duty (the Church at one time had sold off some of its land in this way to raise money). Others were rented by relatives of landowners who ran several small farms as a single unit and collected the rent (in the Highlands these men were called tacksmen). Most commonly, farms were rented collectively, each tenant cultivating for himself and contributing a carefully specified share of the rent. A farm village or 'toun' (a word much misunderstood by English travellers, who castigated the Scots for thus grandiloquently, as they thought, describing a huddle of huts) consisted of the dwellings of all the tenants of one particular farm.

The plan of the farm was invariable. Immediately adjacent to the toun lay the land known as 'infield' – the only area to be consistently fertilized with dung or seaweed. It was never allowed to lie fallow, but cropped every year, first with bere and then with oats. Beyond the 'infield', and separated only by temporary barriers removed after harvest, was the 'outfield' – fertilized by wandering cattle and divided into sections, which were cultivated in rotation, though unenclosed. Beyond the 'outfield' again lay natural grassland or moor where the cattle pastured in summer 'except in the Highlands where they were taken to the high meadows known as shielings).

'Infield' and 'outfield' were divided into long strips of land varying from a quarter to half an acre in breadth, known as rigs. These were the basis of the Scottish system, runrig, designed to allow each tenant a portion of both good and poor land. It worked like this: Suppose a farm to have some good land with natural drainage or a sunny, gently sloping hill. The problem of who is to farm this prime site is solved by dividing it into rigs, each the length of a ploughgate (the distance a team can pull the plough without having to rest); some rigs are then allotted to each tenant, but not contiguously, so that every man gets his share of the best. On stony, steep hills and in sunless glens, rigs are likewise allocated. To make the arrangement even more equitable a redistribution takes place every three years at most, but biennially or even annually on some farms.

It is easy to see the Scots democratic temperament at work here; but though the motive was praiseworthy, there were certain clear disadvantages. Since rigs were too numerous and too small to be hedged or walled, runrig was a major obstacle to enclosure. In addition, the frequency of reallocation discouraged people from trying to improve the soil; even when they did attempt it, much time and energy was wasted where men often had to walk miles to cultivate all their land. And whilst allocation was easy when a village had few inhabitants, as the population increased subdivisions became necessary, and eventually only the landcourts could untangle the rights of each tenant.

It is, of course, impossible to generalize about the condition of farms in different parts of Scotland before 1707. But a few facts are common to all. First, they were totally vulnerable to weather and crop diseases: drought, flood, or an invasion of pests rapidly brought everyone to the same level of destitution. Second, poor transport and communications tended to isolate even neighbouring regions from each other, so that though one community might flourish while another starved, no help could get from one to the other. Third, one of the greatest continuing obstacles to agricultural development was lack of money. 'Nothing is scarce here except money' wrote a 16th-century French traveller; consequently, almost everything farmers produced went to pay rent to the landlord and tithes to the Church.

Grain was the chief commodity. In good years it was even exported, but it was the landlord, not the farmer, who got the profit. Once all dues had been met, and enough put by to feed the family, very little often remained for next year's seed, and there was no question of selective breeding. This pressure on farmers was also the reason why land was neither enclosed nor allowed to lie fallow – they simply could not afford it. The same pressure affected every branch of agriculture, for landlords could, and did, claim rent in the form of poultry, eggs, milk, butter, fruit, and wool.

Even time was a feudal commodity. Whatever agricultural tasks needed to be done, those on the landlord's farm must come first: his was the first land ploughed, the first seed sown. The many other feudal obligations – peat-cutting, transport of goods, road-making and mending, hunting services, fighting in time of war – left tenants ultimately with very little opportunity to look after their own crops adequately. Small wonder Defoe found them dull and stupid; their predetermined role over centuries, in the face of climate, land and society itself, had been one of passivity.

By the end of the 17th century, this structure, outdated and wasteful of resources, had caused the collapse of the country. It had been a difficult period for the whole of Europe, politically and economically; but in Scotland alone there seemed no basis from which recovery could begin – the Exchequer was empty, the people exhausted, the land without resilience. And thus, 1707, the year of the Union of Parliaments, can be seen as a watershed in the history of farming as in much else. It was not that no efforts to change the system had yet been made, for throughout the previous century various Acts aimed at reform had been passed. Rather was it that the general level of interest, even among educated men, had been very low; and the lack of money for investment in agricultural improvements had blocked every path forward.

The effect of Union was slowly to remove the obstacles. The gradual development of trade put money into the coffers of landowners and merchants. At the same time, it allowed Scots and English to move more freely from one country to the other, and encouraged the dissemination of new ideas. Politicians too (forced to travel much more frequently from Edinburgh and Glasgow to London) were made aware of the latest trends in farming. Above all, educated Scots were able to keep in touch with the movement towards agricultural reform which is one of the notable characteristics of 18th-century Europe.

Slowly at first, then with increasing momentum, an interest in land cultivation spread through the aristocracy. Improvers, these men and women came to be called. They spent their lives experimenting, discussing, questioning, writing – and working. Like their counterparts in France, they discovered the charm of rural life but, being Scots, they did not arrive at happiness through play: Marie Antoinette and her model dairy were not to their taste. Their commitment was serious, and lasting. Side by side with their farmers they dug ditches, planted hedges, built dykes, and sowed turnip seed.

Most innovations – the consolidation of runrig land, the abandonment of rent payment in kind, and especially the introduction of enclosures – met with considerable resistance from mistrustful tenants. So did the new crops; potatoes, turnips, and different varieties of grass for cattle-food. The only measure which found immediate favour was the substitution of long leases – up to 38 years – for the previous short terms.

This book is concerned with the story of Scottish food, not of farming. At this point it becomes necessary, therefore, to look no longer at the farm, but rather at its produce, and to discover how traditional foods have changed or developed up until our own times.

It is probably Dr Johnson who is responsible for the widespread belief that oatmeal has always been the predominate cereal in the Scottish diet, a misconception which had defied facts for over 200 years. His famous definition of oats as 'a food given in England to horses, and in Scotland to men' – together with Lord Elibank's almost equally celebrated riposte, 'Where will you find such horses, and such men?' – did much to publicize a relationship between Scots and oats which, although very ancient, was only in Johnson's own time assuming that prominence which is now considered traditional.

It is true that the grey oat, together with bere, had for centuries been a major constituent of the diet of poorer people. But the former was described in 1808 as 'the worst and least productive grain in Europe'. It was bere which was the more extensively cultivated, especially in the Highlands, and travellers' accounts suggest strongly that bere was more appreciated as a food even than as a source of malt. Bere broth and bere bannocks nourished townsfolk and peasants alike until well into the 17th century.

Early documents display a certain confusion between the words 'bere' and 'barley'. Barley does not do well in acid soil; liming seems not to have been practised until the 17th century (and then only in East Lothian and the Forth Valley), so bere must be the cereal referred to by early writers even when they speak of 'barley'. Once the importance of lime had been established, and improved communications developed, barley began to supplant bere as a crop. By this time, however, it was falling from social grace anyway; new, more successful varieties of oats were increasing the popularity of oatmeal, and more attention was also being directed to the cultivation of wheat.

By the early 1700s, though bere bannocks and bere porridge were still common in the Highlands, in the Lowlands they were only eaten by the very poor, a situation which remained stable for at least a century. Dr Johnson tasted bere, though he was also given wheat bread and oatcakes, when he visited Skye in 1773. He disliked oatcakes and later wrote to Boswell

Tell [my friends] when you see them, how well I speak of Scotch politeness, and Scotch hospitality, and Scotch beauty, and of everything Scotch but Scotch oatcakes and Scotch prejudice.

But he approved the bere-bannocks, which he described as thicker and softer than oatcakes: 'I learnt to eat them without unwillingness; the blackness of their colour raises some dislike, but the taste is not disagreeable.'

Fifty years after Johnson, the Wordsworths were encountering barley bread, with a certain dismay:

These cakes are as thin as our oat-bread but, instead of being crisp, are soft and leathery, yet we being hungry and the butter delicious, ate them with great pleasure, but when the same bread was set before us afterwards, we did not like it.

If barley was doomed to an increasingly subsidiary role in the kitchen, however, one invention of the 18th century ensured that it would at least continue to survive – as the principal ingredient of that most loved and most Scottish of dishes, Scots broth. The old method of husking barley was a process known as *knocking* – placing the grain in a specially hollowed-out stone or a wooden trough, and pounding it. Knocked-barley was a standard article of diet for most people in Northern Europe, so much so that the Dutch, resourceful as always, finally devised special mills which did the job neatly and quickly, and much more easily.

One of the earliest Improvers, Andrew Fletcher of Saltoun (patriot, landowner, traveller, and a man of extraordinary ability marred by wild temper and an impulsive nature) had spent several years in exile in Holland before returning to Scotland with William of Orange, and had noted the barley-mills. Accordingly in 1710, he sent his wheelwright, James Meikle, to learn

the perfect art of sheeling barley, both that which is called French barley, and that which is called pearl barley, and how to accommodate, order, and erect mills for that purpose, in so far as he can, with his uttermost industry, and the recommendations given him.

Having accomplished this, Meikle was to return by the first fleet or man of war; but, if forced to wait, 'he shall endeavour to instruct himself in any useful trade or manufactory'. (He did, in fact, bring back an invention of utmost importance, the winnowing fan.) The Articles of Agreement are very explicit: all his wages and expenses are to be paid, also his ransom if taken prisoner on his travels, and in the event of his death 'Saltoun shall be obliged to give his wife and children 100 merks'. Furthermore, on his return, Meikle is to be master of the new mill if he so wishes, if not, he is to teach the method to someone appointed by Fletcher, and then to leave, and 'renew his obligation not to make use of this art himself, nor teach it to any other.'

Such was the success of the mill, operated by Meikle and Fletcher's brother Henry, that 'Salton barley' became famous all over Britain. Henry's wife took the orders and guarded the door, ensuring that no spy penetrated the secret, to such effect that no similar mill was built in Britain, Ireland or America for another forty years: then production increased so rapidly that 'Salton barley' became known all over the world.

Today, barley has lost its position as food for humans. More than half the world's crop fattens cattle, and the bulk of the remainder goes to brewers and distillers. If, once again, it is the predominant cereal grown in Scotland almost the entire crop goes for the manufacture of malt, either at home or abroad. And if barley- and bere-bannocks do survive (just) in the north and the islands, they are mainly eaten by older people who prefer them to the mass-produced white bread shipped from the mainland. There is, too, some conscious attempt to maintain tradition, and a minority are aware of its value as a health food. As one old Caithness lady told a researcher: 'A bit of bere-bannock every morning keeps me right all day.'

It is not easy to see exactly why barley lost ground as it did towards the end of the 17th century, nor why, having held a central position on stage for so many centuries, it never achieved the folk food status which was to make of oatmeal one of the most potently evocative symbols of the Scots way of life.

Part of the explanation may be that oatmeal keeps longer than barley, is much more versatile, and more nutritious. It also has greater potential as a convenience food – as Froissart observed, having noted the poke of oatmeal attached to every Scots cavalry- man's saddle. Whenever a quick meal or a pick-me-up was called for, these 14th-century soldiers would put a metal plate to heat over a fire, and mix their meal to a thick paste with water:

When the plate is heated, they put a little of the paste upon it, and make a thin cake, like a cracknel or biscuit, which they eat to warm their stomachs.

Here (despite the absence of fat) we have the first recorded recipe for oatcakes. It is an uncomplicated dish, but for real simplicity, the prize should go to another – *drammach* to Highlanders, *glug* or *gluggo* to Orcadians, *krul* (with the refinement of a lump of butter) to Shetlanders.

Though it is but cold water mingled with oatmeal, yet it makes a good enough dish for a hungry man; and where there are no means of making fire, or (as in our case) good reason for not making one, it is the chief stand-by of those who have taken to the heather.

Thus David Balfour, the hero of *Kidnapped*. For him, as for thousands of others, oatmeal proved its worth as food for travellers – those too poor or too disreputable to stop at inns; those, like shepherds and hunters, whose business lay in the hills; and those who, fleeing the soldiers or the law, depended for their lives on a bed of heather and the secret silence of the moors. Raw or cooked, oatmeal is portable, palatable, and nourishing.

Another reason for the rise of oats was agricultural development. Land reclamation and more informed attitudes to soil enrichment coincided with the introduction of improved varieties of seed, tolerant of both soil and climate, returning a higher yield than the old grey oat. It may be that additional supplies met an already existing demand. People turned to oatmeal, in fact, because they had always preferred it.

Lastly, patriotism may well have influenced taste. Animosity between Scotland and England had by no means ended with the Union of the Crowns in 1603. Resentment of the English, fuelled by their own attitude to Scotland as well as by envy of their economic and social stability, culminated in real hatred when the Darien venture, on which so much had hinged, collapsed due to English obstructionism and greed. Just as it became every Scot's patriotic duty to drink claret rather than port because England (trying to cut trade links with France and encourage those with Portugal) wished the contrary, so eating oatmeal may well have been considered an assertion of independence, of difference of character, of national pride. The English ate barley or wheaten bread; the Scots would shun that. The English mocked the Scots dependence on oats; Scots would make a virtue of it.

The 18th and 19th centuries were without doubt the golden age of the oat. In its many forms it was present at almost every meal in all classes of society. The wealthy and the middle classes breakfasted upon porridge and oatcakes, dined on meats stuffed with oatmeal, and supped on vegetable and oatmeal soup, haggis, or fish cooked with oatmeal. The poor virtually lived on porridge, brose, and sowens – an economical dish made from the inner husks. When, during the famines at the end of the 18th century, East Lothian farmers voluntarily raised money to buy grain for the starving, they found that the price of oats was rising so much beyond that of other cereals that they were compelled to buy barley, wheat and peasemeal. They continued, however, to purchase some oats,

as much as was sufficient to make at least one meal a day for the younger part of the families, to whom, from their having tasted scarce any other food for breakfast from their infancy, it was indispensable.

Young country boys coming to town to study or serve an apprenticeship brought their bag of meal with them. There exists a letter from Burns to his parents, written in 1781 from Irvine, where he had gone to serve under a flax-dresser, which has a touching little postscript: 'My meal is nearly out, but I am going to borrow till I get more.' Meal Monday, that day in January when classes in universities were suspended so that students might return home and replenish their meal bags, was abolished as an anachronism only in the late 1950s.

Not only was oatmeal a food; it was also currency, and had been since the Middle Ages. Though the practice was diminishing by the end of the 19th century, farmworkers in many parts of the country were still receiving bags of meal, pease and barley as wages. The schoolmaster's pay and minister's stipend were supplemented with meal. Highland fishermen bartered their catch for it; there is in Glenlochay, near Killin, a Herring Stone where farmer and fisherman are said to have exchanged their wares. Even dowries included bags of the precious grain.

No wonder, then, that every virtue possessed by the Scots, from good health to good brains, and courage to canniness, has at some time been attributed to oats. In 1800 the English divine Sidney Smith proposed a motto for Jeffrey's *Edinburgh Review* which might have served for the whole nation: *Tenuit musam meditamur avena* – we cultivate literature on a little oatmeal. And not literature alone for, if enthusiasts are to be believed, oatmeal takes the credit for the philosophers and judges of the Enlightenment, the scientists and explorers of the Victorian age, the inventors and business men of today.

Its physical effects can hardly be denied. Most farmworkers rarely if ever ate fresh meat, butter or cheese. They had peasemeal, and it is now known that pulses and cereals complement one another to produce an adequate form of protein. For about nine months of the year they could get calcium in the form of milk, from cows, sheep or goats. The stone-grinding process preserves much of the oat's inner kernel, with its minerals and vitamins. Such a diet, therefore, though monotonous and lacking in vitamins A and C, was low in cholesterol, high in calcium and carbohydrates, and provided reasonable nourishment at least for adults. In his *Tales of a Highland Parish* (1929) T. D. Miller writes of the capacity for endurance of the 19th-century labourer:

The shepherds of Glenshee, before the advent of the railway, walked to Lanark to buy the sheep. They walked the eighty miles to Edinburgh in two stages, spent the night there, and next day completed the remaining fifty miles to Lanark. Returning with their flock of lambs they travelled by easy stages; for the whole week, they never had their clothes off. These long journeys could only be done by men in the full vigour of life, and the sustaining power of their endurance was oatmeal.

In 1879 the total Scottish acreage under oats reached almost its highest figure, 1,004,535 acres, compared with 278,584 under barley and 76,613 given over to wheat. Again, in the early years of the Second World War, production peaked with an acreage of 1,010,895 in 1943 (barley 213,619 and wheat 170,623). The figures seem unbelievable when we see those for 1986: 28.3 thousand hectares for oats and mixed grain.

The reason for the decline is, of course, the disappearance of horses from daily life. Their peak years had coincided with those of oats, for it was during the early 1800s that Clydesdales emerged as a breed to replace the old ox or mixed teams. The great era of the draught-horses extended from the 1860s to the 1920s. At one time there were no less than 140,000 horses on Scottish farms, pulling ploughs and reapers, carting grain, milk, turnips, potatoes – all the farm's produce – and providing power for the threshing-mill. A fully grown Clydesdale doing regular heavy work could get through 20 lbs of oats a day when not out at pasture, but the figure is somewhat artificial since most farmers supplemented oats with hay, turnips, even crushed whins; bothy ballads also refer to mean farmers who mixed in straw and chaff as well. The horsemen rose early – 5.30 was the usual hour – and went straight to the stables to groom and feed their charges. Only when this had been done would they have their own breakfast, of porridge if they lived at the farmhouse or in married quarters, of brose (boiling water poured onto the raw oatmeal, to be eaten with a little salt and milk) if they looked after themselves in the bothy. Almost literally then, oats were the lifeblood of the farming communities in the 19th century and the early years of the 20th.

Diesel-powered machinery put an end to the power of the oat, though petrol shortages during the Second World War brought back the horses for a while. But Johnson's linking of men, horses and oats proved to have been part of a circular chain, and the dwindling numbers and eventual disappearance of cart-horses lost us the waving fields of golden grain forever. With a yardful of tractors, the modern farmer is more interested in oil shares, and if he eats oats for breakfast, they are almost certainly in the form of some patent packaged cereal.

Wheat, by contrast, which for so many years held modest third place in the tables of crops, has now moved up, though its acreage is still unimpressive compared to barley (89,100 hectares as against 418,800). If it remained for so long a secondary crop, it was not from lack of interest, but rather because soil and climate were not favourable for its cultivation.

Even in very early communities wheat was grown wherever the land was sheltered, well drained, and fertile. Such conditions existed in the south-east and in part of Fife, but also further north, and by the Middle Ages we find it growing in Angus and the narrow lush strip of land known as the Carse of Gowrie, which runs between Perth and Dundee. There were also wheatfields in Morayshire near the coast, whence seaweed could be brought to fertilize them. Where no wheat was grown and the country was difficult of access, even the rich ate barley bannocks and oatcakes, but grain could be shipped to many areas. Defoe praised the wheaten bread he found at John o' Groats in 1705, and in most towns wheat bread, often made from imported grain, was sold at the bakehouses.

But even on the farms which cultivated it, until the late 18th century wheat was strictly a cash crop. The farmer kept none for his own use, except under very special circumstances – as part payment to shearers coming in to help with the harvest, for instance, or to offer to guests at weddings, baptisms, and wakes.

It was an age of changing patterns of cereal cultivation. Oats were replacing barley, but wheat was the subject of much experimentation, chiefly along the east coast. In Sutherland it was still at the trial stage as late as 1812, but in the neighbouring county of Ross and Cromarty Sir George Steuart Mackenzie was observing a difference in the diet of his tenants:

Wheat bread is more used in this country now than it was a few years ago. The scarcity of oatmeal this season has induced many of the common people to use wheat flour, made by coarse grinding in an ordinary oatmeal mill. This they made into bannocks, sometimes with a little yeast, and they seem to be very fond of it. Several of them have expressed to me their fears of their families liking this bread too well, and eating more than could be afforded.

Much further south, where wheat had been grown for centuries, there were also changes. In Fife:

In nothing almost does the progress of luxury in this country appear more remarkable than in the increased production of wheaten bread . . . there is not a family however poor, that does not use wheaten bread more or less.

The reporter to the *General View of Agriculture for East Lothian*, Robert Somerville, was a conservative man who disliked the new ways. He complained:

Manufacture of Bread: In the towns and large villages, wheaten bread is almost the only kind now in use; even in the country parts, except in the case of the farmer's servants, it is very generally used. A comparison of the present consumpt, with what was required 40 years ago, will, in some degree, explain the high price of that particular article and, at the same time, afford a convincing proof of the infatuation of the lower ranks, in persisting in the use of wheaten bread, notwithstanding its high price, in opposition to what is made from a mixture of oats, pease and barley, which besides its being equally wholesome and nutritive, can be had a great deal cheaper.

Almost every volume of the *GVA in the Counties of Scotland* tells the same tale: wheat bread was more accessible, whether people baked it themselves in the new coal-burning ranges installed in 'improved' cottages, or bought it from bakers' shops.

The increased availability of wheat flour, coinciding with falling prices of sugar, tea and eggs, were to lead to the development of baking skills among all classes of housewives. From enriched breads and spicy currant loaves it was but a short step to the scones, the shortbreads, the gingerbreads, and the diet loaves which were to become the pride of every Scots kitchen.

The adoption of turnip husbandry revolutionized British farming. It facilitated winter feeding of stock, the conversion of straw into yard manure for the improvement of the soil, and the reclamation of light and medium soils which had been previously unproductive under a system that depended on bare fallowing as the means of restoring fertility and freedom from weeds.

So says the *Encyclopaedia Britannica*. What it fails to say, is that in Scotland the turnip revolution was by far the biggest single factor in transforming agriculture from (in general) a subsistence activity into a productive industry. Without turnips, Scotch lamb and Aberdeen Angus beef would not be in butchers' shops today, a great part of the dairy industry would be underdeveloped, and – because turnips, like oats, are eaten in England mainly by animals and in Scotland by men – a number of distinctive Scottish dishes would never have come into existence. 'Nothing,' wrote Sir John Sinclair (editor of *The GVA in the Counties of Scotland*) 'has so much contributed to the improvement of agriculture as this valuable root.'

It is as well, perhaps – the turnip being a protean vegetable – to begin with a definition. Two varieties are commonly grown in Scotland: the globe turnip, *brassica rapa*, and the *rutabaga* or swede, a distinct type having its own characteristics but sometimes confusingly referred to as the swede turnip. It is the latter of which most Scots are thinking when they speak of turnips; it is widely cultivated, as much to be seen on the greengrocer's shelf as in field and byre, and perhaps the only vegetable except the potato which they consistently eat with pleasure – rightly, for it has an agreeable if pronounced flavour, and is highly nutritive.

The need for a food which would allow cattle to remain in good

condition during the winter was felt far more acutely north of the
border than in England. Whereas by the late 17th century English
farmers had become accustomed to having enclosed fields for hay
or winter pasturage, there was no such practice in Scotland until
the mid- or even late 18th century. Cattle were turned into wild
grassland during the summer and brought in to feed on stubble
after the harvest. The best animals, designated 'mart beasts', were
selected for slaughter at Martinmas (11th November). The remainder, kept in fields near the farm or in a byre over the winter, were
lucky to survive until the following spring. If they did, they were
often so weak that they had literally to be lifted out to pasture. It
took weeks for them to regain anything approaching reasonable
condition, with two consequences: cows calved not annually but
biennially, and draught oxen were so puny and undernourished
that it needed from eight to twelve animals to draw the heavy Scots
plough. In its turn, this dependence on a large number of work
animals for simple tasks led to overgrazing of the limited grasslands,
fertilized only by the dung deposited during the short summer
season. Defoe summed it all up:

The greatest thing this country wants is more enclos'd pastures by which
the farmers would keep stocks of cattle well-foddered in the winter and,
which again, would not only furnish good store of butter, cheese, and
beef to market, but would, by their quantity of dung, enrich their soil,
according to the unanswerable maxim in grazing, that stock upon land
improves land.

Turnip husbandry was to achieve precisely these desiderata. The
land had first to be thoroughly cleaned of weeds and fertilized,
then enclosed to protect the crop from cattle until the winter. When
that season arrived, the animals could be fed and even fattened, so
that they were in good condition all year round. Larger and heavier
cows, calving annually, could give a perpetual supply of milk and
good quantities of fresh meat to any farmer prepared to take a little
trouble. Almost all Scottish soils were suitable. As a bonus, the
extra manure would enrich the soil 'according to the unanswerable
maxim in grazing'.

Events which may be told in minutes often take years to unfold.
The turnip revolution took long to achieve, and not until the 1830s

could it be described as an accomplished fact. While Improvers such as the Earl of Rothes and John Cockburn of Ormiston began growing turnips as early as 1716, their influence, in this respect at least, was not widely felt, perhaps because the scope of the new agricultural theories and experiments was too enormous to be taken in all at once by uneducated tenants. Enclosures, tree-planting, drainage, liming, rotation of crops, introduction of cultivated grasses, new implements – it was all too much to assimilate quickly. Not until about 1754 was the beneficial effect of fattening stock on turnips demonstrated convincingly. Even after that, though it might be spoken of and written about, and enthusiastically practised by a few, the majority learnt very slowly. The situation is well exempli-fied by two passages from James Hogg's *Highland Tours*, written between 1802 and 1804 in the form of letters to his friend Sir Walter Scott. Writing from Perth in 1802, he tells Scott:

I often looked for turnips, in vain, for many miles altogether. For the rearing of this excellent root the banks of the Tay are admirably calculated and what a pity it should not be generally cultivated; the profits arising from its culture are now well ascertained, the crop being lucrative and the soil pulverized and enriched.

Here is the voice of the enlightened farmer (and, indeed, Hogg was awarded a prize for a paper on the diseases of sheep). But two years later, with that disarming honesty which makes him so attractive, he recounts a journey from Hamilton to Glasgow in the public coach, with two friends:

We also, very kindly, endeavoured to entertain our fellow travellers with appropriate remarks on the infallibility of the turnip husbandry succeeding to a miracle on such lands, and of its infinite superiority to their present modes of agriculture; unfortunately none of us could authenticate it, by an appeal to the abundant profits which we ourselves had reaped from that excellent plan.

Nonetheless the turnip – or swede – field was by this time a fairly common sight in many regions. Swedes made their appear-ance, according to Sir John Sinclair, in 1781–2, when a Mr Knox from East Lothian, who had settled in 'Gottenburgh' sent some seeds to his friend Dr Hamilton. A little later, probably in 1788, they were introduced into Dumfries. They were known as rutaba-gas, and even today the true East Lothian man will speak of *bagies*.

Most reporters to the *GVA* (1793–1816) referred to turnips as a field crop, and believed that swedes would do even better in the cold Scottish climate. Though all were impressed by the benefits to cattle and sheep, hardly any mentioned their value as food for humans – but we must remember that *brassica rapa* had been a garden vegetable for over a century. In the Hebrides, where swedes were enthusiastically received, 'passengers passing through the fields cut holes in them', but whether this was from curiosity or to take home pieces for family or cattle, will never be known.

In Sinclair's *Account of the Systems of Husbandry adopted in the more improved Districts of Scotland* (1812), he wrote that

Mr Kerr observes that the Swedish turnip is perhaps the best winter vegetable we have except the potatoe. 5 pounds weight of beef or mutton will make richer Scotch broth, along with Swedish turnips, than 7 pounds along with an equal quantity of any other turnips. It is fully equal to a mixture of carrotts and turnips in that respect, and much sweeter.

This is useful evidence that just thirty years after the arrival of the first seeds, swedes were becoming part of the standard diet. It is curious to reflect that Burns, who died in 1796, and whose enjoyment of haggis has almost attained mythological status, prob-ably never saw, let alone tasted, its now inseparable companion.

About the 1820s, nomenclature becomes confused. *Rutabaga* gradually disappears. *Swede* remains in the language but is increas-ingly used more by farmers than by ordinary people. It is some-times difficult to determine which is meant in literature dating from that time, but earlier references must allude to *brassica rapa*. Smollett, who returned from London for a brief visit to his native Dumbartonshire in 1766, and whose book *Humphrey Clinker* provides us with a delightfully biased portrait of Scotland, makes one of his characters write to a friend:

You know we used to vex poor Murray of Balliol College, by asking if there was really no fruit but turnips in Scotland. Sure enough, I have seen turnips make their appearance, not as dessert, but by way of hors d'oeuvres, or whets, as radishes are served up betwixt more substantial dishes in France and Italy; but it must be observed, that the turnips of this country are as much superior in sweetness, delicacy and flavour, to those of England, as a musk-mellon is to the stock of a common cabbage. They are small and conical, of a yellowish colour, with a very thin skin; and over and above their agreeable taste, are valuable for their anti-scorbutic quality.

Smollett was probably exaggerating less than we think. Lord Henry Cockburn (the judge, not to be confused with Cockburn of Ormiston, the Improver) was also talking of turnips in his vignette of the philosopher Adam Ferguson who, broken in health by a stroke and suffering from palsy, but still of venerable bearing and appearance, never dined out except with his relative Dr Joseph Black. Then, although a vegetarian and teetotaller, he ate largely and drank milk in huge quantities. 'It was,' says Cockburn, 'delightful to see the two philosophers rioting over a boiled turnip.'

Cockburn's *Memorials of his Time*, though published posthumously, was written between 1821 and 1830, by which time both turnips and swedes had become part of the agricultural pattern. In some areas, such as the north-east, turnips were preferred. In the Lowlands, swedes predominated. In Orkney and Shetland first turnips, then swedes were cultivated. Only the Highlands and the north-west showed little interest. One reason was demoralization subsequent to the Jacobite Rebellion of 1745 and the disbandment of the clans. Few landlords, and even fewer tenants, were prepared to expend the time and effort necessary to change from the old runrig system to consolidated, enclosed fields, and to abolish the custom of turning all the cattle onto the arable land after harvest – changes which were essential for turnip cultivation. A second, more potent reason, was that another new vegetable was being introduced into the country; a vegetable which, though it was slow at first to gain acceptance, eventually became almost as important to the Western Highlands as it did to Ireland.

This new vegetable was of course the potato. But if now we think of it very much as one of our national foods – and plenty of recipes substantiate the notion – initial attitudes were very far from enthusiastic.

Educated Scots became aware of potatoes in the second half of the 17th century. The gardening expert John Reid was recommending them and giving advice for their cultivation as early as 1683, and in that year also they were grown in the physic garden of Edinburgh's School of Medicine, the forerunner of the Royal Botanic Gardens at Inverleith Row. A few noblemen were interested enough to try the plant, but no prophet among them forecast that it would, in time, avert famine in the Highlands and, by making it possible for a large family to live off a relatively small piece of land, would help to inhibit emigration; that later, failure of the crop would in its turn cause famine, and force an unprecedented number of Scots to leave their homes; or that, later still, Scottish potato varieties would become world-famous and constitute a useful article of export; and that in our own day it would be estimated that Scots obtain up to 50% of their daily requirement of vitamin C from 'tatties'.

Whatever their place in the gardens of the wealthy, field cultivation began slowly and patchily. In the south-east, Cockburn of Ormiston seems to have grown them in a tenant's field in 1726. Two years later, a Kilsyth man was trying them. By 1739 another Kilsyth farmer was actually renting fields so that he could grow potatoes, creating considerable interest among his neighbours. Not until the 1760s did field cultivation become general in the Lothians. Gradually, the eastern Lowlands generally began to recognize the vegetable as 'a very bulky and valuable food for the whole of the lower ranks, and a substitute for bread at the tables of all the superior ranks', in Somerville's supercilious judgment. They were not yet grown for market, remaining very much a subsidiary crop in this part of the country; for the success of turnips, the cultivation of new types of oat, and the spread of wheat, were to prevent their adoption as the dominant – almost the only – food as was happening in Ireland and was about to happen in the Highlands.

Somewhat surprisingly the Highlanders did not at first take at all kindly to the new vegetable. The story is often told (though it seems to be apocryphal) how Clanranald, returning from a visit to relatives in Antrim in 1743, brought with him some tubers for his tenants on Benbecula. They refused to plant them and some suffered imprisonment. Clanranald had his way; but when the crop was eventually harvested, his tenants brought the potatoes to his door, remarking that though they might be forced to grow them, they could not be made to eat them.

This hostility seems to have been fairly widespread in the west and we may infer that it was one of the topics of conversation in Dumbarton when Smollett came home, for another character in *Humphrey Clinker* expresses surprise 'that the cultivation should be so much neglected in the Highlands, where the poor people have not meal enough to supply them with bread through the winter.'

The prejudice was dissipated as farmers observed that potatoes throve in the stony, peaty soil of the north, and that lazy-beds, already used to grow bere, were ideal for the new vegetable. Soon, on the Isle of Lewis, potatoes replaced bread for more than half the year; while on the western mainland, they were part of the staple diet of all classes by the 1780s. Johnson noted in 1773 that on Skye, although he was offered no great variety of garden vegetables, 'potatoes at least are never wanting, which, though they have not known them long, are now one of the principal parts of their food.'

They certainly seemed to provide the answer to many pressing problems. Social and economic structure in the Highlands was now in disarray, scarcely alleviated in the 1780s by the return of confiscated estates to men who had spent perhaps 30 years abroad; they were no longer in touch with affairs at home, some indeed preferring to remain absent and have an agent collect the rents – a system clearly open to abuse. The policy of eviction now adopted by some landlords, who saw greater profit in sheep than in the miserable crofts, forced thousands of families from the hills onto the narrow strips of land along the coastline. Such land could not, under any system of husbandry, yield enough grain to feed the wretched people trying to scrape a living from the hostile earth. Already, there was a moderate but steady emigration to the industrial towns of Scotland and England, and further afield.

Into this situation potatoes brought three qualities of great importance. They grew well on poor soil and liked the damp climate. They seemed to be resistant to disease and continued to thrive when other crops failed. And one acre of potatoes could provide three or four times as many meals as one acre of oats or bere.

As a result, dependence became almost as extreme in the Highlands, as in Ireland. Paradoxically, of course, far from ameliorating the condition of the people, such a dependence perpetuated it, by allowing a dramatic rise in population. One writer suggested that some mysterious element in potatoes actually enhanced the fertility of people; the truth is that it was less a matter of magic vitamins than of greater calorific yield per acre, inhibiting immigration to the towns and allowing earlier marriage and parenthood. So long as the lazy-beds did well, the people would be free from famine. More, they did not expect.

Meanwhile, potatoes were making some advance in the rest of the country. Where other crops did well they gained little ground. In the north-east, for example, it took the failure of the grain harvest in 1782 to persuade farmers that here really was a valuable food for horses, cattle, sheep, pigs and poultry. (That humans might enjoy it was not envisaged.) In Moray and Nairn, the strange tubers were 'eaten only thro' necessity, never thro' choice, by the poor; and in many families the servants refuse them wholly as a meal'. Yet the time was not far away when the fisher-folk of the north-east, and of the rest of the country, discovered the affinities of fish with potatoes, and 'tatties an' herrin'' became a well-loved food.

In Ayrshire and Dumfries, where climate and soil seemed specially designed for the crop, it was widely cultivated, especially as the population of the Clyde towns and ports provided a market. Ayrshire was to become a major potato region, but there were always other crops, and dairy cattle, to prevent overdependence. Nonetheless, by 1803 when the Wordsworths were touring, Dorothy noticed potato patches on almost every stage of the journey from Dumfries to Ballachulish. One gave her particular pleasure:

We passed by one patch of potatoes that a floreist [sic] might have been proud of; no carnation-bed ever looked more gay than this square plot of ground on the waste common. The flowers were in very large bunches, and of an extraordinary size, and of every conceivable shade of colouring from snow-white to deep purple. It was pleasing in that place, where perhaps was never yet a flower cultivated by man for his own pleasure, to see these blossoms grow more gladly than elsewhere, making a summer garden near the mountain dwelling.

That was at Inversneyde. At the ferry-house at Loch Creran, other emotions were excited:

They had just taken from the fire a great pan of potatoes, which they mixed up with milk, all helping themselves out of the same vessel, and the little children put in their dirty hands to dig out of the mess at their pleasure.

Soon enough, however, Dorothy's essential kindliness and cheerful composure reasserted themselves, and she was able to reflect

How light the labours of such a house as this! Little sweeping, no washing of floors, and as to scouring the table, I believe it was a thing never thought of.

What would her reaction have been, had she accompanied the young Osgood Mackenzie and his mother to the Isle of Harris in the 1850s? There they had an experience which the boy would never forget, nor can anyone who has read his book:

The goodwife, like all Harris people, had most charming manners, but she was busy preparing the breakfast, and bade us sit down on little low stools at the fire, and wait till she could milk the cow ... There was a big pot hanging up by a chain over the peat-fire, and a creel was heaped with short heather ... The wife took an armful of the heather, and deposited it at the feet of the nearest cow, which was tied up within two or three yards of the fire, to form a drainer. Then, lifting the pot off the fire, she emptied it on the heather; the hot water disappeared and ran away among the cow's legs, but the contents, consisting of potatoes and fish, remained on top of the heather. Then, from a very black-looking bed, three stark-naked boys arose, one by one, aged, I should say, from six to ten years, and made for the fish and potatoes, each youngster carrying off as much as both his hands could contain. Back they went to their bed, and started devouring their breakfast with apparently great appetite under the blankets.

By now – the mid-19th century – the great promise of the potato had turned out to be a mirage, and the discovery sent what remained of the Highland way of life crashing. A vicious disease, blight, swept Ireland and Scotland in 1845 and again in 1846; both seasons' crops were destroyed within a few days. In Ireland it was catastrophic, with thousands of deaths from starvation and associated causes. In the Highlands and Islands similar calamity was prevented by the relatively small size of the area and quick action by relief committees from Glasgow and Edinburgh. The fact that the rest of the country could send grain and other foods saved Highlanders from the terrible sufferings of the Irish; but the situation was bad enough, and many landlords risked impoverishment trying to help their destitute tenants. Those who did not were denounced by name in newspaper articles and from the pulpit. Even so, the courage and morale of the people failed almost irretrievably, and the isolation and independence of communities ended forever. The population dwindled as whole families of embittered, exhausted crofters sought work in Glasgow, Birmingham, and abroad.

It is one of the more unfair twists of history that these events, so catastrophic for many, actually advanced potato cultivation in the rest of Scotland, where the lessons of blight were so well learnt that within a few years the country became one of the major centres of seed potato culture. The importance to a small country of mixed agriculture was the first lesson; the second – that potato varieties become less resistant to disease as they get older – stimulated growers to experiment with new breeds. In Angus, Fife, Orkney, the Lothians and Ayrshire, breeding became and has remained an important activity, producing many famous names – Orkney Reds, Champion, Up-to-Date, Majestic, Eldorado, Kerr's Pink, Ben Lomond, Great Scot, and latterly the whole Pentland and Maris ranges.

In our own day, there is no doubt that the Scot prefers potatoes to oats. Although less knowledgeable and less demanding than formerly – a recent survey by the Potato Marketing Board revealed the astonishing fact that shoppers consider the two most important qualities to be freedom from blemish and low price – there are still strong regional preferences for different types. In the west, white-fleshed potatoes are popular, whereas in Angus the yellow-fleshed Record is favourite, and the Aberdonians like Duke of York. Further south, regional loyalties create demand for 'East Lothians' or 'Ayrshires' under the mistaken impression that these are named varieties, but perhaps also based on the correct observation that the fresher the potato the better it tastes. Whether used for champit tatties and served with haggis, for clapshot (Orkney's national dish), or for the potato cakes and stovies of Aberdeenshire, the potato remains the Scots' most-loved vegetable.

— RECIPES —

BARLEY

A friend who was a young girl on Lewis just after the 1914–18 war recalls watching her father's farmworkers harvest the barley. It was very carefully treated; each stalk was precious, none was clumsily cut or allowed to lie unnoticed on the ground, for from it was to come their daily bread. Her own father's father remembered seeing the first loaves (i.e. wheat loaves made with yeast) appear on the island but, still in her youth, barley bannock, not wheat loaf, was standard fare.

Today, on the islands, older people like new-baked bannocks with their fresh fish. It is long since plain barley- or bere-meal was used – the addition of a little wheat flour (some recipes call for half and half) lightens the texture and is now traditional. An Orkney recipe substitutes baking powder for the more traditional buttermilk which is sometimes hard to find.

Bere Bannock

½ lb (250g) barley or bere meal
2 oz (60g) self-raising flour
1½ teaspoons baking powder
½ teaspoon salt
1 teaspoon treacle

Set the girdle to heat on a medium flame. Mix 1½ cups water with the treacle. Sieve the dry ingredients, then stir in the liquid to make a soft pliable dough. Shape it on a floured board, handling it as little as possible, and rolling it into rounds. Sprinkle the girdle with meal, then place a bannock on it and cook until the underside is nicely brown, then turn it over to brown the other side.

Scotch Broth

For this, one of the world's great soups, barley is the one indispensable ingredient. You may do without meat, you may substitute one vegetable for another; but barley you must have. Scotch broth has received many accolades since Dr Johnson ate several platefuls declaring that he had never eaten it before, 'but I don't care how soon I eat it again'. H. V. Morton wrote what is surely its definitive description, and followed that with an authoritative recipe which cannot be improved upon, though he was clearly not aware that the use of fresh peas had been recommended by Meg Dods a hundred years before him.

If a man encounters nothing in Scotland but broth – that porridge of the evening – thick with peas, barley, leeks, carrots, and almost everything that was in the kitchen at the time, he has not travelled in vain. He can return to his own land with the boast that he has met real soup . . . No unintelligent woman could make this soup. Its appearance is itself a guarantee of a wife's taste and skill: it is a perpetual compliment to her judgment . . .

This is how it is done: The night before take a quarter of a pound of Scotch barley and allow it to soak until the morning. Scotch barley is not the inadequate, microscopic pearl barley common in England but fat generous grain almost as large, when softened, as a pea. At the same time take quarter of a pound of dried peas and soak them in a similar way. If you like peas, throw in an extra handful. Now the cookery books, which as an earnest student of Scotch broth I have, of course, read, tell you to use fresh peas when they are obtainable. Do not be misled by such nonsense: dry peas are infinitely better, and, as I like them slightly hard, I decline to soak them overnight. When you have made this soup once or twice you will be in a position to decide for yourself whether my taste is yours. I think that the slightly hard peas give to the soup a richer accent . . .

The important day dawns. You are about to make divine soup. You find in the kitchen the barley and the peas soaked and ready. Now take half a pound of mutton and if anyone says that any other meat will do give him a crack over the head with the nearest frying pan! This is rank heresy. The mutton to use is called in Scotland 'flank' and, I believe, in England 'the best end of neck'. Place this half pound of mutton in a fairly roomy saucepan and cover it with cold water. Throw in a tablespoonful of salt and bring to the boil. Then let it simmer at the boil for one hour.

During this hour take two, or even three, leeks, two carrots, one fine turnip and a good-looking young spring cabbage. Chop the carrots and the turnip into small squares, chop the leeks and the spring cabbage and mix them all together. You now have a beautiful raw, red, white, and green salad. When the mutton has been at the boil for an hour take the barley and the peas which, you remember, are already soaked, and empty into the pot; then add the pile of chopped leeks, carrots, turnip and cabbage. Give them a stir with a wooden spoon. You are now well on the way.

The soup must now boil for another hour. Soon it will begin to smell like Scotch broth and you will become ravenously hungry. The great temptation at this stage is to dip into the brew with a spoon and start reducing the number of peas; but resist this temptation because you may upset the balance of power. Instead, during this second hour and in intervals of watching the soup, take a small handful of parsley, chop it finely and keep it ready on a plate. Take also a carrot and crush it over a grater into a pink mush. Keep this ready on another plate.

At the end of the hour which elapsed since the introduction of the vegetables add the chopped parsley and grated carrot (this carrot merely gives the soup a delicate pink flush) and stir gently. In fifteen minutes the soup will be ready.

A recapitulation of the ingredients may help the reader:

¼ lb (125g) Scotch barley
¼ lb (125g) dried peas (or more)
½ lb (250g) flank mutton
water
2 tablespoons salt
2–3 leeks
3 carrots (one reserved for the final stage)
1 turnip or swede
1 small spring cabbage (curly kale is not only more
    traditional, but better – 5–6 leaves will do)
1 oz (30g) parsley

Barley Soup

This is a very delicate soup with the texture of thin cream. Good stock, made from knuckle bones and chicken carcase, is vital.

2 oz (60g) Scotch barley
1 pt (500 ml) water
2 pt (1 l) well-flavoured white stock
salt and pepper
a little butter

Soak the barley overnight, then boil in water for about an hour, or until soft. Pass it through the blender, then through a nylon sieve. Add the stock, stirring well, and reheat. Season. Just before serving a little cream or butter may be added.

OATMEAL

If wheat is the most versatile cereal, oats must run a close second. From the farmworker's morning brose, which was simply meal with boiling water added, to the merchant's haggis and the laird's cranachan, oats can find their place at every course of every meal in every household.

Even brose has its variants. There is kail brose, where the boiling liquid contains chopped cooked kail and perhaps a piece of meat as well. Beef brose calls for the oatmeal to be well toasted before having rich stock poured over it. Mussel brose brings together the harvest of fishermen and farmer, and is too good to be allowed to fall into oblivion.

Mussel Brose

3 lb (1½kg) carefully cleaned mussels
3 pt (1½ l) fish stock
1 pt (500 ml) milk
1 handful of oatmeal per person.

Scrub the mussels well and remove the beards, then put them in a pan with a well-fitting lid, and shake over heat until they are all open. Take them out of their shells and remove the black parts (they are tough). Mix the stock and milk, add the mussels and simmer for about ten minutes. Toast the oatmeal. Put a handful of meal in each soup bowl and quickly stir in a good cupful of brose so that knots are formed. Return the mixture to the pan for two minutes, then serve.

A different affair altogether is Athole Brose, which Stevenson described in *Kidnapped* as made of 'old whisky, strained honey, and sweet cream slowly beaten together in the right order and proportion'. He omitted the oatmeal which many consider essential, and added cream which, strictly speaking, turns it into Gromach, to be eaten with a spoon rather than bottled and drunk at Hogmanay or other festive occasions. But there are many variants. Two I like particularly come from a small book called *The Scot and His Oats* by G. W. Lockhart.

Athole Brose (as an apéritif)

Soak a quantity of pinhead oatmeal in water overnight; drain off the liquor and add to it honey to taste; add an equal amount of whisky, and serve with some of the oatmeal in each glass.

Athole Brose (as a dessert)

To a lightly toasted tablespoon of pinhead oatmeal add 1 tablespoon of honey and 2 tablespoons of whisky; mix well; gently fold this mixture into a pint of stiffly beaten cream.

During the summer, a common breakfast food in place of brose was crowdie, for though we think now of crowdie as a type of soft cottage cheese, originally it consisted of sour milk or buttermilk mixed with raw oatmeal to the consistency of soft porridge – a dish both refreshing and healthful. Later, crowdie was adapted for use as a main dish in the middle of the day. In this context it was made with meat or poultry stock and, unlike brose, the oatmeal was cooked in the liquid. This is the crowdie Burns had in mind when he described the cares of a family man:

> Ance crowdie, twice crowdie,
> Three times crowdie in a day;
> Gin ye crowdie ony mair
> Ye'll crowdie a' my meal away.

Crowdie (Oatmeal soup)

2 pt (1 l) meat or chicken stock, well skimmed of fat
2 oz (60g) fine oatmeal
1 finely chopped onion

parsley or chives to garnish
pinch each pepper, sugar, and salt

Bring the stock to the boil. Mix the oatmeal with enough cold water to make a slightly runny paste. Pour into the boiling stock, stirring well. Bring to simmering point again, add onion, season and cook for about 30 minutes. Sprinkle with chopped parsley or chives before serving.

The most celebrated dish made from oatmeal is porridge. By tradition, porridge is 'them'.

'Hoot-toot!' said Uncle Ebenezer, 'dinna fly up in the snuff at me. We'll agree fine yet. And, Davie, my man, if you're done with that bit parritch, I could just take a sup of it myself. Ay' he continued, as soon as he had ousted me from the stool and spoon, 'they're fine, halesome food — they're grand food, parritch.'

Robert Louis Stevenson, *Kidnapped*

Also, by tradition, they are eaten standing (though not by Uncle Ebenezer). This curious custom is variously accounted for:

1. It allows the eaters to remain alert in the event of a surprise attack.
2. 'A stauning sack fills the fu'est.'
3. (A corollary of 2.) Porridge is more easily digested this way. Anyone who has had porridge in bed will corroborate this.

It is common nowadays and quite acceptable, to use rolled oats when making porridge. My own preference is for pinhead oatmeal, so coarsely ground it almost looks like finely chopped nuts; soaked overnight, it requires fifteen minutes' attention in the morning, and the flavour is superior to rolled oats.

Porridge

1 fistful pinhead oatmeal per person
water to cover
1 teaspoon salt per 4 persons
1 little thin cream or top of the milk

The previous night, soak the oatmeal in water in the saucepan in which it is to be cooked. Next morning bring it slowly to the boil, stirring to avoid lumps. When it begins to bubble slowly it needs less attention, but an occasional stir should be given, and if it becomes very thick a little boiling water may be added. After about five minutes, add the salt, and continue to cook until it spits and belches 'until it says "Gargunnock and Perth"' goes the saying.

Pour it into cold plates, which will encourage it to set. Have thin cream or top milk for each person to dip his spoonful of porridge into before conveying it to his mouth.

This is the classic approach. In the 18th century many people took ale or porter to their porridge, and in some families children were allowed honey or syrup to sweeten it. An old man whose childhood was spent on Skye remembers that on wintry mornings his mother added a spoonful or two of whisky to the bowls of those who had a three-mile walk to school ahead of them.

There are also more spartan traditions. Shepherds, it is said, made their porridge once weekly and poured it into a drawer to set, cutting off a slice or two each day. The custom was continued by country people who came to Glasgow to work in the factories in the 19th century. Cold porridge, disagreeable as it sounds, is actually not unpalatable if carefully made and well salted; it has satisfactory rib-sticking qualities which sustain one until the next meal, even if that is many hours away.

Haggis

Strange that, while porridge was easily accepted throughout the British Empire – some would say it was an integral attribute of it – haggis remains a curiosity outside Scotland, an unfamiliar object which calls forth defensive ribaldry in its own country. It was not always so, for in one form or another it was eaten in England until about the 18th century. Part of the fault lies with Scots themselves: contests in haggis-bashing and haggis-hurling are unlikely to engender respect. This is a shame, for as well as being a first-class food which few people of good sense would reject, haggis has a very ancient history.

Its origins are obscure. Some writers refer to Aristophanes, others to the Gauls; some kind of meat stuffed into an animal paunch to be steamed, is an old way of making ingredients which look unpromising, palatable. In its present, Scottish form, haggis is well documented from the mid-18th century for, within the space of a few years, we find Boswell and Johnson eating it ('Sir Alexander stuck his fork into a liver-pudding'); Smollett recording, tongue-in-cheek, the English reaction to it:

a mess of minced lights, livers, suet, oatmeal, onions and pepper, enclosed in a sheep's stomach, had a very sudden effect upon mine, and the delicate Mrs Tabby changed colour, when the cause of our disgust was instantaneously removed at the nod of our entertainer. Scots in general are attached to this composition with a sort of national fondness.

and Burns celebrating it with an ode.

The Wordsworths do not seem to have encountered it, probably because nearly all their meals were taken at inns or in the houses of the very poor, but Queen Victoria tried it and 'really liked it very much'.

Nearer our own times, haggis was approved by a Professor of English literature at Edinburgh University, George Saintsbury, whose writings on wine and food are still readable, declared that:

The people who regard haggis and sheep's heads as things that the lips should not allow to enter them and the tongue should refuse to mention are (begging their pardon) fools. I believe it to be a fact generally and know it to be one in some actual cases, that haggis extracted from its bag and presented as mince, or a cold sheep's head pie offered as a sort of galantine, do not fail to deceive and delight the average Southerner.

He was right, of course. Those who enjoy *civet de lièvre*, braised ox heart, fried brains, and other such delicacies, accept them without knowing the process of preparation; and those who shudder at the mention of a sheep's stomach are often the same people who eat with relish the innumerable variations on minced pork stuffed into an animal's intestine which we call sausages.

The final word rests with Marian McNeill, whose genius has encapsulated all the essential attributes of haggis in four sentences:

It is a testimony to the national gift of making the most of small means; for in the haggis we have concocted from humble, even despised ingredients, a veritable plat de gourmet. It contains a proportion of oatmeal, for centuries the national staple, whilst the savoury and wholesome blending of the cereal with onion and suet (met with in its simplicity in such dishes as Mealie Puddings, the Fitless Cock, and Skirlie-in-the-Pan) is typically Scottish. Further, it is a thoroughly democratic dish, equally available and equally honoured in castle, farm and croft. Finally, the use of the paunch of the animal as the receptacle of the ingredients gives the touch of romantic barbarism so dear to the Scottish heart.

Haggis is rarely home-made these days. It can be bought ready for reheating in a slow oven (or in water at a gentle simmer) from any good butcher, who probably uses his own recipe. My own favourite is made with pig's liver, not lamb's, and originated in Mauchline, near the site of Burns's farm, Mossgiel.

If you wish to try making it yourself, the following is one of the standard recipes.

> 1 sheep's pluck (lights, liver and heart)
> ½ lb (250g) pinhead oatmeal, toasted till brown
> ¼ lb (125g) minced suet
> 2–3 onions, finely chopped
> 1 tablespoon salt
> ½ teaspoon cayenne pepper
> 1 sheep's paunch, thoroughly scrubbed and soaked
>   overnight in cold salted water

Wash the pluck well, put in a pan, and cover with cold water, leaving the windpipe hanging over the edge. Boil for 2 hours, then cool in its liquid. Reserving the liquid, remove the pluck and cut away the pipes and all the gristle. Mince heart, half the liver, and the lights, mix in all other ingredients and check the seasoning. Add enough of the reserved liquid to make a softish mixture. Stuff the paunch with it, till it is slightly over half full (the oatmeal will swell and the bag, if too full, will burst). Sew up the orifice with strong thread, and put the haggis in a large pan of boiling water. When it begins to swell, prick all over with a large needle. Boil gently without the lid for three hours, topping up the water as necessary. Serve with mashed potatoes (champit tatties) and finely chopped boiled turnips or swedes (bashed neeps), both lavishly flavoured with butter and black pepper.

Pan Haggis is kinder to the squeamish, simpler than real haggis, but very nearly as good.

Pan Haggis

1 lb (450g) pig's or lamb's liver
3 onions
5 oz (150g) minced suet
½ pt (250 ml) water
3 oz (100g) pinhead oatmeal
1 teaspoon salt
½ teaspoon pepper

Simmer liver and onions in stock for 30–40 minutes. Put oatmeal in a heavy pan over heat or under the grill, and toast until nicely browned. When the meat is cooked, remove from pan, keeping liquid. Mince liver and onions, add oatmeal, suet, salt and pepper. Moisten with sufficient liquid to give a softish consistency, put into a greased pudding basin and cover with a double lid of foil, and steam for 3 hours.

Recipes using oatmeal in many other ways – in soup, with vegetables, with meat, and in desserts – appear elsewhere in the book. This section, however, would lose all credibility if it did not include that most typical of Scottish products, the oatcake.

When Fergusson and Burns wrote of the Land o' Cakes, it was oatcakes they meant. In fact, oatcakes were long made in other parts of Britain too; yet not even haggis has such evocative powers for Scots of all ages and in all parts of the world. To generations, they have symbolized home, rural life, the traditional values of thrift, honesty, hard work and simple godliness. In some households porridge has been replaced by instant cereal, and haggis is only eaten on Burns Night; but oatcakes remain an integral part of daily life.

They are, perhaps, an acquired taste. As we know, Dr Johnson disliked them. Perhaps he was unlucky in his experience, because not all are made to the same recipe. W. G. Lockhart says that in the north a finer grind of meal is preferred for a floury, hard cake, but in the south the crunchy mixture of pinhead is appreciated. Proportion and type of shortening vary too, some cooks using dripping or goose fat, some butter, and in the Trossachs the Wordsworths had excellent oatcakes which had been kneaded with cream.

Really first-class oatcakes need no accompaniment other than best fresh butter, as every devotee acknowledges. Nonetheless, each person finds his favourite spread or accompaniment, whether it be sardines, cheese, broth, or treacle. In *Huntingtower*, Buchan's heroes, offered high tea by an elderly lady, are urged to 'try hinny and aitcake . . .' I would myself put forward a modest claim for fresh butter and crab-apple jelly.

It is possible to find in the shops many good commercially made oatcakes, and if one lives in Scotland it is merely a matter of experimenting to see which one prefers. Elsewhere they are harder to buy, and making them may be the only solution. They are not difficult, though it needs practice to gauge correctly the amount of water needed.

Oatcakes

4 oz (125g) oatmeal
1 pinch bicarbonate of soda
1 pinch of salt
1 teaspoon melted lard, bacon fat, or poultry fat
hot water

Mix the dry ingredients. Place a perfectly flat heavy frying pan or girdle on the stove to heat. Add the fat to the dry ingredients with just enough hot water to make a stiff dough. Sprinkle plenty of meal on the baking board and roll out the dough as thinly as possible, sprinkling more meal if it shows signs of sticking. Cut dough into rounds or quarter rounds, place on the girdle over a moderate heat, and when the edges begin to curl, remove carefully and finish by cooking the top under a grill for a few minutes.

Sowens

These were a by-product of oats, and have been variously described to me as 'a delicious dish' and 'horrible'. Whatever their appeal or lack of it, sowens played an important part in rural diet throughout the 18th and 19th centuries.

They were made, thriftily, from the husks or sids left behind when the oats had been ground and sieved. First, the sids were set with water in a wooden dish and allowed to stand for a week or more, until mild fermentation had taken place. Occasional stirring encouraged the loosening of any particles of meal sticking to the husks. When the mixture was ready, the swats, or liquid, was carefully poured off without disturbing the sediment, providing a not unpleasant and refreshing drink. Then, the sediment itself was pressed and washed through a cloth or fine sieve. The pale liquid in the bowl was now raw sowens, and could replace milk or beer when times were hard, or could be given as a cooling drink to patients with fever. In Ross-shire, raw sowens could also accompany a dish of boiled sowens, the combination being designated 'sowens and sowens to them'.

The next stage of preparation was to boil the sowens until the mixture thickened. They were then ready to eat, hot or cold, with milk, cream, or even beer.

Though undoubtedly a rural delicacy, sowens were not eaten only by farm labourers. Nor do they have particular associations with a specific meal: in some areas they were eaten at breakfast and supper, in others they constituted the mid-day meal, and in others they were a festive dish. In Angus and Caithness they formed supper dishes even in quite well-to-do families.

Further refinements were possible in the preparation. They could be dried into a paste which, rolled in raw oatmeal, provided many a 'piece' for Orkney school-children. In this form they could even be sent to relatives in the big towns, to be dissolved in water and boiled up, re-creating the pleasures of home. Sowens scones, made by mixing oatmeal, milk and eggs into raw sowens and dropping spoonfuls of the batter onto a hot girdle, were popular in Caithness and Orkney.

In the north-east, Sowens Nicht was an established part of the Christmas period as late as 1905, with young people gathering to drink sowens and ale, and eat bread and cheese, in each others' houses. For many years Christmas morning itself had been the statutory Sowin Morning, when, as an Aberdeenshire farmer put it,

many people delights in running about from Town to Town, and drinking sowins and getting fun and making a noise.

Few traditional foods can have disappeared so rapidly and so completely from daily life. Within the space of 50 years, sowens have become unknown to all but researchers and the very old. Their only trace now is in proverbs and sayings, one of which at least deserves to survive. It expresses the feelings of many a hostess towards the late-departing guest:

Our Sowins are ill sour'd, ill seil'd, ill salted, ill sodden, thin, an' little o' them. Ye may stay a' night, but ye may gang hame if ye like.

WHEAT

In the Middle Ages, when wheat was scarce and often had to be imported, it was an ingredient accorded respect, and for which imaginative recipes were devised. The wheaten bread of the wealthy was frequently enriched with eggs, butter or cream, and a strong continental influence encouraged the addition of spices and dried fruit. This strand of the Scottish baking tradition leads to the gingerbreads, seed cakes and diet loaves we know today.

The other strand originated in the late 18th century, when home production of wheat took a step forward. There was coincidentally a marked fall in the price of the sugar coming into the ports on the Clyde, and tea too dropped in cost, so that it was no longer the prerogative of the upper classes. In the neat new stone houses of the emerging rural middle-class, equipped with kitchens with coal-

burning ranges and proper ovens, ale was no longer fashionable for
the 'four hours'. Instead, tea was drunk, and little delicacies to
accompany it soon became popular. Many were based on the older
traditions of peat fire and iron girdle – and so we get the variety of
scones, crumpets, and pancakes which housewives still take pride
in if they live in the country.

Most baking recipes belong under the heading high tea, and may
be found in the chapter which deals directly with this and other
meals; recipes in this chapter are mainly for yeast breads and rolls.

Aberdeen Rowies (Buttery Rowies, Butteries)

It is pleasing to be able to use the alphabet as an excuse for putting
these little rolls first, for they are really outstandingly good. Many
writers have remarked their similarity in texture if not in appearance, to French croissants, which are supposed to have first been
made in Budapest in 1686 when the Turks were defeated by western
armies. How and when the method reached Scotland, why it
became a speciality of Aberdeen, are questions yet unanswered, but
the real mystery, in my opinion, is why butteries are not more
often made at home. Although there are some complicated recipes
about, this simple one works well:

> 1 lb (450g) strong white unbleached flour
> 1 teaspoon salt
> 6 oz (150g) butter
> 1–2 teaspoons sugar
> 2 gills (280 ml) tepid water
> ½ oz (15g) fresh yeast
> 2 oz (60g) lard

Set aside the lard and two-thirds of the butter on a flat board or
plate. Add the salt to the flour and rub in the remaining butter.
Melt the sugar in a little of the water and add the yeast. Cream
well. Leave for a few minutes, then cream again, and pour into
the flour. Adding as much tepid water as will make a softish
dough, mix well by hand and knead it until it is elastic and
smooth. Cover and leave in a warm place for 1–1½ hours, until

well risen. Meanwhile, with a round-ended knife blade, mix the butter and lard until they have softened to an easy spreading consistency.

Sprinkle a work-surface with self-raising flour and knead the dough again. Roll out fairly thin, spread on half the fat mixture, dust lightly with flour, and fold in three as if making puff pastry. Seal the ends, give a half turn, roll again. Spread on the rest of the fat, dust again, and fold. Roll out into a square this time. Cut into squares – you should get about sixteen – and bringing the corners of each square to the centre shape roughly into rounds without over-handling. Dust a baking-tray with flour, put the butteries on it, and leave to rise for 30–40 minutes. Bake at 400° F (200° C) gas 6 for 15–20 minutes.

They can be baked for 10 minutes only and frozen when cold. Five minutes' baking, after defrosting, gives a good result. They are sensational partially split while still warm and filled with raspberry or cherry jam – no butter is needed.

Baps

These are soft white rolls, traditionally served warm for breakfast.

> 1 lb (450g) strong white flour
> 1 small teaspoon salt
> 2 oz (60g) lard
> 1 oz (30g) fresh yeast
> 1 teaspoon sugar
> ½ pt (300 ml) tepid milk and water, mixed

Sift flour into a warm bowl and mix in the salt. Rub in the lard. In another bowl, cream yeast and sugar, add the liquid, and strain into the flour. Make into a soft dough, kneading until it is elastic, cover, and set to rise for 1–1½ hours in a warm place. Knead lightly again, and divide into pieces of equal size to form ovals about 3 in (5 cm) long and 2 in (3–4 cm) wide. Brush with milk, then dust with flour. Place on a greased and floured baking tray and set in a warm place, to prove, for 15 minutes. To prevent blisters, press a finger into the centre of each before they go into the oven. Bake in a hot oven 425° F (220° C) gas 7.

Just as a mixture of barley and wheat came to replace pure barley in the making of bannocks, so oatmeal and wheat were often combined in the manufacture of bread. It made the wheat go further. Moreover it increased the fat content of the loaf, making it softer, and gave it also an interesting flavour. Oats contain almost no gluten, and dough made from oatmeal alone will not rise, so if a heavy loaf is to be avoided, care must be taken with the proportions of the flours. Fine meal is best, but a tablespoon or so of pinhead sprinkled over the loaves when they are proving makes an unusual and delicious crust even if the dough itself contains no oatmeal.

The following loaf is made without yeast. It is not one for everyday, but it makes a pleasant change from standard wheat bread.

Oatmeal Loaf

½ lb (225g) oatmeal
10 oz (280g) plain strong white flour
1 teaspoon bicarbonate of soda
2 teaspoons cream of tartar
¾ pt (375 ml) milk

Soak the oatmeal in the milk overnight. Sift the dry ingredients and stir into the oatmeal mixture, which should be very soft. Butter a loaf tin very thoroughly, and pour in the mixture. Bake in a moderate oven, 350° F (180° C), gas 4.

POTATOES

In *The Scots Kitchen* Marian McNeill gives ten recipes for 'dishes of vegetables'. Eight concern potatoes. If Scotland can be said to have its own brand of *cuisine bourgeoise*, much of that undoubtedly owes a very great debt to the potato, which was exploited almost to the limit of its possibilities.

Early in its history, its compatibility with fish was noted.

Potatoes and herring go especially well together, the mealy softness of the vegetable absorbing and enhancing the oils and firm flakes of the fish if fresh, counterbalancing the saltiness of the pickled variety.

Tatties an' Herring

Traditionally this was made with salt herring and cooked over a peat fire. Here is a modern version:

> 1 lb (450g) mealy potatoes
> 2 onions, thinly sliced
> 4 fresh herring, boned
> 2 fl oz (50 ml) milk
> salt and pepper

Scrub potatoes well, but do not peel. Slice them thickly. Peel and slice the onions. Grease a heavy flat-bottomed pan, and in it put half the potatoes, then half the onions. Sprinkle with salt and pepper. Lay the herrings on top, flat if they are small, rolled up if they are large. Cover with the rest of the vegetables in layers. Season again. Pour in the milk. Cover, bring just to the boil, then keep on a very low heat until the potatoes are cooked, about one hour.

Another good fish and potato combination is Findon Fish Pudding. It comes from Catherine Brown's splendid book, *Scottish Traditional Recipes*. The inclusion of tomatoes shows the recipe's recent origins, but it is a good example of the adaptation of traditional ingredients and methods to meet contemporary taste.

Findon Fish Pudding

> 2 lb (1 kg) potatoes
> 1¼ lb (625g) Aberdeen fillet
> 1 oz (30g) butter
> 2 tablespoons milk or cream

1 tomato for the top
1 oz (30g) grated cheese

Preheat the oven to 350° F (180° C) gas 4. Peel potatoes and put on to boil. While they are boiling put the fish onto a greased baking tray, dot with butter, and sprinkle with milk. Cover with a piece of paper or foil and bake for 20 minutes. Remove from the oven and leave to cool.

The potatoes can now be drained and mashed. Drain the cooking liquor from the fish into the potatoes, then flake the fish in on top. Mash all together and season well. Put into a greased 2½ pt (1¼ l) dish. Put sliced tomato on top and cover with grated cheese. Heat through in the oven and serve with leeks in cream sauce.

Another very popular main dish combines potatoes with cabbage or other greens, in a sort of vegetarian Bubble-and-Squeak. It is given different names in different regions: in the Highlands (as in Ireland) it is Colcannon, in the north-east, Kailkenny, while in the Borders it has the splendid appellation of Rumbledethumps. The basic recipe is the same, though some versions add leeks or onions – an embellishment I would recommend – and opinions differ as to the relative merits of butter or cream.

Rumbledethumps

1 lb (450g) potatoes, thickly sliced
1 lb (450g) white cabbage, spring cabbage, or kale, also sliced
3 oz (75g) butter or ¼ pint (125 ml) cream
white part of 2 leeks, or 1 onion, sliced
pepper, salt

Boil the vegetables separately in as little water as possible. Drain. Mash the potatoes roughly. In a large heavy pan, melt the butter or heat the cream, and add the leeks or onions. Heat for a few minutes, then add the potatoes and cabbage. Sprinkle with salt and black pepper, stir well, check the seasoning. Beat with a wooden spoon for a minute or so, and serve.

Stovies

Even potatoes cooked on their own can be treated in more interesting ways than by plain boiling or roasting; credit for one of the best and simplest potato recipes belongs firmly to the person who invented Stovies. This dish brings out the flavour of the vegetable, so good quality potatoes only should be used. The word Stovies comes from the French *étuver*, to sweat, i.e. to cook in its own steam.

Peel and cut potatoes into even-sized pieces, or use new potatoes, well scrubbed. Put a very little water, just enough to cover the bottom of the pan, into a heavy pan. Add the potatoes, sprinkle with salt and pepper, and add about 1½ oz (30–45g) butter cut into small pieces. Cover tightly and cook over the lowest possible heat for about an hour, shaking often and checking at intervals that they have not dried. A tablespoon or two of boiling water may be added if you are nervous.

Wigtown is in the heart of potato country (Dumfries and Galloway), so the following recipe needs no puff from me:

Wigtown Potatoes

1½ lb (750g) small new potatoes, well scrubbed
4–6 oz (125–150g) mushrooms, sliced but not peeled
1 tablespoon each chopped thyme and chives or parsley
salt and pepper
1½ oz (40g) butter

Melt the butter in a heavy pan, add the potatoes and shake well. Add the mushrooms, herbs, and a little seasoning. Put a piece of well-greased foil on top, cover with a close-fitting lid, and cook over a very low heat, shaking frequently, for about 30 minutes. Serve immediately with any kind of grilled meat or by itself as a supper dish.

Tatties and Crowdie

In this context 'crowdie' has the meaning of cottage cheese, made from naturally soured milk. In summer, when the cattle grazed in the Highland shielings, they produced good milk and this dish was a popular way of using it.

> 1 lb (450g) potatoes, peeled and boiled
> 1 oz (30g) butter
> 2 oz (60g) crowdie
> 1 tablespoon chives or parsley, finely chopped
> 1 tablespoon double cream
> salt and pepper

The crowdie is mixed with cream and herbs and well seasoned. It is then handed round with the potatoes, which have been put in a covered dish with plenty of butter. An alternative version carefully scoops out the centre of the cooked potatoes and puts the crowdie mixture in.

Victor McClure, a writer of the 1930s whose books on food, alas, are out of print, describes an Aberdeenshire way with potatoes:

The potatoes were simply washed and their outer skin removed with a rough cloth. After a final rinse they were dropped into boiling water, not salted until the potatoes were practically cooked. The water was strained off and the pot placed at the back of the stove. A little finely diced onion was made transparent in butter in another pan, and the dry potatoes were rolled in this, being sprinkled at the same time with fine oatmeal touched with ground pepper. The potatoes were shaken in the buttery flat pan until this new jacketing was almost dry.

Potato scones are, I suppose, an acquired taste, being flat and somewhat leathery unless absolutely freshly made. Even so, they are delicious and I acquired the taste long ago. The very sight of them recalls to me Edinburgh in the 1950s. Before the Clean Air Act, when a sun the colour of a blood orange dimly lit the wintry streets, I used to grope my way home after lectures, stopping on the way to buy these satisfying little pancakes. Warmed in front of my gas fire and spread with butter, accompanied by a hot cup of tea, they were very comforting objects of my life during these first months away from home.

They are much better freshly made in one's own kitchen.

> ½ lb (250g) potatoes, boiled and sieved
> 2 oz (60g) flour
> a little milk
> salt

Place all ingredients except the milk into a bowl, and mix well. Be careful with the flour – you may need a little less than 60g if the potatoes are the mealy kind. Add sufficient milk to make a very stiff dough. Roll out thinly, about ⅛ of an inch (¼ cm), into rounds the size of a small plate. Cut each round into four. Prick all over with a fork. Heat and lightly flour a heavy frying pan or girdle, and bake the scones on it until they are opaque and nicely speckled on both sides.

TURNIPS

The most usual way with swedes is to peel and dice them, boil them in a little salted water until soft, then drain them and serve them with a generous piece of butter and a few good grinds of the pepper-mill. Excellent. But there are other ways. Orkney's most celebrated writer of the 20th century, George Mackay Brown, describes Clapshot, the island's national dish for which all exiles yearn:

Clapshot is one of the best things to come out of Orkney, together with Highland Park and Orkney fudge and Atlantic crabs. I have it at least once a week, sometimes more. It goes with nearly everything – sausages, corned beef, bacon, mealy puddings.

The other day, by way of a treat, I bought a piece of steak for grilling. Would clapshot go with grilled steak? No harm in trying. I peeled carefully the precious 'Golden Wonders' – and thought what a shame, in a way, 'Golden Wonders' being so delicious boiled in their thick dark jackets. And while the tatties and neeps were ramping away on top of the electric grill it came to my mind that somewhere, a while back, I had read a recipe for clapshot that advised an onion to be added . . .

In no time at all I had an onion stripped and chopped and delivered

(my eyes weeping) among the neeps and tatties in the rampaging pot
. . . Fifteen minutes later the probing fork told me that all was ready.
Decant the water into the sink, set the pot on the kitchen floor on top
of last week's *Radio Times*, add a golden chunk of butter and a dash of
milk, then salt and plenty of pepper, and begin to mash . . .

Everything about clapshot is good, including the smell and the colour.
I think this particular clapshot, with the onion in it, was about the best
I've ever made. And it blended magnificently on the palate with the
grilled steak. And it made a glow in the wintry stomach.

Glazed Swedes

All root vegetables respond deliciously to this method of cooking,
but swedes most of all, in my opinion. There can be no finer
accompaniment to a roast or to any kind of white fish, or to a game
stew. Because they contain sugar of their own, there is no need to
add sugar to produce the glaze.

> 1 lb (450g) swedes, peeled and diced
> 1 onion, sliced
> 2 oz (50g), butter or dripping, or two tablespoons
>   vegetable oil
> salt and pepper

Melt the fat in a heavy pan, then add the onion and the swedes.
Cook, uncovered, stirring frequently, until the vegetables are
browning and beginning to stick to the pan, even to burn slightly.
At this point, add enough hot water to cover the bottom of the
pan, and cover tightly to finish cooking. If water still remains
when the vegetables are tender, turn up the heat and let it
evaporate. Season. This is a good moment, if you feel inclined, to
add one tablespoon of whisky, but do not let it catch fire, the
object is not to *flamber*, simply to gild the lily in the matter of
flavour.

There is also Spiced Turnip Soup. Swedes and spices go particularly
well together, because the swede is a strong-flavoured vegetable in
its own right. (It is the sulphur in swedes which give them that
peculiarly 'hot' flavour so noticeable in the raw vegetable. They

also, as a matter of interest, contain arsenic – the only vegetable apart from cabbage to do so.)

Spiced Turnip Soup

1 lb (450g) swedes
1 medium onion, chopped
2 oz (50g) butter
½ pt (250 ml) water
½ pt (250 ml) milk
¼ teaspoon ground ginger
¼ teaspoon grated nutmeg
½ teaspoon caraway seeds
salt and pepper

Peel and dice the turnips, blanch in boiling water for 2–3 minutes, then drain, reserving the water. Melt the butter in a heavy pan, add vegetables and seasonings, cover, and cook over very low heat for about 10 minutes, stirring occasionally. Add the reserved water, bring to the boil, and simmer until tender, about 30 minutes. Cool slightly, then liquidize. (For really good results, it is best to pass through a fine sieve after liquidizing.)

Add the milk to make the soup the consistency of thin cream. Reheat but do not boil. Serve with sippets of fried bread or a little cream, or both, in each bowl.

— 4 —

LIVESTOCK

'He that has a shilling may have a piece of meat.'

Dr Johnson, *Journey to the Western Isles of Scotland*

From very early times the Scots have eaten mutton. Even before the agricultural improvements of the 12th and 13th centuries, sheep grazed the Border hills and those of the Highlands. Mostly, they were there to provide wool and milk, but occasionally animals were slaughtered for fresh meat, or to be salted down for the winter. In addition, men ate 'braxy' – sheep which had died from that disease, or by accident, or from old age.

It was, however, in the 12th and 13th centuries that sheep-farming in the southern and eastern Lowlands developed into an industry. Members of continental monastic houses settling in Scotland under the aegis of the Canmore kings, showed the way, bringing a quite new measure of prosperity to the whole area.

The great abbeys of Melrose, Jedburgh, Kelso and Dryburgh, built up flocks and established an export trade with Flanders, France and Italy. There was great demand for wool and skins from Scotland, and the agricultural pattern of the Borders was thus set: sheep in the hills, arable in the valleys. The culinary traditions which developed in conjunction were to continue more or less unchanged for 600 years, and though the great Ram which gazes majestically over the market square in Moffat is a tribute to the power of wool, in the kitchen mutton was unconditionally king, until well into the 19th century.

The main consumers were townspeople, who could buy at market the quantities which suited their purse and their needs. Even so, only the aristocracy regularly ate meat. As Dr Johnson wrote of the Highlands, the majority

seldom taste the flesh of land animals; for here are no markets. What each man eats is from his own stock. The great effect of money is to break property into small parts. In towns, he that has a shilling may have a piece of meat; but where there is no commerce, no man can eat mutton but by killing a sheep.

Under the circumstances, the acceptability of braxy mutton becomes less surprising. In John Buchan's *John Burnet of Barns*, set in the 17th century, the fugitive hero is sheltered by a shepherd who offers to 'pit up some cauld braxy and bread for ye, for it's a' I have at this time o' year'; possibly Buchan had eaten braxy himself, in his wanderings across the Lammermoors and the hills of Galloway, for it had certainly not disappeared even at the end of the 19th century. A journalist of the 1930s, Ian Macpherson, recalled life in the Central Highlands around 1900:

My grandmother often lodged as many as 30 drovers in a night, and baked to feed them all, besides a dozen smearers and her own family . . . there was no tea, except a quarter of a pound at the New Year, very little sugar, some flour, but they had braxy mutton, as black as coal with unlet blood, salmon, kippered for the winter, salt herring, oatcakes, milk, butter and cheese, venison killed with some ancient muzzle-loader . . . There was piping and fiddling and whisky ran like water. You could buy smuggled whisky or make it yourself.

As we have seen, the reforms of the 18th and 19th centuries completely altered the agricultural system. They took effect most rapidly in the Lowlands, where runrig was replaced by bigger, more efficiently organized units, owned or leased by one man with others working for him. The system of enclosures favoured large flocks of sheep, and crofters were no longer able to run a few animals on unfenced moorland. Fewer, larger farms brought unemployment – one of the things Cobbett criticized when he visited Scotland – but there was a gradual rise in the prosperity of all those who stayed on the farm, with better housing and better food. By the 1850s even the cottar's Sunday broth might have a bit of fresh mutton in it, to be eaten with potatoes when the soup had been supped. The rest of the week's meals were still meatless. At the employer's house, fresh meat was probably eaten every day – not always mutton, sometimes chicken, perhaps pork, or an occasional joint of beef; but mutton was favourite, and rightly, for by that time a Scotch leg of lamb was appreciated even in London.

In the Highlands, where there had been no monastic houses to generate commercial enterprise, keeping sheep continued to be a subsistence activity until almost the end of the 18th century, the animals providing wool and milk rather than meat.

The native sheep were small and generally ill-fed, since they grazed only on the sparse natural vegetation, without any supplement to fatten them. Captain Edward Burt, who in the 1720s travelled extensively throughout the region and was a connoisseur of Highland mutton, blamed the custom of milking the ewes for the leanness of the meat:

... when sold in the Low-Country they are chiefly used, as they tell me, to make Soups withal; and when a Side of any one of these Kinds hangs up in our Market the least disagreeable Part of the Sight is the Transparency of the Ribs.

But the meat, 'when fat, is delicious and certainly the greatest of luxuries'.

Because of the need for ewe's milk, and also because of wolves, Highlanders had been accustomed to fold their sheep at night and to keep them indoors during the winter. By 1743 the last wolf had been killed, but not until the 1760s, when farmers from the north of England moved to Scotland in search of new grazing, did the old habits lose their hold. The incoming Blackface sheep, used to staying out all winter on the high Northumbrian moors, withstood Scottish conditions remarkably well. Throughout the winter they grazed on heather, supplemented by turnips imported from the Lowlands, and a little hay. Gradually it became clear that even in the Highlands, sheep-farming could be profitable.

The change of fortune which, by slow degrees, was bringing easier times to the farmers of the Lowlands was not affecting the North. Here, soil and climate were harsher, less susceptible to attempts at improvement. The way of life was very different: there were no large towns and there had never been much trade except at the fishing ports. The concept of producing for a market was not properly understood, even had the land allowed it. Inverness possessed a market, but there can have been few traders in such a small town surrounded by great self-supporting estates. Captain Burt was moved to pity (or was it scorn?)

When the Highlanders bring their Commodities to the Market: but, good God! you could not conceive there was such Misery in this Island. One has under his arm a small Roll of Linen, another a Piece of coarse Plaiding: these are considerable dealers. But the Merchandise of the greatest Part of them is of a most contemptible Value, such as these; viz, – two or three cheeses, of about three or four Pounds weight a piece: a Kid sold for sixpence or Eight pence at most; a small Quantity of Butter, in something that looks like a Bladder, and is sometimes set down upon the dirt in the street; three or four Goat skins; a Piece of Wood for an Axletree to one of the little carts, &c.

The disruption of the clans after the '45 had destroyed the old ways. Men whose lives had been based on a careful balance in society between service and protection now found themselves in a tenant-landlord relationship; they were often unable to meet rent demands, whether in kind or cash, and the banishment of many clan chiefs removed all probability of sympathetic treatment. The desperate poverty remarked by Burt grew, if anything, worse, and only the introduction of potatoes prevented real disaster.

We have already met Sir John Sinclair, first President of the Board of Agriculture. A man of immense enthusiasms, with a talent for organization, he was deeply concerned about Highland conditions (he was himself a Caithness man). In an attempt to combat the situation, he initiated a scheme which, ironically, finished by increasing the hardships suffered: convinced that it would be the salvation of the region, he introduced the concept of large-scale sheep-farming.

Sinclair was certain that Cheviot sheep could thrive on all but the highest farms and restore the Highland economy. Their wool was superior to that of the Blackfaces, their meat also was good, and Sinclair contended that for every pound weight of beef, a shepherd could bring at least three of mutton, besides having the fleece to sell. With the assistance of turnips and a little winter hay, he felt crofting could be made profitable and, to prove it, in 1792 he placed a flock of 500 ewes on a farm in Caithness. Within eight years the number of animals had risen to 3000, meat and wool both fetching high prices.

What Sinclair did not realize was that not only were the crofters too demoralized to attempt anything new and untried in the way of agriculture (their resistance to potatoes should have alerted him), but they could afford neither sheep nor turnips to try the experiment. It was the landlords and tacksmen, and their agents, the wealthy men willing to take a small risk, who learnt the lesson. A crofter who could not pay his rent was a liability; sheep cost almost nothing and yielded high returns. Thus began the Clearances, when men, women and children were turned off the land which was all they knew, in favour of sheep.

From about the 1830s to 1874, when the price of wool suddenly fell, the sheep runs were immensely profitable. The wool was excellent, the meat (thanks to turnips and hay) superb. The fame of Scotch wool and Scotch lamb exceeded anything Sinclair could have wished. The sweet Highland mutton was renowned for its quality all over Britain and it was not mere chauvinism which made the judge, Lord Cockburn, write in his journal in 1853

Castleton, Braemar, Wednesday night, 28th September 1853:
I think it my duty to record the unmatched merits of a leg of mutton which we had to-day at dinner. It was a leg which stands out even amidst all the legs of my long and steadily muttonised life. It was glorious. A leg of which the fat flats of England can have no idea, and which even Wales, in its most favoured circumstances, could only approach. It was a leg which told how it had strayed among mountains from its lambhood to its death. It spoke of winter straths and summer heights, of tender heather, Alpine airs, cold springs, and that short sweet grass which corries alone can cherish. These were the mettle of its pasture. It left its savour on the palate, like the savour of a good deed on the heart.

Had the landlords resisted the temptation to overstock the land, had they remembered that even the poorest croft had contributed to the fertility of the soil on which the sheep now grazed, and that this fertility must be renewed, their prosperity might have lasted a little longer. But they ignored the warning signs of erosion, whilst other factors were conspiring to reduce the money to be made from sheep.

Parts of the Empire, notably New Zealand, were beginning to produce excellent mutton which, thanks to fast vessels and the innovation of refrigerated containers, could be imported cheaply into Britain. Consumer taste was altering, too, asking for smaller joints from younger animals not hardy enough to survive on the high hills in winter. All this coincided with the growing fashion among southern aristocrats and industrialists for owning deer forests. In this new craze, which reached its peak round about 1900, Highland landlords saw an opportunity to recoup their losses; and so began the second round of Clearances, of sheep and shepherds, making way for the deer. By 1912 nearly four million acres of land was given over to deer forest – almost double the 1883 figure.

During that period, surprisingly, the total number of sheep in Scotland, far from diminishing, increased, albeit minimally. Demand was still high enough to encourage Border farmers to improve their breeding stock and add to their flocks. Since 1925, figures for sheep population have remained remarkably steady, but if anything the slight upward trend has continued. Three different breeds – Cheviots, Blackfaces, and a hybrid, the Border Leicester – form the basic stock today, with the emphasis always on quality. Now that the superiority of natural fibres over synthetics is again acknowledged, Scotch wool fears little competition; Scotch mutton is harder to find. Even Lord Cockburn, though, would still enjoy Scotch lamb and recognize it as among the finest in the world.

Medieval cattle, like sheep, were not farmed primarily for meat. Their chief functions were as draught animals and to provide milk, an important item in everyone's diet. Some animals were slaughtered at Martinmas and salted, but fresh beef was the prerogative of the very rich.

Captain Burt also mentions that in the Highlands when meal began to run short in spring, cattle were bled and their blood was boiled into cakes, which, 'together with a little Milk and a short Allowance of Oatmeal, is their Food'. The inevitable effect on animals already weakened by lack of winter fodder was that 'in the Morning they cannot rise from the Ground, and several of the Inhabitants join together to help up each others Cows &c'. The quality of the milk in spring is not difficult to conjecture, and it comes as no surprise that cows calved only every second year. In summer, the poor animals had a chance to regain some flesh and strength, for whole villages would move into the mountains for the grazing of the high pastures, or shielings. There, all recuperated from the severities of the previous season, milk was once more abundant, and butter and cheese were made. In August or September came the move back to permanent quarters.

It was then, says Burt, that 'the Beef is extremely sweet and succulent, which, I suppose, is owing, in good Part, to their being reduced to such Poverty in the Spring, and made up again with new Flesh'. The animals were small (they reminded him, when full-grown, of large Lincolnshire calves) but the quality, or at least potential, of their meat had been recognized a century earlier, when farmers from Northumberland and Cumberland began buying Highland cattle to fatten them on the rich English pastures.

By the end of the 17th century there was already a substantial trade with England. Defoe writes that 'above an hundred thousand pounds a year was paid into Scotland every year, for cattle only'. From the Highlands came the small, half-wild native breed. The larger black cattle of Galloway – larger chiefly because their summer pasturage was richer and they were fed on hay during the winter – were also much in demand and very profitable. According to Defoe again:

The people of Galloway . . . are in particular breeders of cattle, such as sheep, the number of which I may say is infinite, that is to say, innumerable; and black cattle, of which they send to England, if fame lies not, 50 or 60,000 every year, the very toll of which before the Union, was a little estate to some gentlemen upon the borders; and particularly the Earl of Carlisle had a very good income by it . . .

The gentlemen generally take their rents in cattle, and some of them have so great a quantity, that they go to England with their droves, and take the money themselves. It is no uncommon thing for a Galloway nobleman to send 4,000 head of black cattle to England in a year, and sometimes much more.

Traces of the drove roads exist today, a romantic reminder of those times. Bordered by stone dykes or hedges, winding over moorland and through lonely valleys, they linked all the major market towns in the Lowlands with their English counterparts on the one hand, and the highland shielings on the other. They were used for over two hundred years, some for much longer. Both Scott and Stevenson knew them and the men who walked them; Stevenson's hero St Ives, when making his way to England in the company of that memorable pair of drovers Sim and Candlish, 'travelled for long upon the track beaten and browsed by a million herds, our predecessors'. It is a happy invention of Stevenson's which allows 'the Shirra' – Scott himself – to appear on the road and speak to St Ives and his guides, for Scott must have been a familiar figure on those Border byways. Today, long stretches of road are yet distinguishable, either by the half-ruined dykes flanking them or simply as a greener swathe lying ribbon-like across the moor. No one who walks even a short distance on one can do so unmoved: the memory of those tough, lonely men and their flocks lingers like the faint mist over a forest at the end of an autumn day.

Though the English knew so well how to fatten Scots cattle, at home there was a reluctance to try their methods. William Mac-Intosh of Borlum, an Improver and fervent Jacobite who from a prison cell in Edinburgh Castle published pseudonymously a pamphlet on farming, castigated the apathy of his countrymen:

In an enclosed country, all Months of the Year affords the Mercats with Meat always in Season; not as now where in many Towns in Scotland, for almost half the Year, there is no Beef nor Mutton to be seen in their Shambles and, if any it is liker Carrion than Meat, yet dearer than ever I saw the best Beef in England cost. Nor can it be otherwise in the supine Ignorance our Farmers are in, in the Method of choosing the right Ages of putting up to fatten their Beasts, and the want of every Provender fit to raise them; for they generally never stall any but such Oxen as are no longer fit for the Yoke; or Cows, but such as the Goodwoman tells her husband are no longer good to breed or milk; These, for eight or ten weeks, they blow up with scalded Barley, Chaff, and Malt-Grains; that lean Rickle of Bones is all the Butcher can pick up in Fife and Lothian, from Candlemas to June, even for our Metropolis. No other town is so well served.

The breathless indictment is just a little misleading for as early as the 1680s efforts to improve livestock were being made, in particular by Sir David Dunbar of Baldoon. This was the man on whose life Scott based *The Bride of Lammermuir*; but, before his tragic death, he had amassed a thousand animals which he kept in enclosed pastures and had begun, by careful feeding and selective breeding, to establish a herd whose cows calved annually and in which all the animals were very much larger than others in the country at the time. Other reformers were looking at the problems and while MacIntosh's strictures are generally correct, clearly there were isolated and sporadic early efforts at systematic improvement.

Throughout the 18th century the momentum increased. By 1800 the average weight of cattle was twice what it had been 100 years before. At the market at Crieff, the number of beasts sold annually more than tripled between 1723 and 1800. The way was being paved for the real successes of Scots cattle in the 19th century.

The soil of Aberdeenshire had been discovered to suit turnips particularly well, especially if the fields were enriched with bone meal. As a result, production of fat beef cattle became the chief agricultural enterprise. The development of two major breeds, the Scottish Shorthorn and the Aberdeen Angus, was the outcome of work by a number of single-minded and brilliant farmers obsessed with the idea of breeding first-class cattle. The first Aberdeen Angus beasts sent to Smithfield in 1829 created a sensation. Since that date, the breed has continued to gain in quality and fame, and it is pleasing to note that the descendants of the first breeder, William McCombie, are still in the business. The name of the breed itself has become synonymous with excellence of flavour, texture, and tenderness. Wherever 'Scotch beef' is on a restaurant menu it comes – or will be said to come – from an Aberdeen Angus animal. As for the Shorthorns, their progeny are to be found on almost every ranch in the United States, testifying to the genius of the men who first bred them.

Meantime, in the south-west, dairy cattle were preparing to change expectations and standards for dairy produce in the whole of Scotland.

Milk and milk products had always been an important food for all communities except those which, living by the sea, relied on fish. Cows, ewes, and goats were all milked. Most milk was taken in its natural state, but a number of different regional ways of using it had been devised in addition to butter and cheese.

Butter was to be found in most areas, but seldom in marketable quantities. At the time of the publication of the *GVA* it varied greatly in quality. In Argyll, for instance, it was thought to be good, probably because of that county's proximity to Ayrshire where butter was already something of a speciality. But in Moray and Nairn it was still at a primitive stage, according to the Reverend William Leslie:

The knowledge of this branch of husbandry had made such little progress so late as the year 1770, that on many farms along the coast, no better way of making butter was known, than by a woman whisking about the cream, with her naked arm in an iron pot . . . considerable quantities of butter, made up into the form and bulk of a middle-sized globe, partly wrapped in the allantois of a calf, and partly without any covering, were imported on open boats from Caithness. The pastry of the bakers' shops at Elgin and Forres, were then enriched with this importation.

Nation-wide, the position was more or less as described by the Shetland Reporter.

In certain cases, Shetland butter, when carefully made, is equal to that of any country: but when made in part payment of rent, the chief purpose for which it is manufactured, the quality is bad to a proverb.

(Rent-butter, it should be observed, was not simply a tenant's way of getting even with his landlord; it had a specific function, for a blend of butter and tar was believed to protect sheep against scab, and the beasts were smeared with the mixture once or twice a year.) Fresh butter was naturally only available in summer, but salt butter kept reasonably well, and in some areas it was churned again with fresh milk in the winter, so that the salt was carried away with the butter-milk. One method of keeping butter sweet was to put it down a well or bury it in a peat-bog, as various finds of forgotten 'bog-butter' testify even today. In the main, a farm wife took care with her butter, and offered it to visitors with pride.

The development of a specific Scottish tradition in cheese-making was principally held back by the small quantity of milk available, and the lack of over-wintering facilities for cattle. A skimmed-milk cottage-type cheese, crowdie, had actually been made from a very early date. A writer in 1605 claimed, somewhat rashly perhaps, that the Highlands could supply the Lowlands with ample cheese if the crops there failed. But, though appearing frequently in charters and rental books (the word *kain*, meaning a rent payment in kind, actually came to mean a specific weight of cheese), it could only be made in small quantities for a short period each summer, and very little went to market except in Ayrshire.

Nonetheless, it was a valuable food for home consumption, under the generic name of kebbock. Scott once described kebbock as a mixture of cow's and ewe's milk, but the word seems to have had much more general application to any hard cheese.

A farming manual of 1665 (Skene of Hailyard's *Manuscript of Husbandrie*) advises the novice in the dairy:

Kys milk is best for butter, and yows milk best for cheiss, for kys milk will give both more butter and better butter than yows milk, and yows milk will give both mor cheiss and better cheiss than kys milk. They use in Cunninghame to make cheiss of kys milk, but it is not good.

Cunninghame was to retrieve its reputation in years to come. The story goes – it is probably untrue, because Ireland had no reputation for cheese-making at the time – that in the 1680s a woman called Barbara Gilmour was sent to Ireland to escape the Covenanting troubles, and returned eventually with the recipe for a full-cream hard cheese which both kept and travelled well. What we do know is that she and her husband settled on a farm near Dunlop in 1688, and that shortly afterwards the first Dunlop cheeses were produced. Their sweet, nutty flavour, firm consistency, and deep gold colour, guaranteed success. The milk of Ayrshire cows was rich in butterfat, proving to be the perfect basic ingredient for a cheese which rapidly became celebrated, as local farmers learnt the 'Dunlop method'.

Neighbouring districts, including Cunninghame, began exporting Dunlop cheese to the growing industrial towns of the Clyde coastline. If Scott is to be believed, Dunlop cheese was renowned right across Scotland by 1737, the year in which the events in *Heart of Midlothian* are supposed to have taken place. Jeanie Deans was a Midlothian lass, but she yielded to none in her claim to the cheese-maker's skill: 'we have been thought so particular in making cheese,' she boasted to the Duke of Argyll, 'that some folk think it is gude as the real Dunlop.'

It is fact, not fiction, that by the 1790s Ayrshire cheeses met with a very ready sale everywhere, and in 1812 there were even Ayrshire women in Caithness making cheese from Ayrshire cows' milk though apparently not for export. (Caithness might send its filthy butter to Moray and Nairn, but it kept its cheese to itself, and the inhabitants of those counties had to content themselves with Cheshire and Gloucester cheeses brought from England.)

Ewes' milk cheese was growing steadily rarer; it was highly valued, but expensive where it competed with cows' cheese. Only in the Lammermoors and in the Highlands did it survive for a while. An author's note in *Heart of Midlothian*, remarks with Scott's usual enthusiasm

the hilly pastures of Buckholm . . . which the author now surveys . . . are famed for producing the best ewe-milk cheese in the South of Scotland.

Dr Johnson had seen both goats and sheep milked in the Highlands. 'In the penury of these malignant regions nothing is left that can be converted into food.' Sheep milk, very liberal of curd, was formed into small cheeses by the natives of St Kilda, using the ashes of seaweed as a curing agent instead of salt. Elsewhere, salt was often only added after the cheese was made; oatmeal, mashed potatoes, caraway seed, or mustard might also be used for flavour.

In Ayrshire, the success of Dunlop led to experimentation with other cheeses in the early part of the 19th century. Stilton was a failure, but Cheshire cheese became part of the repertoire, principally because 'a person from Cheshire' and his family settled on a farm in the parish of Hodden and instructed the local people how to make it.

By the mid-19th century the hazards of mass-production and

fame had caught up with Dunlop cheese. Overall quality had deteriorated. Accordingly a well-known cheese-maker in Somerset, Joseph Harding, was invited by the Ayrshire Agricultural Association to visit Scotland with his wife and teach his skills. The venture was highly successful: Scottish Cheddar of excellent quality was soon on the market and joined Dunlop as a major dairy product. This led to the establishment of a permanent Dairy School at Kilmarnock in 1889, where farmers' wives and daughters could learn the methods. For many years, it was possible to buy farm-produced cheeses made to the highest standards, even into the 1930s and despite the setting-up of co-operative creameries for commercial manufacture.

In a sense, the very popularity of Dunlop and Scottish Cheddar militated against their survival as farm-made cheeses, for commercial concerns concentrated on mass-production. With hindsight, one cannot help regretting that the Dairy School and the Board of Agriculture had not tried to encourage farmers to produce other cheeses as well.

In any event, all farm cheese-making stopped during the Second World War. It did revive for a short period afterwards, but then declined very rapidly. The last farmhouse Dunlop was made in the 1970s, and even traditional round Scottish farmhouse cheddar made from unpasteurized milk is disappearing, being made for demonstration only.

Fortunately, recent revivals and innovations may be providing the base of a future tradition, at least in soft cheeses. From the Borders, Bonchester cheese, made from full cream unpasteurized Jersey milk, is justly and increasingly acclaimed; on a farm at Blairliath in Ross-shire, two cheeses, Caboc, a full-cream soft cheese rolled in oatmeal, and traditional Crowdie, are made by the old methods and sold countrywide. Barac, a ewes' milk cheese from Dumfriesshire is a hard cheese worth searching for. Even Scott's problematic Kebbock of mixed milks can be bought in specialized shops, giving us a chance to enjoy a flavour familiar to our forebears. The success of these cheeses, proves that there is still a market for the product made in traditional ways, and that the trend towards standardization is gradually being reversed.

* * *

Traditionally, dairy industries and pig-keeping go together, but Scots attitudes to pigs and pork have always puzzled researchers. Tenants of the medieval abbey farms kept pigs, as we know from surviving lease records. In many parts of the country, however, for no clearly identifiable reason, there seems to have been great prejudice against eating pork. The Bible was certainly an influence, exerting pressures on communities like the fishing villages, where pigs, together with ministers and women, were regarded with deeply superstitious dread. In other areas pigs may have been disliked on improperly understood grounds of hygiene, or because they could cause a great deal of damage on unenclosed land; or perhaps because, in Sinclair's words, 'it is a doubtful question whether they can be fattened to much advantage, by those who have to purchase every article of their food.'

Prejudice, then, seems to have been most prevalent on the coasts and in parts of the Highlands; yet even in the Highlands there were villages where the cottager's pig was almost part of the family, and might be seen tethered to a leg of the kitchen table. In Edinburgh, it was not uncommon for wealthy families to keep a pig in the sty at the stair-foot of a Royal Mile tenement – yet a common 18th-century term of contempt for the English was 'pork-eaters'. After the Darien collapse in 1701 an English visitor to the city was plagued by small boys who pulled at his sleeve, then ran away shouting 'A Pill for the Pork-eaters' – which happened to be the title of one of the most violently anti-English pamphlets of the day.

The problem is to identify the extent and strength of the prejudice. As late as 1814 it is discussed in the *GVA*, though most writers assert that it has disappeared, or is about to disappear. The Reporter for Galloway writes that although many of the inhabitants still retain a prejudice against eating pork, 'almost every cottager keeps one, the farmers two or three each and frequently a much greater number. The villages swarm with them.' And Sinclair corroborates:

They are to be found on almost every farm, and in several counties at almost every cottage. In several of the western counties, where potatoes are extensively cultivated, particularly Dumfries-shire, and in the districts where dairy husbandry prevails, their numbers are considerable ... Almost every town and village in Scotland are regularly supplied with pork and bacon; and even in the northern counties, the prejudice against the flesh of swine has greatly subsided.

In some parts there never had been any prejudice. Pigs were numerous in the Northern Isles, running wild in Orkney during the winter, rooting about in the meadows and corn lands in search of food, so much so that 'many a time has the Orcadian farmer sown his lands, without bestowing any other preparation than that given by the snouts of his pigs'. Aberdeenshire, away from the coast, was also a great pork-producing area. A 19th-century bothy ballad sings of a servant lass's ideal of married bliss:

> A dainty cowie in the byre
> For butter and for cheses.
> A grumphie feedin' in the sty
> Wad keep the hoose in greases.
> A bonnie ewie in the bucht
> Wad help to creesh the ladle –
> And we'll get tufts o' cannie woo'
> Wad help to theek the cradle.

Significantly, only from these two counties, Orkney and Aberdeenshire, do we find recipes for pork which can in any way be described as indigenous. From the rest of Scotland, nothing, not even a regional sausage. What was happening to the meat from those swarming pigs?

Defoe discovered part of the answer when he watched Dutch East Indiamen and men-of-war loading in Aberdeen harbour. The barrels going abroad were filled with pickled pork, 'the Aberdeen pork having the reputation of being the best cur'd, for keeping on very long voyages, of any in Europe'. Sinclair too mentions the value of pigs to the income of people in eastern counties, who sent carcases to Berwick or Aberdeen for salting and export. The prejudice, that is to say, far from dying out, had gone underground; pigs were still not eaten at home, but they *were* being reared for commercial gain.

Nonetheless it would be foolish to assert that no fresh pork was being eaten, as the lack of recipes might suggest. The pig is a particularly useful animal in that almost every part can be cooked very simply indeed, so although pork was beginning to enter the diet, nearly all the ways in which it was being used were common to the whole of Britain. By the mid-19th century a new element had entered the situation, in that beef and mutton, now available all year round and accessible to more of the population, were satisfying the demand for meat. Thus regional dishes never had the chance to develop.

The biggest pig-rearing regions were also those where potatoes and dairy-farming were predominant – Ayrshire and Galloway. Here, as in Aberdeenshire, the emphasis was rather on cured than fresh meat, and Ayrshire soon began producing a distinctive type of bacon, which is still the most popular with Scottish housewives. The rind is removed after the meat has been cured, and the bacon is tightly rolled and tied with string; this allows an even distribution of fat and lean when the bacon is sliced.

Although nowadays bacon is universally eaten in Scotland, the ancient prejudice against fresh pork has never, sad to say, entirely disappeared. Possibly the fact that during the Second World War pigs had to be fed largely on fish-meal, which slightly flavoured the meat, reinforced the old dislike. At any rate, Scotland still accounts for only four per cent of the British market despite the excellent quality of home-produced pork now on sale.

Every farmer, cottager, and crofter from medieval times to our own kept a few poultry. The 'kain hen' was an important part of the rent, but generally speaking farmers resented the presence of poultry in the farmyard, even though it was largely from the profits of the chicken-run that their wives were able to clothe the families. Still, there was a feeling that 'hens aye die in debt', and that they consumed three times as much food as they produced.

Contrary to belief, poultry and eggs were neither very plentiful nor very cheap before the 19th century – if they had been they would certainly have formed part of the peasant diet. Almost all went to pay the rent, small tenants giving perhaps one or two hens a year and an egg a week, bigger farmers liable for anything up to four or five dozen hens, capons, or geese, or a selection of the three, plus a large number of eggs. For landlords, and for those with money, no doubt eggs were cheap enough, but the large number often called for in old recipes is chiefly an indication of their small size; as for the price, one may quote Dr Johnson:

When Lesley, two hundred years ago, related so punctiliously that a hundred hen eggs, new laid, were sold in the Islands for a penny, he supposed that no inference could possibly follow, but that eggs were in great abundance. Posterity has since grown wiser; and having learned, that nominal and real value may differ, they now tell no such stories, lest the foreigner should happen to collect, not that eggs are many, but that pence are few.

Among the upper classes, poultry and eggs formed part of the everyday diet, and they were also standard fare at inns. Experienced travellers knew that, however inedible the rest of the menu, there was a chance that an old hen would have been stewed into tenderness, and eggs could usually be relied on, as first Burt, then the Wordsworths, quickly learnt. Near Bothwell Castle, the latter were offered nothing but eggs. At Tarbert, there was 'Nothing but salt meat and eggs for dinner – no potatoes', but next morning they

desired the landlady to roast us a couple of fowls to carry with us. There are always plenty of fowls at the doors of a Scotch inn, and eggs are as regularly brought to table at breakfast as bread and butter.

In certain places geese were more common than hens, notably in Orkney where they were smoked in the chimney like fish and pork; and goose feathers were a significant 18th-century export.

As the change from rent-payment in kind was effected, attitudes to poultry-keeping altered. It was to market that most birds and their eggs went now, but the fact that they were the farmer's property rather than the landowner's, allowed occasional relaxations, and eggs began to find an infrequent place on the crofter's table. He himself, as a hard-working man, had priority, and many a 19th-century child regarded it as a great Sunday treat to be given the top of the only egg on the breakfast table.

Yet even the lowly hens benefited from the general improvement in living standards. Potato peelings, bits of turnip, old bread, and a handful or two of grain began to supplement the scraps coming from the kitchen – and as the poultry fattened laying too improved.

By the beginning of the 19th century, almost everyone in the south-east was eating chicken on important occasions or feastdays, and eggs were in common use for baking as well as at breakfast or tea. In Fife, they were recognized as food for all classes – no cottager was without his brood of hens. In Banffshire too, though beef and mutton were preferred, 'fowls are reared in every dwelling, from the greatest down to the very least . . . "Not to have a cock to crow in the day" is a phrase denoting the utmost extreme of poverty,' wrote the *GVA* reporter.

Turkeys and ducks were also widely reared. They, of course, were unequivocally destined for the tables of the gentry, a status to be maintained even into the early years of this century. A crofter's grandson from the north-east, who never tasted turkey until he went to the United States, remembers that the birds were bred in scores by his grandparents, but never for their own use. To eat one themselves would have been 'the most ridiculous thing you could possibly conceive of'.

Poultry were the last of the farmer's products to receive attention in the agricultural revolution; the idea that keeping hens could ever be really profitable was not one that even the 19th century entertained. It is really only since the Second World War that large-scale rearing has become commercially possible. From improved genetic strains producing heavier, faster-maturing birds (developed at the University of Wisconsin), a few eggs smuggled into Britain in 1946 became the basis for entirely new breeds and a new approach. In Scotland, as elsewhere, the 'sixties were unfortunately the age of the battery egg and the frozen chicken. Now, in the 'eighties, eggs from battery farms still predominate both in the supermarket and the corner grocer's.

But since about 1970 poultry-farming has taken enormous strides, with one of the country's largest groups employing over 2,500 people and producing 100 million birds annually. Bred from the company's own stock, and fed on a carefully controlled diet of grain and soya, they live in large, well-ventilated sheds with room to run and even fly, and die a quick and painless death. No cages, no hormones, no unnatural additives are involved at any stage from hatching to table. The result is birds of a quality which not even the most ardent of free-range champions can deny. Poultry-farming is one of the big success stories of Scotland in the 1980s, and consumers are recognizing this as increasingly they turn their backs on frozen chicken and opt for the fresh birds reared and processed under immaculate conditions of quality control and hygiene.

Yet, contemplating the near-disappearance of that traditional standby in much Scots cooking, the boiling fowl, one must feel a pang. It is still possible to make howtowdie, cock-a-leekie and chicken stovies – indeed it takes about half the time now that there is no longer the need to stew some tough old hen into tenderness – but the result is not quite the same. Who is to say whether what is lacking is the flavour of an old bird, or simply that of the past?

— RECIPES —

MUTTON

Good Scotch lamb, whether from the Highlands (like the animal which inspired Cockburn to ecstatic admiration) or from the seaweed- and heather-fed flocks of Shetland, or from the great sheep-runs of the Border hills, holds its own against all other. Yet while the best cuts – gigot or loin – need little art to complement their intrinsic excellence, their quality can be destroyed by careless treatment; as always, the better the ingredients, the more respect they deserve.

When roasting lamb or mutton, therefore, one must get the heat and cooking time exactly right. It is best to seal the meat and keep the juices in by starting it off in hot fat in a hot oven 400°F (200°C), gas 6 for 20–30 minutes, then reduce the heat to 325°F (160°C), gas 3, for the rest of the time. Total time should work out at about 20–30 minutes per pound, plus another 20 minutes. If, like me, you prefer the meat slightly pink, the shorter time is the one to choose. It is most important to let the meat stand in a warm place for 15 minutes before serving, as this allows the juices, which retreat to the centre during cooking, to redistribute themselves evenly.

Before the mid-19th century, when coal became more readily available, roasting was not a method widely used, except by the very rich – it took too much fuel and required someone in constant attendance at the spit. Boiling and braising were the more popular methods, and a good cook could produce wonderful results even if the animal were of mature age. Boiling is of course a misdescription of the process: boiled meat, generally speaking, is tough meat. The following recipe, reproduced by Theodora Fitzgibbon in *A Taste of Scotland in Food and Pictures*, imposes simmering since it uses milk instead of water. The result is superb.

Boiled Gigot of Mutton in Milk with Caper Sauce

1 leg of mutton or lamb, about 4–5 lb (2–2½ kg)
2 large onions
2 carrots
1 sprig rosemary
1 bay leaf
1 sprig each parsley and thyme
milk, about 2½ pt (1½ l)
salt

Remove as much fat as possible from the meat, place in a deep saucepan, and pour in milk to come three-quarters of the way up. Put in the sliced vegetables and herbs and season to taste. Cover and bring gently to the boil, then simmer for 2–3 hours or until the meat is tender. Now take out the meat and keep hot. Skim the fat from the milk and strain off about 1½ pt (800 ml) for sauce.

Caper Sauce

2 tablespoons flour
2 tablespoons butter
3 tablespoons capers and a little of the juice
1½ pt (800 ml) of the lamb stock
salt and pepper

Melt the butter, stir in the flour, and cook for one minute. Add the warm stock stirring all the time to prevent lumps. Add the capers and the juice and stir again until well mixed and creamy.

Carve the lamb in a hot ashet, cover with the sauce, and surround with small boiled potatoes sprinkled with parsley and carrots cooked with a pinch of sugar and sprinkled with chopped mint.

Lady Clark of Tillypronie collected many recipes for lamb and mutton. She was a woman who saw clearly the essential points of each method, and cared sufficiently to note them down. She begins the second of three recipes for braised mutton, 'The secret is to cook it *very slowly* – to let it simmer, *never to boil*. For 7 lb fully 4 hours steady cooking is needed.' Here is how Mrs Sherwood, a cook employed by Lady Clark, made Braised Mutton:

Braised Leg of Mutton

4–5 peeled, quartered onions
3 carrots
1 turnip
1 stick celery
bunch of sweet herbs
1 pt (500 ml) stock or cold water
1 leg of mutton

Put all the ingredients into a heavy stewpan. Cover first with buttered paper, then with the lid. Cook very slowly over low heat. When cooked, take the mutton out of the pan, skim and strain the gravy. Dish it like a roast leg of mutton.

Lady Clark adds, 'We like it tender but not rich, so we often use no stock and never use bacon.'

A similar attention to detail makes a recipe for Broiled Mutton from the same source worth recording. (Interesting how that word, *broil*, evidently still common at the end of last century, has virtually disappeared from the British vocabulary, being replaced by *grill*. In the United States, it is of course still widely used.)

Mutton Broiled

Cook *over* (*not before*) a very clear fire. Rub the gridiron well with suet. Melt a little butter, divide the meat, beat and trim, and dip each chop or steak into the butter – first one side, then the other. Take the chop or steak up with steak tongs and put it on the gridiron; turn it over when brown, that both sides may colour equally. If you do not turn it often, one side of the chop will always bulge out and the other side will be hollow and it will be deficient in gravy. Cut all fat ends off the chops. *You can hardly turn the meat too often* if it is to be kept juicy. Do not pepper them till you dish them up. If you season before you cook it, the meat will be very hard.

The Clarks must have been very fond of sheep's head – there are no less than six recipes for it, apart from those for Powsowdie or Broth. The following Sheep's Head Pie may well have been the one of which Saintsbury was thinking when he wrote of 'a sheep's head pie being offered, cold, as a sort of galantine'.

Sheep's Head Pie

2 Sheep's heads and trotters, singed and well cleaned,
   then soaked overnight
1 carrot
1 onion
1 turnip
1 head celery
parsley
1 bunch sweet herbs (thyme, marjoram, rosemary)
salt and pepper
4 hard boiled eggs
½ lb (250g) sliced ham
¾ lb (350g) shortcrust pastry
1 beaten egg

Put meat, vegetables, herbs and seasonings into a pan with water and boil very slowly until the meat will easily separate from the bones, 3–4 hours. Then strain, allowing the jelly and meat to stand till quite cold. Take a pie dish, and in it put first a layer of jelly, then neat slices of the meat, then of ham, then of hard boiled eggs. Fill up the dish with the remainder of the jelly.

Cover it with pastry, brush over with egg, and put into the oven at 425°F (220°C) gas 7, for about 30 minutes.

Boiled sheep's head in its own broth makes a full meal by itself. It was a popular Sabbath dish in the days of strict observance, because it could be cooked on the previous day, or put on, early on Sunday morning, to simmer very gently at the side of the stove – the longer the better – to provide a hot meal 'between sermons', as Cockburn put it.

Many are the associations of sheep's head broth, or Powsowdie, with Scottish life. One of the nicest stories is of the twelve-year-old Grisell Home (later Lady Grisell Baillie) who helped her mother care for her father when he lay in hiding in a vault of the parish church near his home for several months, having been proscribed after the Restoration. One of the little girl's responsibilities was to take food to her father. He was very fond of sheep's head, and one day when the Powsowdie was on the table, Grisell took advantage of a diversion to remove the head and hide it under her apron. Her young brother cried out: 'Mother, will ye look at Grisell: while we have been eating our broth, she has eat up the whole sheep's head.'

It was also the first Scottish dish encountered by the Wordsworths and Coleridge on their tour. Dorothy was delighted with it:

This first dish was true Scottish – a boiled sheep's head, with the hair singed off; Coleridge and I ate heartily of it; we had barley broth, in which the sheep's head had been boiled.

The trend to ease and speed in cooking nowadays means that sheep's head is rarely on any menu. It is good to know, though, that apart from its literary and political credentials, it has the endorsement of the Law, one of the most eminent members of the modern Scottish Bench having acquired fame almost equally for the sagacity of his judgments and the excellence of his Sheep Head dinners.

Sheep's Head Broth (Powsowdie)

1 sheep's head
4 sheep's trotters

1 lb (450g) stewing mutton, trimmed of fat
¼ lb (125g) Scotch barley
½ lb (250g) dried peas
1 tablespoon salt
2 carrots
2 small white turnips or ¼ swede
2 onions, chopped
1 oz (30g) parsley

Ask the butcher to singe the head and remove the eyes. Soak it and the trotters overnight in water. The butcher should also have cleaned the head and cut out the tendons, and split the skull.

Take a large pan, and in it put the head and trotters and the stewing mutton, with the barley, salt, and dried peas. Add plenty of water to cover, and simmer for two hours, skimming occasionally. Then add the sliced carrots, turnips and onions, and the parsley and simmer again for about one hour. Serve all together if liked, or the broth may be eaten first.

The next recipe is not Scottish at all. It is so extraordinarily delicious, however, and has such pleasing affinities with the old Scots gastronomy, that I cannot leave it out. Its name, in the first place, is appropriate, reminding us that housewives and butchers still use the old French term for a leg of lamb or mutton. Then, the method has great simplicity and is perfectly designed to enhance the qualities of such an animal as sent Cockburn into transports. Again, it is the closest equivalent to spit-roasting we can achieve, and the dish of potatoes set beneath to catch the dripping juices was a device well loved by 19th-century Scots cooks. Even the herbs and olive oil do not go against tradition: herbs were extensively used from medieval days and we find olive oil mentioned in *Lady Grisell Baillie's book of Household Accounts*. All in all, there is little doubt that Scots travelling to France in, say, the 18th century would have brought this recipe back for their own use had it existed. It is entirely suitable that its inventor (Sophie Tanner, Best Young Cook in the *Sunday Times* Best British Meat Dishes competition for 1976) should be half French.

Gigot qui Pleure

5–6 lb (2.25–2.72 kg) leg of lamb
8 cloves of garlic, chopped
fresh thyme
rosemary
mint
olive oil
salt and pepper
3 lb (1.35 kg) very good potatoes,
    peeled and thinly sliced
butter

Make deep diagonal slashes in the lamb (rather like the criss-crossing in a baked ham) and push three-quarters of the garlic and some of the herbs into pockets; put some of the herb mixture aside to sprinkle the leg of lamb at the end of the preparation. Brush with oil, sprinkle with salt, pepper and the remaining herbs.

Layer the potatoes in a buttered baking dish with salt and pepper, the rest of the minced garlic and dots of butter between each layer. Set the dish on the bottom rack in the oven. Place the lamb above the potatoes directly on the oven rack so that the drippings fall onto the potatoes, hence the name – crying leg of lamb.

Roast in a hot oven at 400°F (200°C) gas 6 for 1½ hours for medium rare; if it is preferred more thoroughly cooked, reduce heat to 325°F (180°C) gas 3 for another ½ hour. Slice the meat and arrange on top of the potatoes, which are already impregnated with delicious juices from the roasting lamb.

All these dishes having been made and enjoyed, obviously a good deal of the sheep was still left unaccounted for. In the days before butcher's vans and deep-freezes, when no man could get meat but by killing a sheep, families often clubbed together to make the most of the animal; but even where the household was large, waste was unthinkable and every part was used. Those uncertain how to proceed might have been helped by Lady Clark's advice:

How to use a Whole Sheep or Lamb

The blood makes Black Puddings, with sieved oatmeal, or groats, or rice, and the fat under the loin round the kidney can be used in the way 'fleed' is used with pig's blood in making ordinary Black Puddings.

The head, trotters and breast of mutton, with some of the superfluous fat on this last cut off, make, with vegetables, the best broth, and afterwards all the meat is useful in other ways.

The sheep's head, whole, is served with the feet ('trotters') round as garnish and with broth as sauce; or cut up in squares in dressed sauce as an entrée, vegetables in centre and fried brains as garnish; or can be boiled and turned out of a mould solid.

The trotters require long boiling and, after removing the bones, you can make fritters of the meat for breakfast as if they were pettitoes.

For Sheep's Trotters, see also Sheep's Head recipes.

The boiled breast of mutton used to boil with Sheep's Head No 2, can afterwards be crumbed, with mixed herbs, and broiled or baked a nice brown, to eat hot.

If for upstairs, serve a sharp sauce in a boat with chopped gherkins or capers in it.

Kidneys can be sliced for breakfast, with bacon, or in an omelet, and the liver sliced and fried, and served with bacon and fried potatoes.

The sheep's heart is hard if roasted; it is better stuffed and braised – but must be eaten at once – it chills so immediately.

A sheep's sweetbread is not worth cooking though in a lamb it is excellent.

A lamb's head can be served upon a 'fugie', a mince of heart, sweetbread, liver, &c., but *no* kidneys. Make it savoury.

Much of the rest is used for Haggis. Any bits not otherwise wanted are very welcome additions to the scraps set aside for the keeper's dogs.

BEEF

The gaffer inspected a small pot of potatoes that were boiling in their skins, on top of the brazier. Then he picked up a worn shovel from the side of the watchman's box, and fell to cleaning it thoroughly with the trench sand. He made it shine. He gave it a final dusting with his snuffy bandana, then he set its blade on the lip of an upended pipe.

From the back of the Hut's interior he brought a parcel, from which he unwrapped a piece of meat something more than half-an-inch thick and about 8 inches by 5 in irregular area. I fancy it was what we Scots call a 'popeseye' steak – a fat-surrounded core from the thigh of a bullock. He dropped his knuckles lightly on the heating shovel, was apparently satisfied with the temperature, and laid the steak on it. Quickly producing a huge 'gully' pocket-knife, he opened out the blade and with it prized the steak from the shovel and turned it over. He gave this raw side as much of the shovel's heat as he had allowed the other, and turned the steak again. By this time the surface of the shovel was fairly greased, and he kept turning the steak over at increasingly long intervals. He now poured the water off the potatoes, and hooked the pot by its handle on the side of the brazier with its lid half-on, half-off. Finally, he drew the shovel off the brazier, letting it balance between the drain-pipe and the brazier's rim, and allowed the steak to finish cooking on the shovel's residual heat. I did not mark the minutes then, but I would say they were little over five for the whole process.

'By the time I salt an' pepper that, laddie,' he said to me, 'What wi' the tatties in their jaikets, it'll be fit for a king's son to eat. An' that's the way to brander steak, no ha'ein' a brander. Jist an invilope – jist an invilope – a' the nait'ral juices sealit up inside wi' yon first heat.'

Victor McClure, *Good Appetite my Companion*, London 1955

Nowhere, in any recipe book, will there be found a more characteristic account than this of Scots beef cookery – simplicity itself, but with a careful attention to detail worthy of the care given to the animals themselves.

The same concern is evident in another beef dish, already given the status of a national dish by Meg Dods in 1826. The following recipe dates from 1712 and comes from the manuscript of Lady Castlehill's *Receipt Book* in Glasgow's Mitchell Library:

To make Scotch Collops, either Beef, Veal, or Mutton

Slice thin your meat, beat it with a rolling pin till it be tender, season it with salt; frye them without any other Liquor but their own gravy; serve them up with some melted Butter mix't with your Gravy, a little Vinegar Verjuyce, and the Juice of a Lemon, some Anchovies beaten therein over the Fire until they be dissolved. Rub ye bottom of ye Dish with Garlick.

Minced collops is a dish much spoken about, which often disappoints. It is, quite simply, mince, and when treated correctly is a good, if everyday, Scots dish. The addition of water, mushroom ketchup, and breadcrumbs or flour turn it into a barbarian mockery of what is a respectable and tasty meal – not perhaps to be offered to guests at a dinner party, but certainly to be shared and enjoyed with old friends in a relaxed atmosphere. Here is the best recipe I know:

Minced Collops

> 1 lb (450g) steak mince
> 1 large onion, peeled and sliced
> 1 small teaspoon salt
> 1 handful oatmeal, toasted
> ½–1 oz (20–25g) butter

Melt the butter in a heavy saucepan, then add the meat. Cook it over *low* heat, pounding it well – an old-fashioned wooden potato masher is the best implement – to avoid the meat coagulating into lumps. When it is all a light greyish-brown and nicely crumbly, sprinkle in the salt and add the onion. Cover with a tight-fitting lid, and cook over *very low* heat for about one hour. *Good beef* as Lady Clark observes, *should make its own gravy*, and the small signals of steam escaping will indicate its presence. If there is no steam and you hear sizzling, a tablespoon of stock or water must immediately be added. If desired, vegetables to be served with the collops – carrots or leeks – may be cooked on top of the meat in the steam, and will add to the meat's flavour, but must not be mixed with it. Just before serving remove the vegetables and stir in the oatmeal. There should be no liquid in the pan, and none required. All the flavour remains in the beautifully tender meat. The only accompaniment necessary is steamed mealy potatoes in their 'jaikets'.

All cheap cuts of beef respond well to very gentle, slow cooking. Boiled beef, like boiled mutton, should scarcely shiver in its pot of water over the lowest possible heat, for several hours; vegetables and salt to be added three-quarters of an hour before serving.

Potted meat loaves and brawns originating in the same need to produce good food economically, were for long a Scots speciality and source of pride. Nowadays they are not often home-made, which is a pity because they are very little trouble and well repay the effort. Potted Hough (shin) can be bought at most butchers', but is nice to make at home. It is a lovely summer lunch dish with salads.

Potted Hough (Jellied meat mould)

> 2 lb (approx 1 kg) shin of beef
> 1 nap bone
> 1 pig's trotter
> 2 cloves
> 1 blade mace
> 6 peppercorns
> 3 teaspoons salt (approx)
> hard boiled eggs

Put all ingredients except the salt into a large pan and cover with cold water, bring gently to the boil, and remove the scum. Simmer very gently for about 5 hours, continuing to remove the scum periodically. Add the salt, and simmer for one more hour. Remove the meat and bone and strain the liquid into a bowl. When the meat is cool enough to handle, cut away fat and gristle, and chop the flesh into neat small pieces, or mince it if preferred. (Chopping gives a nicer appearance.) Put the meat into another bowl, cover both bowls and leave in a cold place overnight. Next day, remove any fat which has solidified at the top of the liquid. Put meat and liquid into a pan, bring to the boil, and simmer for about five minutes. Check the seasoning – dishes for eating cold should be quite strongly flavoured. Wet the insides of two or three moulds with cold water, then strain a little of the liquid into each and swirl it round the edges. Put slices of hard-boiled egg at the bottom and round the sides, and when these have 'set' carefully pour in the rest of the meat-and-liquid mixture in the pan. Leave to set. Unmould onto ashets and garnish with green salad.

A cold meat loaf which is more strongly flavoured, and baked like a terrine, is the oddly named Baby's Leg. This recipe is from Dione Patullo's *Scottish Cooking in Colour*, which is an interesting blend of traditional and modern recipes.

Baby's Leg

½ lb (250g) minced beef
½ lb (250g) minced ham
1 small onion, minced
3 oz (75g) + 1 oz (25g) oatmeal
1 egg
2 teaspoons Harvey's sauce
black pepper
¾ cup + ½ cup beef consommé

Mix 3 oz (75g) oatmeal with all ingredients except the half cup consommé, by hand. Grease a 1 lb (450g) loaf tin or stone jar thoroughly, using lard or good dripping. Put in the mixture and stand tin or jar in a baking dish with hot water halfway up. Cover with a double layer of foil. Bake in a moderate oven 350°F (180°C) gas 4 for two hours. Remove from oven and pour in remaining consommé. Cover with foil and put a weight on top. When quite cold remove from tin and sprinkle with remaining oatmeal, toasted.

Knowing that even wealthy Scots, before the Age of Improvement, had to content themselves with salt meat for the greater part of the year, one would expect a large number of recipes to have survived. In fact, there are few. But I like to think that Miss Menie Trotter of Mortonhall might have enjoyed Jellied Pickled Brisket. Miss Trotter was one of the strong-minded old Edinburgh ladies whom Lord Cockburn described in *Memorials of His Time*, setting down for all posterity how she generally sacrificed an ox to hospitality every autumn, which, according to a system of her own, she ate regularly from nose to tail; and as she indulged in him only on Sundays, and with a chosen few, the animal feasted her half through the winter. This was at Blackford Cottage, a melancholy villa on the north side of Blackford Hill, where the last half, at least, of her life was passed. I remember her urging her neighbour Sir Thomas Lauder, not long before her death, to dine with her next Sunday – 'For eh! Sir Thammas! we're terrible near the tail noo.'

Jellied Pickled Brisket

3 lb (1½ kg) boned rolled brisket
2 tablespoons oil
2 chopped onions
2 chopped carrots
2 pig's trotters
¼ pt (150 ml) water
6 peppercorns
1 cup port wine
1 bay leaf

Ask the butcher to soak the brisket in mild brine for only 48 hours. Put some oil in a pan, and brown the meat. Remove from the pan, brown the vegetables and remove them. Take a heavy casserole only a little larger than the meat, and in it put brisket, trotters, vegetables, water, port, peppercorns and bay leaf. Simmer slowly for about 4 hours. Strain off the liquor and allow to cool. Then pour a little liquor over the meat. Put the meat in a clean pot which, again, just fits it. Pour a little more liquor over it, and do this again after about an hour. After a further hour, pour in all the liquor, put a weighted plate on top, and allow to set overnight in the refrigerator.

POULTRY

Domestic poultry were the last of the farm animals to attract specific attention in the period of agriculture reforms. But though the farmer might have resented and ignored the greedy, demanding birds clucking at the back door, his wife did not, for it was they and their eggs which provided the money to keep the family clothed. Whatever could be spared in the way of leftovers went into the hens' pail, besides handfuls of grain quietly abstracted from the barn.

Young birds presented few culinary problems: they were stuffed and steamed or roasted. Inevitably, the stuffing was oatmeal-based, proving once again that natural law by which ingredients from the same locality are right for each other. Old birds had to be boiled – but what a flavour then exuded into the richly simmering liquid! It is one of the saddest gastronomic facts of 20th-century Britain that unless you actually live on a farm, it is next to impossible to get a good boiling fowl. Young battery birds taste of blotting-paper and old ones of cardboard – therein is the only difference. And while free-range roasting birds are available to those who seek, I should like to know where the old ones go.

Oatmeal Stuffing for Poultry

This, under the name of Skirlie, is a useful dish in its own right, traditionally served with potatoes and a glass of sweet milk. As a stuffing, it is excellent.

> 2 oz (50g) suet
> 1–2 finely chopped onions
> 4–6 oz (150–170g) medium oatmeal
> salt and pepper

To make stuffing, prepare a hot pan, melt the suet, and add the other ingredients. Stir well and allow to cool before putting it into the bird.

For Skirlie, follow the same procedure, but allow the mixture to cook for a few minutes before serving.

Stoved Chicken

Like stoved potatoes, this is cooked pretty well in its own steam, and served with a savoury sauce. Lady Clark's recipe for 'Fowl – stoved' with slight adaptations for modern conditions, is very good:

1 young plump chicken 2½–3 lb (1–1¼ kg)
3–4 oz (75–100g) butter
1 onion, peeled and finely chopped
3 oz (75g) Ayrshire bacon in the piece, diced
2 tablespoons beef consommé (tinned consommé will do
    perfectly well, unless you are lucky enough to have some jelly
    left over from a roast)

For the sauce

A little consommé, a pinch of sugar, a squeeze of lemon juice, 1
    teaspoon mushroom ketchup (optional)

Truss the fowl as for boiling. Melt butter in a heavy pan, add the
onion and bacon, then the fowl, first lying on its breast, but to
be turned every 10 or 15 minutes. Cover the pan and cook over
very gentle heat. After about half an hour, add the consommé.
Cook for another half an hour or until tender.

Remove the bird and keep it hot. To the liquid in the pan add
one more tablespoon of consommé, a pinch of sugar, and the
lemon juice and ketchup if used. Boil fast for a minute or two,
then strain and pour over the bird. Serve at once.

A richer, older version of this comes from Meg Dods, who calls it
'a very nice small Scots dish'. If the second epithet surprises – by
modern standards the dish is small neither in size nor in flavour –
one cannot quarrel with the first. 'Howtowdie' probably comes
from an Old French word for pullet, but the recipe is based more
on international medieval cuisine than on anything specifically
French. 'Drappit eggs' is the graphic Scots term for poached eggs.

Howtowdie wi' Drappit Eggs
(for 6 people)

2 young roasting chickens, 2½ lb (1 kg) each
12 button onions or shallots
4 oz (125g) butter
6 black peppercorns

1 blade mace
1 bunch sweet herbs (marjoram, thyme, a bay leaf, parsley)
½ pt (275 ml) approx boiling stock or water
1–2 chicken livers
2 lb (1 kg) spinach
6 small eggs

Stuff the birds with a mild-flavoured stuffing like the Skirlie. Put them in a heavy casserole with butter, onions, spices and herbs. Brown on all sides, then add the stock. Cover closely and cook over gentle heat for about ¾ of an hour. Meanwhile, wash the spinach very well, and cook gently in butter, then drain it, season and chop it. Arrange it round the edges of a dish, cover and keep in a warm place. Poach the eggs carefully in stock or water and put them on mounds of spinach. Poach the liver for a few minutes, and put through the blender with a little of the stock. Place the chickens in the middle of the dish. Reheat the liver-stock sauce slightly, then pour over the chicken, and serve.

The most popular method of dealing with an old bird was that used also for beef and mutton, boiling in a large pot with plenty of vegetables to turn it into a one-dish meal. From this evolved the celebrated Cock-a-Leekie, though when, or where, is unknown. James VI of Scotland and I of England is said to have been very fond of it, and one of the most memorable last lines in English language fiction comes from Scott's *The Fortunes of Nigel*: 'And, my lords and lieges, let us all to dinner, for the cockie-leekie is a-cooling.'

Cock-a-Leekie

1 boiling fowl, 2–3 lb (1–1½ kg)
1 onion, quartered
1–2 lb (450–800g) leeks, cut into inch-long (2–3 cm) pieces, white and green kept separate
3–4 pt (1¾–2 l) beef or veal stock, or use water with 2 stock cubes
1 bay leaf, some parsley

6–12 prunes, soaked overnight (optional)
salt and pepper

Put the bird in a large pot with the onion and nearly cover it with cold stock or water and stock cubes, add the herbs and salt and slowly bring to the boil. Skim, cover and simmer until tender, about 2 hours. Remove the bird and allow to cool slightly. Meanwhile add the green part of the leeks and the prunes, and continue to simmer. Cut the white meat from the chicken into neat pieces, and return them to the soup with the white part of the leeks. Simmer for about 10 minutes, check the seasoning and serve.

Rice is sometimes also added to this soup, but not in the version given by Marian McNeill from which the above is adapted.

Rice is an ingredient, however, in the next recipe, which is another good way with a boiling bird if you are lucky enough to find one.

Happit (wrapped) Hen
(serves 4–6)

1 boiling fowl, 2–3 lb (1–1½ kg)
1 lb (450g) each of young carrots and young white turnips
8 oz (225g) long grain rice
3 fresh sage leaves
salt and pepper

For the sauce:

2 oz (50g) butter
1 onion, finely chopped
1 oz (25g) flour
2 tablespoons cream
1 beaten egg
salt and pepper

Cover the bird with cold water, bring slowly to the boil and skim. Add 2 teaspoons salt, simmer for about 1¾ hours. Meanwhile wash the rice thoroughly in at least 8 changes of cold water. Peel the vegetables and cut them into neat pieces, add to the meat, and simmer again until they are cooked. Turn off the heat, remove the bird, and allow to cool until you can handle it, then cut the meat neatly and put in a covered pan with a little of the stock to keep warm. Strain the rest of the stock over ice or through linen to hold the grease, and put about 1½ pt (850 ml) into a pan and bring to the boil. Put in the rice and sage leaves, and cook for 20–25 minutes until tender.

Meantime, prepare the sauce. Melt the butter, sweating the onion in it for 5 minutes, add the flour, stir thoroughly, and still stirring add enough chicken stock to give it the consistency of thin cream. Strain into a clean pan and keep warm. Arrange the rice in a layer on a warm dish, put the pieces of chicken on top; quickly add the cream and beaten egg to the sauce and reheat slightly but on no account allow to boil. Pour the sauce over the chicken, arrange the vegetables round it, and serve.

More chicken recipes will be found in the chapter on foreign influences.

DAIRY PRODUCTS

Despite the absence of milk during the winter months, it was always an important item of diet for the Scots. There is some evidence that at times people in the Highlands and Islands depended almost totally on it for their nourishment. Thus, not far from Inverness, Boswell and Johnson met a woman who told them that she considered oatmeal an expensive food and that, in spring, when the goats gave milk, her children lived without meal. An earlier traveller, Martin Martin, wrote that the Western Islanders, in times of adversity, lived for months off a dish called Oon, consisting of milk or whey, boiled up and then frothed with an implement called a fro'stick. (Such sticks are to be seen today in the National Museum of Antiquities; they have a small cross-stick at the lower end, round which a horse-hair band was fixed.) Bulked up in this manner, even a small quantity of milk or whey could satisfy hunger and give at least a modicum of nourishment.

In Shetland, a whole range of milk dishes formerly existed, with strange Nordic names. *Strubba* was coagulated milk whipped to the consistency of cream and eaten with rhubarb or other fruit. *Blaund* was whey strained off buttermilk, considered at its best at the onset of fermentation, when it had a slight and agreeable fizz: it was thought valuable in the treatment of consumptives, and was also much drunk by fishermen at sea. *Kloks* – an extravagant dish for special occasions – was new milk simmered for several hours, until it became clotted and yellowish-brown (there is a very similar dish to be found in parts of India). Kloks was flavoured with cinnamon and sugar, and tasted much like what is, in fact, its modern equivalent, condensed milk. *Klabba* was junket, another popular dish to set which, when rennet was not available, butter-wort juice was used. *Whipcoll*, another special party dish, was eaten at Yule. Egg-yolks and sugar, well beaten, were combined with thick sweet cream and a not insignificant quantity of brandy, rum or whisky. The similarity with the Dutch drink Advokaat is obvious, the only question being, who influenced whom?

Johnson commented on the large number of milk dishes on offer in the houses where he and Boswell were entertained. The reason was that lack of reasonable roads and transport forced the consumption of milk on the spot. It was drunk in its natural state, it was made into butter and cheese, and it was used in the ways described above, plus many more. Whey and buttermilk were universally drunk during the summer, the latter being particularly popular in Edinburgh, where at a penny the Scots pint (equivalent to at least three English pints) it was within reach of almost everybody's purse. *Soor-dook* was its local name, and the citizens, it is calculated, spent £1000 a year on it, and ascribed to it all manner of health-giving properties.

At least two dishes have survived from those pre-Milk Marketing Board days. Hatted Kit would be worth preserving just for its name, but it makes a perfect companion for stewed fruit, fresh or dried. (Try it, if you can, with the small perfumed apricots from Hunza sometimes obtainable in health food shops.) The original recipe required simply buttermilk and 'a pint of milk hot from the cow', in the proportion of two to one. In the absence of a cow, rennet is required. Cream was usually served in a separate dish, and the two were sometimes eaten alone, sometimes with stewed fruit or with brown bread and (oddly) salt. The following recipe comes from Catherine Brown's *Scottish Regional Recipes*:

Hatted Kit

> 2 pt (1 l) buttermilk
> 1 pt (500 ml) milk
> 3 dessertspoons rennet
> 2 oz (50g) sugar
> grated nutmeg to taste
> ¼–½ pt (125–250 ml) double cream

Put buttermilk and milk into a large pan and heat very gently till just blood heat. Remove from the stove and add rennet. Pour gently into a bowl and leave overnight. By next day the curd will have formed and separated from the whey. Pour through a fine nylon or hair sieve and allow the whey to drain off. Leave for at least 24 hours. The curd should now be fairly stiff. Season this with some sugar and nutmeg.

Whip cream till stiff and add sugar and nutmeg to taste. Mix the two very gently together. Chill and serve with any kind of fresh or stewed fruit.

Probably the best known of all Scottish desserts is Crannachan. Rightly, many would say. Once again, we have a perfect example of the marriage of simple local ingredients, each element tasting of itself yet contributing both flavour and texture to the memorable creation of one of the world's great desserts.

Once Crannachan was an indispensable dish at Harvest Home and G. W. Lockhart says it was customary to serve it at Hallowe'en, with small charms hidden in it. Where it originated, no one knows, but a similar dish of mixed cream and whey, whisked with the fro'stick and then sprinkled with toasted oatmeal, was still a popular dish on the east coast in the 1950s. Crannachan contains no whey, but the oatmeal is there, and honey was often added as sweetener. Which of the other two ingredients was added first, the whisky or the fruit? If whisky, the origin is probably Highland, if fruit, the raspberry fields of Angus and Fife may be the true home of this delicious sweet. There are a number of variations on the basic theme. I prefer the simplest, without honey, which tends to mask the flavour of the other ingredients.

Crannachan

3–4 oz (75–100g) toasted, sifted pinhead oatmeal
½ pt (250 ml) double cream
1 tablespoon whisky
4–6 oz (120–140g) soft fruit (raspberries, brambles or
  blueberries)

Half whip the cream – do not make it too stiff, it should be fluffy but still soft, for the oatmeal will thicken it. Add the whisky. Fold in the sifted meal, then the fruit. Serve in glasses.

— 5 —

THE PLEASANT ART OF GARD'NERY

'No spirited cultivation of the land can be performed by the poor inhabitants of a damp smoky hovel.'

James J. Donaldson, *GVA* Nairn, 1794.

'There's a child among the artichokes.'

Robert Louis Stevenson, *St Ives.*

Scots have a long-standing reputation for not eating vegetables. Partly it is based on ill-natured remarks by early tourists, especially travellers who stayed at inns instead of following the more usual Scottish custom and relying for hospitality on the local gentry. Partly too it is founded on observations by Scots themselves about the diet of the peasantry during the 17th and 18th centuries. In its contemporary form the charge rests on the rather poor showing in greengrocers' shops up and down the country. Yet at no time has the accusation been more than partially true: this chapter will show that at every period there were at least some Scots interested in gardens, and in the cultivation of vegetables and fruit to as high a standard as anywhere else in Britain.

If the blanket charge, covering all classes at all times, can be said to be accurate, it must be so of the Highlands. Here the poor soil, uncertain climate, and short growing season have always enforced upon the inhabitants the application of their entire energy to producing the most basic food, grain. Any time and energy remaining could be more profitably used to harvest the sea than to equip the soil to grow vegetables – which, having achieved the status of a luxury, were for long held in contempt as unworthy food for heroes. (It is said that Clan Grant earned the disdain of its fellow-countrymen for cultivating kitchen-gardens in the 18th century – for many years they were habitually referred to as 'the soft, kail-eating Grants'.) Before potatoes became popular, High-landers avoided the worst effects of scurvy by making soup of young nettle leaves in spring, while in summer and autumn they ate wild fruits. As late as 1808 the Reporter for Inverness remarked that though the monks of Beauly Abbey had tended their gardens with skill and care, they exerted little influence on the local population, 'being despised by a warlike people as something less than men'.

Undoubtedly, this indifference to vegetables, still observable in the Highlands, was once common to the poorer classes throughout Scotland. Few medieval peasants were disposed or able to emulate the monastic labours in orchard and *potager* (vegetable garden). There might be vines at Melrose Abbey, cabbages and apricots at Arbroath; Culross had its plum trees, the Haddington orchards were celebrated even in the 13th century, and the Rental Book of Dunkeld provides evidence of the purchase of seeds of onions, beans and cabbage. Every monastery and abbey had also its salad and herb gardens, the latter chiefly for medicinal use. Even so the peasants, hampered by the limitations of poor soil, short leases, and the necessity of providing both agricultural labour and military service, were unwilling to expend extra effort trying to coax fruit and vegetables from the unco-operative land. (In this they resembled their counterparts on the Continent more than is sometimes realized. The marvellous illuminations we admire, in, for example, the *Très Riches Heures du Duc de Berry*, show peasants working on their master's estate to produce food for *his* consumption. There was not very much to distinguish between the diet of a labourer in northern France and that of his Scottish contemporary.)

Yet the medieval monasteries did leave their mark. In the first place, the monks brought to Scotland many hitherto unknown varieties of fruit and vegetables – apples, pears, spinach, leeks, carrots, cabbage and salads. Secondly, 'a gardener is Scotch, as a French teacher is Parisian', in the words of George Eliot; and the foundation of this tradition lay in the abbey gardens, where monks and lay apprentices worked side by side. We can only conjecture that the first royal gardeners were trained by monks, but it seems a reasonable assumption. David I, who endowed the abbey at Holyrood just outside the walls of Edinburgh, laid out orchards and gardens at the base of the Castle Rock. What more natural than that he should ask the monks, experts in horticulture, for advice and training for his men?

These Royal gardens provide the first record we have of non-monastic cultivation. The garden at Stirling Castle is well documented and was fully productive in the mid-15th century, though remodelled towards the end of that period. Papers for 1584 name the head gardener as John Modane; he was responsible for both Stirling gardens and those at the newly built Falkland Palace. His contract of employment is direct and explicit: no fruit and vegetables, no pay. (Modane's successor at Falkland was required to produce eight barrels of onions per year before *he* got paid. Perhaps there were grounds for a contemporary traveller's complaint about the Scots 'that nauseate the very aire with their tainted breath, so perfumed with onions, that to an Englishman it is almost infectious'.)

As the wool and skin trade with Europe developed, prosperity began to touch the upper and middle classes, and we can see the first signs of non-conformity to the accepted legend. The towns were increasing in size and wealth, noblemen's houses were no longer built to be fortified barracks against the weather and the enemy. By the end of the 16th century, wherever the land was reasonably fertile and the people at peace, there were gardens: round Glasgow (the 'dear green place'), in parts of the Central Belt, in Morayshire, and especially in Midlothian, described as having many noble residences, 'beautified with fair orchards and gardens'.

But, irritatingly, there were no botanists or gardeners among the early travellers. We know nothing of what was cultivated, beyond the fact that onions, leeks and kail figure often in both royal and monastic accounts of seed purchases; in addition fruit trees, chiefly apples and pears, but also plums and cherries, are often referred to.

* * *

One has to move on almost a hundred years, to the end of the 17th century, to find the first comprehensive and reliable account of what a Scottish garden could produce. It comes, not from a travel book, but a gardener's manual, the detail and sophistication of which show clearly that a high standard had been reached (at least in some parts of the country) in all branches of horticulture. Even granted the relative poverty of the Scottish nobility and the difficulties of soil and climate, it is evident from this book that Scottish gardens were much more in line with what was going on in England than is usually claimed.

The Scots Gard'ner was first published in Edinburgh in 1683. Its author was John Reid; his father, and his grandfather, had been gardeners at Niddry Castle near Edinburgh, but when John was eleven years old his father died, and the boy went to the city to apprentice himself to a wine merchant. His master too died before the term of the apprenticeship was concluded and Reid returned home, where he was, in his own words, 'persuaded to learn the old but pleasant art of Gard'nery'. From 1674 to his marriage in 1678 he worked in three gardens, at Hamilton, Drummond, and 'Lawres alias Forden'. His marriage at Forden, at the age of 23, gave him the advantages of a settled home and its comforts, and he began almost immediately to write his book.

Far from being the 'wise old gardener' described by later editors of his work, Reid seems to have been a vigorous and ambitious young man, and much of this comes through in his writing. He is enthusiastic, knowledgeable, and comprehensive – but, above all, matter-of-fact. His preface is characteristic:

To all Ingenious Planters in Scotland.

I desire you to peruse this Book; for there are many Things in it of singular Use, which I could never find in any, and the Substance of what I could find material (in the Practical Part of Gard'nery) improven and applied home: Whereby I presume it may be satisfactory to you, when you operate in the Choice of Husbandry. Several weighty Reasons induced me hereunto; as, the great Necessity of right Contrivance, whereby you may do your Works, both orderly and cheap; the inexpressible Need of Inclosing and Planting, whereby you may Improve your Estates to the best Advantage, both in Profit and Pleasure. And because so many Books on Gard'nery are for other Countries and climates, and many things in them more Speculative than Practical, this ensuing Treatise may the rather be acceptable;... (though) obnoxious to the undoubted Censure of Criticks, yet when I reflect on my Innocency in the Design therein (the Good of my Country) I receive encouragement. And that my Endeavours may prove successful, is the earnest desire of, John Reid.

The book opens with plans for a formal garden in the fashion of the time, but soon moves to the author's favourite theme: 'The Kitchen Garden is the best of all Gardens.' Reid saw it as a walled area within which vegetables, fruit and flowers could grow protected from the weather and create their own pleasing harmony — for, as on the Continent today, flowers and vegetables were never far from each other in the old Scottish gardens. Aesthetic considerations were important and he attached great value to symmetry:

The Order is to make every sort oppose itself. Example, if you plant a Ridge of Artichokes on the one Hand, plant another at the same place on the other.

Clearly he wished to make his garden an agreeable place to walk in, too, for he recommends edging vegetable beds with thyme, hyssop, lavender, and rue, or with parsley, strawberries, violets and 'July-flowers'.

Fruit trees are dealt with in considerable detail. A proper choice is vital:

The only Fruits for this Country are Apples, Pears, Cherries, Plums (and Apricots and Peaches at the South Side of Walls), Currants, Gooseberries, Raspberries and etc. For Walls are Apricocks, Peaches, Nectarines, Almond, Vine, Fig, ... but you need not take up much with Almond, Vine, Fig, nor Nectarine.

Melons, he thinks, are not worth the trouble — but he gives directions for making their 'Hot-Bed' anyway.

Here we have the first authentic picture of what the educated upper classes living outside the Highlands expected to find at their dinner-tables. The list of vegetables is surprisingly long. Reid gives instructions for cultivating globe artichokes, asparagus (which became especially popular during the 18th century), broad and kidney beans, cauliflower, lettuce and corn salad. To obtain early peas, he says, you should sow in the full moon of November, in a warm place, 'but', he adds with typical realism, 'do not trust too much to them'. He gives (at a surprisingly early date) correct directions for growing and cooking potatoes. Green vegetables include chicory and endive, spinach, spinach beet, sorrel and colewort (kail), celery and cabbage (red, white, and savoy); garlic, shallots, leeks and onions were also grown, as well as parsnip and scorzonera, 'Beet-Rave' (beetroot), carrots and turnips, horseradish and cucumber.

Among the herbs he recommends are the still-familiar parsley, sage, mint and balm, thyme and rosemary, as well as tarragon, chervil, fennel and dill. He also suggests cresses and pennyroyal; burnet, borage and sweet basil; and marigold to add colour to salads and to flavour soups and stews.

Even bearing in mind what every amateur knows – that a gardener's manual is a counsel of perfection – the list is impressive. Other sources such as contemporary household account books detailing seed purchases confirm that most items would have been familiar though many gardeners may have failed to attain Reid's high standard. Although obviously abreast of the latest horticultural ideas, including the cultivation of potatoes, it is clear he was chiefly concerned to set down for his colleagues the best current practice. Nowhere is there any indication that his methods are newly developed or imported.

Before taking leave of his readers, John Reid has a further word for them. Too good a gardener not to care what happens to his produce once it reaches the kitchen, he follows his instructions on cultivation with a chapter on cooking – a real bonus for the culinary historian. Fruit should be eaten fresh or preserved in sugar. Cucumbers are for pickling, gooseberries for baking, boiling, and sauces. Beans and peas must be eaten 'when green', and asparagus before it reaches a height of five inches. Lettuce should be picked young, 'but it's best cabbaged'. After these general directions come some fairly detailed recipes, and he finishes with a 'gardener's calendar', which should really be entitled a 'cook's calendar', for it lists appropriate fruit and vegetables (both fresh and preserved) for each month of the year.

The book ran into a second edition before his death in 1723, showing that demand was high for a work dealing with specifically Scottish conditions. What this suggests is that there was no sudden surge or importation of interest in gardening, but that rather the medieval apprentice working under the monks, and the reader of *The Scots Gard'ner* are linked in a continuous chain of instruction and experiment. That Reid himself had been extremely well trained is beyond question. He is a world away from contemporary farmers in his insistence on deep-digging, manuring and thorough weeding, and in his commitment to enclosing gardens – a matter which he raises both at the beginning and the end of the book as if to emphasize its importance.

In the year in which *The Scots Gard'ner* was published, Reid took his young family to America. He was to become Surveyor-General of New Jersey, and he never returned to Scotland. Nevertheless his book continued to shape horticulture for many years, going through four editions between first publication and 1766.

Thus far, vegetable-growing (and eating) on any scale had been confined to the large private estates. A new type of garden, however, was now beginning to appear. Most medieval towns had their 'town acres' – land on which the citizens were allocated plots to grow barley and oats, and perhaps a little kail. Increases in urban population made the system impracticable, and gradually the plots were being consolidated and leased in blocks to enterprising men who grew what was needed and brought their produce into the city for sale. These were the first market gardeners, and a clue to what they might have grown is given us in manuscripts in the Dalkeith papers quoted in E. H. M. Cox's *History of Gardening in Scotland*.

The papers show that, while the garden at Dalkeith was being laid out at the beginning of the 18th century, the household turned to a 'mail garden', as they were called, to supply the kitchen; and the accounts which survive list payments to a John Arro, who sent vegetables to Dalkeith from December 1702 to September 1703. It makes interesting reading, particularly since it confirms the picture drawn by Reid. Here is evidence, not of what could be cultivated, but of what was actually eaten in a nobleman's household in Midlothian over a period of ten months. Cox's analysis corroborates Reid's 'gard'ner's calendar' in many details. In summer there were artichokes, asparagus, cauliflowers, lettuce, onions, peas, 'spinage' and turnips. In winter, cabbages, carrots, celery, colewort, savoy, scorzonera, spinach and turnips were brought to the Palace. Potatoes were also supplied between December and February.

If the standard of all the mail gardens had been as high, citizens in Edinburgh and Glasgow at least would have thought themselves well off; but until about the end of the 18th century, town-dwellers on the whole were not so fortunate as people living in the country. This may help to account for contemporary reports on the lack of vegetables, for what was to be seen in the markets was inferior to what the gentry were producing on their estates.

The reason for this disparity lay in the historical development of town markets. Medieval markets were strictly controlled by the town councils, or in some cases the Privy Council, and town-dwellers were forbidden to buy produce elsewhere, nor were vegetables cultivated in the 'town acres' allowed to be sold elsewhere than in the market. Everything coming in for sale was taxed, and prices were fixed on the day of sale according to an 'intrinsic just price' which seems to have been unrelated to quality or even to supply and demand. By the time the laws were changed and greater freedom allowed, habit was strong in both producer and consumer; gardeners were unwilling to take risks by trying anything new, or to put any effort into improving quality; for their part, customers were satisfied with little variety and poor produce.

The sharp contrast between town and country conditions must now be set beside the gentry/peasantry and Lowland/Highland polarizations already noted. But there remains a further aspect to the picture of Scotland in pre-Improvement days. The difficult relationship between a master with new ideas and his servant, intent on doing things the old way, is nowhere more clearly visible than in a book which, because never intended for publication, presents one of the most vivid and entertaining glimpses it would be possible to find of such a conflict.

The letters of John Cockburn of Ormiston to his gardener were written over a period of seventeen years, from 1727 to 1744. The son of Adam Cockburn, the Lord Justice-Clerk to Scotland under Queen Anne, Cockburn was one of that first band of Scottish MPs returned to Parliament after the Act of Union in 1707. He became a Lord of the Admiralty and remained in London for many years, but Scotland – Scottish land – was his passion, and as one of the most able and enthusiastic 'Improvers' he probably deserves the title often accorded him, 'Father of Scottish Agriculture'. Though his chief love was farming, nothing to do with the soil bored him, and even from London he kept control of the garden at Ormiston by writing regularly and at length to Charles Bell, his gardener.

Cockburn must have been an infinitely irritating employer. Himself possessing inextinguishable energy and a capacity for total commitment, he was blind to the need of others to remain their own imperfect selves. He *could not* leave people alone; his letters endlessly repeat admonition, advice, complaint. He had firm ideas on every subject, and though he professed open-mindedness, it always ended with his being sure that those who disagreed with him or refused to follow his advice would regret it. Furthermore, he was suspicious of everybody: the seedsmen and postmasters, the captains of the ships by which he often sent plants to Ormiston, carriers, his neighbours, tenant farmers, his brothers, who with him administered the estate – even Charles Bell himself.

With all this, the most casual reader cannot help but be impressed by the man's enthusiasm and intelligence; by his concern for his country and tenants, and by his persistence and meticulous attention to detail. One wonders what he and John Reid, so much alike at least in their passion for doing things properly, would have made of each other.

Bell, unfortunately, was no John Reid. If Cockburn's image of him is to be accepted, he was slow, conservative, unadventurous, inclined to inefficiency and laziness. Yet how much one wishes that even one of his letters to his employer had survived. Despite real or imagined faults, he must have been an exceptional man, to have endured patiently the torrent of injunctions, questions and scoldings arriving without respite from London. (Even when Bell did nothing wrong, Cockburn could still find cause for complaint – 'You should get better ink for the very direction of yours was so pale it could scarce be read'.)

The great proportion of the letters deals with the planting and maintenance of trees; but cultivation of fruit and vegetables (flowers are never mentioned) is also an important topic. Two, or perhaps three, kitchen-gardens are involved: Cockburn's own at the House, that tended by Bell's father who was an estate tenant, and possibly one allocated to Bell himself, though it is not entirely clear whether or not this is separate from his father's.

The following letter is typical of many, and relates to the House garden:

Dont fall short in Onions and Leeks this year as you have commonly done. You had plenty of dung last winter and this and now you have some ashes for heavy ground or for Mixtures where proper for any plants. Get me plenty and good things for the Kitchen. You can now guess of what kinds the greatest demands are. Take care of the Fruit Trees that what fruit we have may be good, well flavoured and tasted. Remember to plant 3 or 4 Rows of Artichokes; don't spare dung upon them in large trenches at first planting. You'll begin to think of Cucumber beds and horse dung or straw litter if to be had. I hope you had good earth for them that we may have plenty and good. Green sage I hope you have got and all sweet herbs commonly used. Don't omit any thing that can help you to a good crop of Garden things that can be got by Labour and care; saving in either is no real thrift, even tho' you should work the ground twice over to open it, if it requires it, or you think it may do service to such crops as may agree with the ground being well opened as Turnips, Carrots etc., several others do. Lose no time in thinking of such things . . .

Don't glance this Letter and then throw it by, as if saying you have read it was enough. Read and consider it over and over for I can't have time to repeat the same things every Post.
3d Feby 1741

The following month he is still insisting on the leeks, 'you know we use many Leeks in Soups when you have plenty', and still badgering poor Bell to dung the artichokes.

When not writing to Bell, Cockburn spent much time at the London seedsmen, and his enthusiasm for trying out something new often got the better of him.

I wrote to Alex^r Wight to tell you about getting the ground ready, and also of my having sent a small vial w^t some hundreds of Crab Apple Seed . . .

Tell Alex^r Wight his Pease and Beans went last week . . . you and he can judge if they come too late or not . . .

I am not sure that Mulberries won't do. If in any place in our climate I believe it will be at bottom of your father's Garden. It is not great matter to try, and if they don't it is only taking them out and leaving the other trees.

(Cockburn was clearly not an imaginative man, and he did not have to do the digging.)

Arch Pringle, who has lost his Wife, talks much of his Onion Seed, so I send you a little of it . . . I suppose you want Melon Seeds for making presents of, so you shall have to stock the whole country, but I never saw any for anything but pickling in Scotland.

(Reid had been of the same opinion.)

Enclosed I send you a second small parcel of seeds which I am sure come from Turkey.

Never shy of giving advice, he sends a message to Bell senior, who evidently tried his hand at market gardening, but not in a manner to win his landlord's approval.

Your father told me himself that he could sell much more than his Garden produces. The people told me they would buy six times as much as he ever had to sell if he had it and would sell at a lower price . . . One great reason for our people's living as they doe and not as they doe in Engld, is the difficulty there is in getting things at all, and if to be gott they pay so dear for them, all sellers w' us thinking of nothing but sharping a high price and sometimes for what is bad and being Idle again till ane opportunity happens for their doing so again . . . Could the Lasie man bring himself to more activity or the Covetous man to a larger way of thinking, they would both gett more business and more money from having more customers. If once by the above method you introduc'd the use of Garden stuff, it would encrease fast and take more and more in the Country, and I make not the least doubt of your finding encouragement and profitt from adding every year considerably, to your Kitchen Garden Ground . . . I am convinc'd for one thing George [the local publican] if he thrives and can gett them, will take more raspberry from you than you can raise, for Brandy every year . . . The very Apothecaries in Edinburgh would take quantities every year. Besides if Gentlemen liked them in punch at George's they would come there to drink it and probably buy the fruit to use it at home. Both ways will encrease the demand upon you if once the use of them is introduced. You know it is a fruit few have in quantities, so you if such a thing takes, will have the market . . . George if he succeeds, may also take Gooseberries Green for Baking or Sauces if Gentlemen come to his house, and also Cherries, Gooseberries, and other fruits ripe, for Gentlemen may like a dish of fruit, or such things Baked may go off, if to be had. Other markets will also take such things. You can't doubt of Artichokes, pease, Beans, parsnips, Carrots and the like going off if you have them at proper seasons . . . I must add to my paper having said more than I designed when I began, as frequently happens when I begin to advise any of you.

The letter of 3rd June 1735 is perhaps the most interesting of all in the context of this chapter, for in it Cockburn, after admonishing Bell's father for selling cabbage at too high a price, goes on to discuss the whole question of commercial production:

May not even better kinds of Pears and Apples yield more than the common kinds – for example a good Nonpariel (sic) and a St German yield more than two common apple trees and two Summer Pears. If so you have more ground free as two trees may bring as much money as four of the common kinds . . . As to people not distinguishing one apple or pear from another, I hope all by North Tweed don't deserve this unsensible character. But there are a world of things not used in Scotld: because not to be had, and if you introduce good kinds such as Nonpariels Russedines and the like and put them into the hands of a few at Eden: [Edinburgh] who know the difference, You'l soon find a demand for all you can have, and by having such you will even get Customers for other things. Depend upon it there are people in Eden: who have taste and if you can once get into the custom of some who have it, will put others upon enquiring where they had good things, and this will hold in your herbs etc as well as in your fruit. Do you think it possible that there are not Families and Taverns in Eden: that would give reasonably for young pease and Beans in July and Augt if they could get them . . . Don't you even think that the people who sell Garden stuff and fruit at Eden: Such as the man who has built a House at Inveresk whose name I have forgot, would deal with you if you could send him in things at uncommon Seasons and better than the common run . . . I remember since little Garden Stuff was to be got to buy at Eden: and Gardeners said why shall we raise them; nobody will buy them The moment they were to be had everybody bought . . . How shall things be carried to Eden: and nobody will buy in the Country are other very good difficulties and convenient enough excuses, wherein excuse is wanted. I don't know if you have a Carrier at Orm: but I am convinced one who understood his business, would get Employment for a Cart . . . If you put your things up in Baskets carefully as Gardiners do here, by which they'l not be wet, Bruised or Broiled in the Sun the Cart being covered as the Garden Stuff commonly is, in carrying to Eden.

There is a reminder here that wheeled carts were still an uncommon sight in Scotland – a hangover from the days of bad roads, or none at all; goods were usually carried in panniers on horses, but the Edinburgh market was supplied from gardens at Musselburgh with fruit and vegetables carried up in creels by women. Not until about 1746 did the first market-garden cart appear in the streets; it belonged to neither of the Bells, incidentally, but to a Henry Prentice who, clearly, like Cockburn, had realized the potential market and set himself to grow large quantities of pease, turnips and potatoes.

Cockburn died in 1759. He had lived 79 years, and the agricultural improvements he so longed to see were just beginning to take effect. Horticulture, on the other hand, seems to have progressed at a steady pace, particularly in private gardens. With labour cheap and money no longer such a problem as it had been before the Union, even the difficulties presented by the climate were being overcome.

Both Reid and Cockburn had been aware of the technique of hot-bed cultivation for raising early vegetables and tender plants (those moonlit peas and despised melons!) but by the middle of the 18th century more sophisticated methods were also in use. First came the hot wall: ovens built at intervals of 150 feet behind the walls supplemented the sun's heat. Then, from mid-century, hollow walls, often with an internal system of flues, provided a more efficient and secure method of retaining heat, generated in furnaces below ground level. Quite delicate fruit could now be forced, particularly if protected by movable lean-to lights. How successful this system was, is uncertain. James Justice, whose book *The Scots Gardener's Director* finally supplanted Reid's in 1754, was an enthusiastic proselytizer. He also invented the pineapple-pit, enabling those exotic fruit to be cultivated, according to him, 'as freely as in their own native land'. Nevertheless one remembers Sydney Smith's backhanded compliment to the Scots, so cleverly managing to hit several targets simultaneously:

No nation has so large a stock of benevolence of heart as the Scotch. Their temper stands anything but an attack on their climate. They would have you even believe they can ripen fruit; and, to be candid, I must own in remarkably warm summers I have tasted peaches that made excellent pickles.

While the gentry were dining on asparagus and broccoli, pineapples and peaches, what was the rest of the population eating? For all the stories of bad vegetables or none at all, the deprivation save in the Highlands, cannot have been severe. There was kail – also known as kale, borecole, or German greens, and so ubiquitous that the word became a synonym for soup and even for the main meal of the day (as in the injunction to a child to 'sup its kail', i.e., eat its dinner; or in the invitation to 'take kail with us'). The kailyard was the kitchen garden: proof enough of the importance of this vegetable, and interesting too for its use of the word 'yard' in precisely the way Americans use it today.

There were leeks – Cock-a-Leekie is a soup of almost antique origin. And of necessity there were the vegetables which go into Scotch Broth – peas, carrots, onions and turnips. (With the scarcity of cooking utensils and the crowded conditions in which most families lived, it is not surprising that most vegetables ended up in soup. The one-pot meal must have been a very attractive idea to mothers of large families, especially given the frequent lack of meat.)

At the very end of the 18th century, the scarcity of hard information about the diet of ordinary people is suddenly succeeded by an almost embarrassing quantity of documentation. We owe this in large part to a man we have encountered before: Sir John Sinclair. To Sinclair are due not only the volumes of the *General View of Agriculture* all of which include notes (sometimes copious, often entertaining, and occasionally misleading) on gardens and orchards between about 1794 and 1814, but also a more accurate and scientific work, *Scottish Gardens and Orchards*, written as part of a government report and published in 1813.

Its author, Dr Patrick Neill, was a printer whose chief interests lay in horticulture, science, and antiquities. He was secretary to both the Horticultural Society and the Wemerian Natural History Society; in addition he played a major part in landscaping and laying out Edinburgh's West Princes Street Gardens, and was largely responsible for the preservation of the 'Flodden Tower' in the 16th-century City wall.

Neill's book has virtues lacking in the *GVA*. He takes enormous pains to be accurate and objective, where some of the *GVA* reporters are clearly either ignorant or, through anxiety to present their country in the best possible light, downright untruthful. Furthermore, his retrospective glimpses into the preceding century are of great service to the researcher. For example, he states that:

The most eminent physicians of the last age were in use to ascribe a remarkable improvement in the health of the Scots peasantry – the alleviation of some prevailing diseases and the extirpation of others – to the general introduction of cottage gardens, and consequent increased use of coleworts, cabbages, and potatoes. The Highlanders still live very much on fish, flesh and the produce of their cattle, with little vegetable aliment excepting oat-meal and potatoes. They are now, however, becoming sensible of the value of other garden-stuffs.

(His subsequent remark, that Scotch Broth forms a considerable proportion of the food of the peasantry, bears real if unconscious tribute to the efforts of the Improvers, almost all of whom included the recipe somewhere in their writings.)

It is also from Neill that we know of a market gardener near Leith who, in the 1750s, was growing asparagus and artichokes. And he gives us a list of the chief vegetables in demand in the Edinburgh market in 1771: cabbages, potatoes, peas, beans, onions, leeks, turnips, carrots and radishes. If none of these is very exotic, at least we see that common esculents (to borrow a favourite word of the times) were not lacking. John Wesley wrote in 1780 that on his first visit to Scotland in 1762 he had been offered no vegetables of any kind, and that now 'they are as plentiful here as in England'. But as Cox points out, it is impossible that so remarkable a change should have been accomplished in only eighteen years, and most evidence suggests that Wesley's first experience was unfortunate and untypical.

Both Neill and the *GVA* reporters convey a picture of established market and cottage gardens thriving beside the private gentlemen's estates:

So well aware are Scottish cottagers how much their comfort depends on gardens, that their choice of a house is often regulated by the size and quality of ground attached.

Especially near the towns and in large villages cottage gardens were well tended and productive. 'Manufacturers and mechanics', Neill informs us, 'generally take delight in them, and their health must be promoted by the exercise and amusement they afford.' In the largest and best cultivated, usually held by feu, the standard was as high as in any south of the Border, and most of the usual vegetables were produced. Often there were apple and pear trees, and bushes of gooseberries and red, white and black currants.

The class least inclined towards horticulture was that of the farmers and farm-workers. Partly, this may have resulted from long habit since gardens are not made overnight, and the system of short leases prevailing until the 18th century would not encourage any kind of forward planning. Yet it is true that even today farmers rarely show much interest in growing vegetables or fruit for themselves. However, when Neill and the *GVA* reporters were making their surveys, the situation varied from county to county, with East Lothian farmers evidently the most advanced in both ideas and execution: in their gardens, broccoli, cauliflower, artichokes, parsnips, celery and even asparagus might appear, together with plenty of berry fruit. At the extreme end of the scale, in Bute 'few farmers have anything that can be termed a garden', while in Argyll, 'he is commonly more than an ordinary farmer who has a few roots and some leeks and onions'.

Certainly this lack of interest was not for want of encouragement. In *The Gentleman Farmer*, a treatise dated 1776, Lord Kames wrote:

The chief accommodation of all is a fruitful kitchen garden. Formerly, oat-meal was the only food of labouring people; and when at 5–6 shillings per boll, there could not be a cheaper food. A kitchen–garden was at that time a sort of luxury . . . by a great advance in the price of oats and oat-meal, a kitchen-garden has become an article of economy . . . well-dressed and cropped, it will afford half the maintenance to a family; and yet this food would not cost much above the third of the price of oatmeal.

Neill, in 1813, reinforced the argument with the candid utilitarianism of his age, remarking that the enlightened farmer would provide cottage gardens for his workers, who should be married, so that he could 'avail himself of the cheap labours of women, boys and girls, in cleaning and hoeing his drilled crops and similar operations.'

Neither Kames nor Neill seems to have been directly conscious of the limitations of soil and climate in much of the country. East Lothian farmers were praised for their gardens which (as the Reporter Robert Somerville pointed out) were tended only after the ordinary day's work was over. But for most of the rural population the ordinary day's work was a dreadful, exhausting grind which left a man too tired to do more than fall into bed once he had eaten his evening meal. Like Cockburn, Kames and Neill could not imagine the physical effort farmers had to make, day after day, to cultivate the sour, stubborn ground. How could they possibly find extra reserves of energy to cultivate kitchen-gardens? The insensitive attitude of the gentry is perfectly expressed in the report of the Reverend Patrick Graham, minister of Aberfoyle, who found the peasantry

deplorably inattentive to the comforts of garden produce. They cannot be made to comprehend the assistance that may be derived from a kitchen garden to the subsistence of a family. The cultivation of carrots, turnips, pease and beans, onions and leeks is very rare amongst them . . . except in the neighbourhood of towns, where a ready sale furnishes a spur to industry.

Indeed, in the towns there was a marked improvement in the provision of vegetables by the end of the 18th century. *GVA* reporters singled out Aberdeen, where all kinds were raised in such plenty in market gardens within two miles of the city that few farmers bothered to bring in their produce for sale. Soft fruit too was plentiful and of excellent quality. Inverness and Nairn had market gardens, as did Dundee where the quality and cheapness of the produce was commented upon.

Neill's descriptions of the Clydesdale and Edinburgh markets are vivid in their detailed analysis of what was sold. Interestingly, many Renfrewshire gardens concentrated on growing vegetables for the ships which now came up the river: 'potatoes, carrots, turnips and onions are the most proper articles for sea-stock. Cabbages which are firm keep long fresh, particularly if placed among the ballast'.

The list of vegetables in demand at Glasgow market hardly suggests a population of vegetable-haters. Early vegetables include potatoes, cabbage and turnips; yellow turnips, onions, leeks, savoys, German greens, Scots kail, celery, late cabbage, cauliflower, broccoli, peas, beans and asparagus all sold well. Parsley and 'the usual salads' were plentiful, and cucumbers were quite popular, but there was little demand for sea-cale, artichokes, beet, endive, French beans, garlic or shallots.

In Edinburgh, Tuesdays, Thursdays and Saturdays were the days for the wholesale fruit and vegetable markets, one on the south side of the High Street near the Tron (the word means a public weighing-machine), the other on the northside, the poet Southey, who toured Scotland with James Telford in 1819, described the scene:

Edinburgh was alive when I entered it; even at that early hour there was a busy greens-market in the High Street. Upon enquiry I learned that everything must be cleared away before eight o'clock – a good, wise regulation.

Lord Henry Cockburn, author of the *Memorials of his Time*, later remembered the 28 stalls with disgust rather than nostalgic approval:

Our vegetables ... were entirely in the hands of a college of old gin-drinking women who congregated with stools and tables round the Tron Church. A few of the aristocracy of these ladies – the burgo-mistresses, who had established a superior business – the heads of old booths – marked their dignity by an awning of dirty canvas or tattered carpet; and every table had its tallow candle and paper lantern at night. There was no water here either, except what flowed down the gutter, which, however, was plentifully used. Fruit had a place on the table, but kitchen vegetables lay bruised on the ground. I doubt if there was a fruit shop in Edinburgh in 1815. All shops indeed meant for the sale of any article, on which there was a local tax or market-system, were discouraged by the magistrates or their taxman as interfering with the collection of the dues.

As in Glasgow, the range was large. Sea-cale and artichokes, both almost unknown in the west, were popular, but salads sold slowly and the quality was inferior.

Silent though he is about the old women at the Tron, Neill praises their suppliers:

It is believed, that no class of men in the country, undergo more continual fatigue and personal exertions, than the Edinburgh market gardeners find indispensable, in order to enable them to support their families and pay the enormous rents now required. To their honour, it may be added, that they are a habitually cheerful and hearty set of men, and very generally of sober habits. A number of the more attentive and industrious, have made a little money; and a few who have old leases, are accounted rich, live in a genteel style, and give their children the best of education.

The attention which Neill and the *GVA* paid to the state of horticulture is symptomatic of a trend which continued throughout the 19th century. Several *GVA* reporters complained that taxing the employment of gardeners on private estates led to deteriorating standards; but in fact throughout the Georgian and Victorian eras all existing classes of garden continued to improve, though, with rare exceptions, there was little change in the attitude of Highlanders and the rural classes.

The most significant 19th-century development was in fruit cultivation. If orchards have hardly been mentioned in this chapter, it is not because they did not exist – especially in the Clyde valley, Stirlingshire, the Carse of Gowrie and the Borders – but because the apples, pears, cherries and plums produced therein, while supplying local needs, contributed little out of the ordinary to either the gastronomy or the economy of the country.

Soft fruit, however, which responds well to a climate such as ours, has always taken a relatively important place in Scottish diet. Far more of it grew wild formerly. From James IV's Exchequer Rolls we know that wood strawberries frequently came to the royal table; many writers, including Mrs Grant in her *Memoirs of a Highland Lady*, speak of the blaeberries and cranberries growing in the hills. The introduction of a 19th-century seedsman's catalogue lists seventeen 'native wild fruits of Scotland', though (rather unfairly) hollyberries, acorns and beech-mast are on the list. And in one of his very rare allusions to food, Hugh MacDiarmid wrote in *Lucky Poet*:

Many a great basket of blaeberries I gathered on the hills round Langholm ... then there were the little hard black cranberries, and – less easy to gather since they grow in swampy places the speckled crane-berries, but above all, in the Langfall and other woods in the extensive policies of the Duke of Buccleuch, there were great stretches of wild raspberry bushes, the fruit of which the public were allowed to pick:

> 'And hoo should I forget the Langfall
> On mornings when the hines were ripe, but een
> Ahint the glintin' leafs were brichter still
> Than sunned dew on them, lips reider than the fruit,
> And I filled baith my basket and my hert
> Mony and mony a time?'

Cultivated soft fruit, long a feature of gentry gardens, became more widely popular as a result of the expansion of the sugar trade, which more or less coincided with the trend to longer leases for cottage and farm tenants. Now it became possible for even cottagers to plant a patch of ground with gooseberries, raspberries and currants; and sugar was cheap enough to allow the making of jams and preserves. Among the upper classes, the use of fruit in this way became a fashion almost amounting to a craze. In Angus, so many gooseberries were grown at the end of the 18th century that families made gooseberry vinegar; Dumfries people were noted for rasp-berry jam and preserved cranberries, which they used in tarts and to give 'the most beautiful colour' to other preserves. Since sugar was considered to have medicinal properties, drinks consisting of sweetened infusions of all kinds of fruit, cultivated and wild, became very popular. The concept, naturally, was soon extended to experiments in the making of wine, referred to by a number of the *GVA* reporters and approved by the Church, if the Reverend John Smith's enthusiasm is anything to go by:

Where there is superfluity of small fruit, and the market distant, it may be converted to a wholesome and palatable drink, by making it undergo a vinous fermentation; and such colour, flavour, and strength may be given it, as to make it resemble and equal imported wine. Raspberries and strawberries, white or red, will help the colour and flavour, and a proper quantity of spirits, with sugar or honey, may be added to make it strong and rich. A respectable family, lately in this county [Argyll], used to make a considerable quantity of such liquor, which was generally preferred to foreign wines, when both were set down on the table . . . wines more wholesome and palatable than most of those that are imported could be made from our own fruits.

The Reporter for Aberdeenshire, even more carried away, seems to have experimented with almost every fruit and vegetable cultivated in his county, including beets, salsify and carrots. He found that scorzonera 'produced a most agreeable flavoured spirit, well adapted for making a liqueur', but the amount of ground required to raise a reasonable crop forced him to conclude, rather sadly, that its best use would only be in making liqueurs 'for the ladies' – who presumably drank less. A patriotic motive was clearly discernible in all these remarks: Napoleon was threatening Britain with invasion.

The result was that some farmers began to grow soft fruit, particularly strawberries and raspberries, for sale. In the early years of the 19th century the region south of Edinburgh was famous for its strawberries, and Neill paints an almost Scott-like vignette of summer delights:

During the season, numerous parties are formed to eat strawberries at Roslin, between 7 and 8 miles South from Edinburgh; a place remarkable for the beauty of its scenery, with a castle hallowed in song, and a Gothic chapel, surpassed by none in the richness of its architectural embellishments.

Nor was this all, for many thousands of pints of the fruit, he informs us, were also consumed in public gardens in the immediate vicinity of Edinburgh.

It was the introduction of steam transport which really improved the market for soft fruit, and as packing and marketing techniques developed, demand increased. (One can almost hear John Cockburn saying 'I told you so!'.) By 1880 the basic horticultural product of Clydeside was strawberries, while Perthshire and Angus were celebrated for their raspberries. Remarkably, despite two world wars, several serious epidemics of plant diseases, and enormously fluctuating labour and land costs, the industry has survived; even today, Scotland is the largest exporter of raspberries within the EEC, while the popularity of the tayberry and the tummelberry show the continuing contribution made by bodies like the Scottish Crop Research Institute at Invergowrie.

The best years of the kitchen garden were during the 19th century and the early 20th. This was so all over Britain, with cheap skilled labour and fuel able to supplement, by art, whatever deficiencies soil and climate might cause. Scots gardeners have been famous since the time of Reid, and perhaps Dr Johnson was right: 'Gardening is much more necessary amongst you than with us,' he told Boswell, 'which makes so many people learn it. It is *all* gardening with you. Things, which grow wild here, must be cultivated with great care in Scotland.'

The Scots gardener is familiar in fiction no less than fact. From Scott to Wodehouse authors have enjoyed depicting him. But one character – Robie, whose attention has to be diverted by 'a child among the artichokes' (R. L. Stevenson, *St Ives*) – had a factual source. Here is the real man, in R. L. S.'s recollection of the manse near Edinburgh where he spent much of his childhood:

He would . . . fill the most favoured and fertile section of the garden with a vegetable that none of us could eat, in supreme contempt for our opinion. If you asked him to send you in one of your own artichokes, 'That I wull, mem,' he would say, 'with pleasure, for it is mair blessed to give than to receive . . .'
. . . It was towards his cauliflowers and peas and cabbage that his heart grew warm. His preference for the more useful growths was such that cabbages were found invading the flower-pots, and an outpost of savoys was once discovered in the centre of the lawn.

Shades of John Reid!

That such men, and such gardens, should now have disappeared is not surprising. The economic effect of two wars is too well known to bear repeating here, and it was inevitable that private gardens large and small should suffer from the disappearance of cheap labour. There is very little gardening on the old scale; and fuel costs ensure that hot-houses, hot-beds and pineapple-pits are now the exclusive province of enthusiastic amateurs, and not designed to produce food for large parties of house-guests or even large families. Obviously the situation is not confined to Scotland, and we need feel no shame in it.

What is far more disturbing is that vegetable cultivation in general has declined dramatically in the last 70 years. In 1935 substantially fewer varieties of vegetable were coming to market than in 1835, and in 1987 there are many fewer still, if we exclude what is grown outside Scotland. Of the vegetables mentioned by Neill, we find now that early turnips have become relatively rare; Scots kail is hardly ever seen, whilst celery, cauliflower, and broccoli are almost always imported from England or the Continent. Peas make a brief appearance but are invariably overgrown and several days old, and broad beans are usually in a similar state; asparagus is generally imported and wildly expensive, sea-cale never appears. Artichokes are imported, so are endive, French beans, garlic, shallots, salsify and cucumbers; skirret and scorzonera are unknown, and curly, plain and cos lettuces appear to be the only varieties with which the unhappy customer may make her salad. It has become a common experience to meet a friend, newly returned from holiday in England or abroad, and almost in tears from frustration at not being able to buy here the basic, good-quality vegetables she has seen every day in some foreign market. It almost seems as though, for town-dwellers at least, there has been a return to the old days of John Cockburn and his gardener Charles Bell.

The reason usually given is that market gardening has become too expensive. Not only is it a labour-intensive activity which requires much work over a relatively short period each year, but also, as we have seen, many plants need special protection, or even a source of heat, to enable them to come to fruition. We are told that the tomato industry, which throve in the 'fifties when market gardeners had acres under glass, is in danger of extinction; that the cultivation of soft fruit like blackcurrants and gooseberries is no longer viable without cheap labour to pick and pack. The only reason that raspberries and strawberries have survived is because, apart from an export market, the pick-your-own system enables farmers to make a profit. These are farmers' arguments: and they do not throw light on the continued existence of market gardeners in England. Is it really for lack of adequate labour that we get our lettuces wilted, our peas and beans past their prime and three days old? Where are the fresh radishes, the seven or eight kinds of salads which the old gardeners grew, the fresh-picked young spinach or the crisp, pink baby carrots? Do they require so much more effort than we can give them? Any allotment owner knows that this is nonsense.

Why this is, would probably provide material enough for a thesis. But it takes no economic genius to calculate that if a market gardener is to sell his produce at a realistic price, it is to his disadvantage to do so through a shop, which will put its own mark-up on the article and probably discourage the customer. Given the high cost of producing good quality fruit and vegetables in this country, the only way they can be sold at prices attractive to a customer is on a market-stall, where the overheads are low. Unfortunately, the daily, or even weekly, market is now only a memory in most Scottish towns. So one by one the gardens also disappear, and the customers are left with mass-produced vegetables brought into the wholesale markets and distributed through the shops, with minimum competition for either price or quality.

— RECIPES —

There are few indigenous or peculiarly Scottish ways with vegetables, apart from some recipes for kale, leeks and turnips; but old recipes often show a surprising familiarity with what we think of nowadays as rather exotic or luxury items. Consider artichokes. The many references in Reid, Neill and other writers indicate that they were not nearly so uncommon in previous centuries as they are now; indeed, they grew in sufficient quantities to allow of them being pickled or dried for the winter. I must admit to having felt extreme scepticism over the claim by Robert Shireff, the reporter to the *GVA* for Orkney and Shetland in 1812, that artichokes were reckoned to do better there than anywhere else in the country. Perhaps he was talking about the Jerusalem rather than the Globe?

Apparently not. Miss E. R. Bullard, of Orkney, says it is perfectly possible to cultivate globe artichokes there – even some placed by her in a 'wild' garden and left untended produced small but edible 'chokes'. She points out that in Shireff's time there seems to have been a period of warmer climate which lasted for perhaps 40 years, and that Osgood Mackenzie, reminiscing about that same period in *A Hundred Years in the Highlands*, wrote of his grandmother's store cupboard in Conon containing 'strings of threaded artichoke bottoms, dried, I suppose, for putting into soup'. So there we are. But even today I suspect that artichokes, asparagus and other tender plants could achieve more widespread cultivation. It would be pleasant to find oneself buying Orkney artichokes one day.

Against that time, here is a recipe from John Reid for pickled artichokes:

Pickled Artichokes

Dissolve two large Handfuls of great Salt (that is dried on the Fire in a Pan) in one Mutchkin of Vinegar, and three of fair Water, mix them while the Salt is yet hot (but put not the Liquor on the Fire), boil the Artichokes till the Leaves come off easily, and while the cleansed Stools are yet warm, you may have three Nutmegs, three Drops of Cloves, 1½ Dram of Mace, ¼ Ounce white Pepper, ½ Ounce Cinnamon beat to fine Powder, and strew upon them; then pack them in the Pot, with 5 or 6 Spoonfuls of the Liquor on each Stratum: when all are potted, pour on the rest of the pickle and stop closs.

Asparagus may be parboil'd and pickled as Artichokes, and so may green Pease with Cods.

Reid's other recipes, though similar, contain many touches showing that he, or perhaps his wife Margaret, was no indifferent cook. Here are some of his other ideas:

Beans and *Pease* are boiled with Savory and Thyme-Fagot, served up with sweet Butter beat among them, and set a little on a Coal or Chafing-Dish.

Boil *Asparagus* in fair water, and serve it up with a little sweet

Butter beat, that is, tumbled in the Sauce Pan above the coals. The young shoots of Colewort will serve the same way. [And taste almost as good. A. H.]

Spinage is excellent Stoves, being boiled with Lamb or Veal, with a little Sorrel therein.

In some Stoves and Broths you may put Arag [?], Marygold Leaves, Violet Leaves, Strawberry Leaves, Bugloss, Burrage, and Endive. In Pottage put Juice of Sorrel, Fagot of Thyme and Parsley, and in most of the Broths.

In the Sauce of Gravy of Rost Mutton and Capon, and in all stewed Dishes, bruise Shallots, or rub the Dishes therewith.

Onions may be baked with a little Butter if you want [lack] Meat. [Do not peel the onions, just scrub and dry them, rub with a buttered paper, and put on a baking sheet in the oven at medium heat for 20–30 minutes or until tender. They acquire a particular, quite excellent sweetness and are good with all egg or fish dishes. A. H.]

Boil *Colliflowers* in Water mixed with a little Milk, then pour it off and mix them in the stew-pan with sweet Butter seasoned with Salt, and so serve them up about boil'd Mutton.

Boil and peel *Parsnips*, chop and bruise them well, pour on Butter, and set them on a Coal, and if you please strew a little Cinnamon upon them.

Potatoes as Parsnips; or for want of Butter take sweet Milk.

VEGETABLE SOUPS

The art of soup-making used to be understood by every Scots-woman. This is no longer the case, for working wives with little time are as much a part of Scots society as of any other. But the recipes remain in the keen cook's repertoire, even if only brought out for special occasions.

Leek and Oatmeal Soup

1 lb (450g) leeks
1 oz (25g) butter
1½ pt (830 ml) chicken stock
½ pt (280 ml) milk

2 tablespoons oatmeal (pinhead grind)
salt and pepper

Wash and chop the leeks, including part of the pale green section.
Melt the butter, add the chopped white of the leeks, cover, and
cook over very low heat, shaking occasionally, for about 10
minutes. Then stir in the oatmeal until it is thoroughly mixed
with leeks and butter. Slowly, still stirring, add the hot stock.
Bring to a gentle boil, and simmer for 15–20 minutes. Add the
milk and seasoning, reheat to just below boiling point, then add
the reserved green leek and serve. This is a very delicate soup, in
both taste and texture.

Nettle Soup

This once popular soup was resurrected during the last war when
food was scarce. It enjoyed a brief vogue but then lapsed into
oblivion. When made with young nettles, it is quite good – but
given the choice most people would probably prefer spinach soup,
which it resembles. Still, it is worth trying and a relief to know that
nettles have some good qualities. The method is the same as for
leek and oatmeal soup, but it should be puréed or blended before
dishing up.

Hotch Potch

One of the classic Scotch soups, but so close to the French stew
called *Navarin de Mouton* that the recipe really belongs in the next
chapter. It makes such good use of the gardener's produce, though,
that we shall allow it to enter this space. Marian McNeill comments
that it makes a famous hot dish after a chilly day on the hill. She is
right. Here is her recipe:

3 lb (1½ kg) neck of lamb
1½ lb (750g) fresh young peas
1 lb (450g) young broad beans
6 young turnips
6 young carrots

6 spring onions
1 cauliflower
1 lettuce
1 handful parsley
salt and pepper
5 pt (2¾ l) water

Put the meat into a saucepan with the water and a little salt. Bring to the boil and skim carefully. Shell the peas and beans, scrape or peel the turnips and carrots and cut them into dice, chop the spring onions, including the green part. Reserve ⅓ of the peas, put the rest of the prepared vegetables into the boiling liquor. Simmer very slowly for 3–4 hours. 'It can hardly be simmered too long,' wrote Miss McNeill. Meanwhile, put the cauliflower and lettuce into cold water with a little salt and let them lie half an hour. Then break the cauliflower into sprigs and chop the lettuce, and half an hour before serving add them to the pot with the rest of the peas and the chopped parsley. The soup should be nearly as thick as porridge. When ready, remove the mutton, season the soup, and serve in a hot tureen.

Elizabeth Cleland, whose *New and Easy Method of Cookery* (Edinburgh 1759) is one of our earliest cook books, has many recipes for vegetable soups. The following one shows no evidence of any lack of greens, though it is called a Meagre Broth ('meagre', from the French word *maigre*, simply refers to the lack of meat).

To make Meagre Broth for Soups with herbs

Set on the Fire a Kettle of Water, put in it some Crusts of Bread, and all sorts of Herbs, green Beets, Sellery, Endive, Lettice, Sorrel, green Onions, Parsley, Chervil, with a good piece of Butter, and a bunch of sweet Herbs; boil it for an Hour and a Half, then strain it off; this will serve to make Artichoke or Asparagus, or Soupe de Sante with Herbs; season it with Salt, Pepper, Cloves Jamaica Pepper; cut the Herbs grossly, and it will be a very good Soup, boiling a good Lump of Butter with the herbs, putting toasted Bread in the Dish, but take out the Bulk of the sweet Herbs

This is really vegetable stock, to be used, as she says, as a base for a soup of some specific vegetable (herbs are green vegetables as opposed to roots or sweet herbs). But if well seasoned, it is very good by itself, either served clear with a piece of toast at the bottom of the plate, or put through the blender to make a thicker soup.

DISHES OF VEGETABLES

Why asparagus is not more frequently cultivated by those who have space for it, defeats me. A friend with an allotment regularly collects 60 lb each summer, and I have heard of an Orkney family who acquired, with their house, such a fertile asparagus bed that they become heartily sick of it by the end of June. For such people, here is Elizabeth Cleland's recipe, easier than Reid's, for pickled asparagus.

To pickle Asparagus

Take the largest Asparagus that is very green, cut off the white, and scrape them lightly to the head, then put them in a Jar, and throw over them some Salt, and a few Cloves and Mace, and pour on them as much Vinegar as will cover them: let them lye nine Days, then put the Vinegar in a Brass Kettle, and put the Asparagus into it, stow them down closs; let them stand a little, then put them in a Jar, and tye them closs.

Celery in Cream

The following recipe for celery from the same author, is a practicable and good lunch dish.

> 3–4 heads of celery
> ¼ pt (125 ml) single cream
> 2 egg yolks
> nutmeg
> salt

Clean the celery and cut into short lengths. Boil till tender, then drain well. Butter an ovenproof dish; beat together the egg yolks and cream, add a little nutmeg and salt to taste. Put the celery into the dish, pour over the cream, and bake in a dish of hot water in a slow oven 325°F (160°C) gas 3, about half an hour or until set.

Most people react strongly to Jerusalem artichokes; John Goodyer, the Englishman who is supposed to have first planted them in Britain in 1621, gave them a bad press:

Which way soever they be drest and eaten they stir up and cause a filthie loathesome stinking winde within the bodie . . . and are a meat more fit for swine than men.

Scots seem to have been unperturbed, for Jerusalem artichokes became and have remained a popular vegetable. They are usually cooked as Palestine soup, but Lady Clark has a deliciously unusual way with them:

Jerusalem Chips

Clean artichoke roots, and peel them; wash them in water with a squeeze of lemon juice; dry them well on a cloth, then cut in slices of 1s or if you prefer of 1d [5p or 2p for today's cooks], and drop them into cold water to keep white; strain them on a sieve; dry in a cloth. Fry in fresh lard to a gold colour like potato chips. Before dishing and when they are still in the frying basket, dust them with salt like whitebait.

If oatmeal is the national cereal, kail is reckoned the national green vegetable, in the Lowlands at least. Burns described the superstitions associated with kail at Hallowe'en, in his notes to his poem about that festival:

The first ceremony of Hallowe'en is pulling each a stock or plant of kail. They must go out, hand-in-hand, with eyes shut, and pull the first they meet with. Its being big or little, straight or crooked, is prophetic of the size and shape of the grand object of all their spells – the husband or wife. If any gird, or earth, stick to the root that is 'tocher' or fortune; and the taste of the 'custoc', that is, the heart of the stem, indicative of the natural temper and disposition. Lastly, the stems, or, to give them their ordinary appelation, the runts, are placed somewhere above the head of the door; and the Christian names of the people whom chance brings into the house are, according to the priority of placing the runts, the names in question.

Scotch curled kail is worth cultivating in any garden. It is a handsome plant, its dark crisped leaves sweeping out from the stem and reminding one of a tree painted by Palmer. It retains its air of vitality during the severest frost and snow, and when spring arrives, put out small tender leaves of palest green as if to assert once for all its determination to *live*. This new spring growth is most delicate in flavour, quite good enough to eat straight from the plant, but also delicious shredded and dressed with olive oil, garlic, salt, and a drop of lemon juice. The darker leaves are always cooked, and can be harvested at any time from November, though the flavour is supposed to be finest when the plant has been touched by the first frost. One must pity the English, most of whom, if rumour be true, feed kail only to their cattle.

After an article of mine in the *Scotsman* some years ago, a reader kindly sent me her recollections of making Lang Kail during the war, when food was rationed. Her recipe is identical to that which appears, under the heading 'Sir John's Luncheon Kail', in *Lady Clark of Tillypronie's Cook Book*, and I give it as she wrote it, adding only that as kail boils down almost as much as spinach, 1 lb (450g) will feed only two or three people, and that anyone who has not tried this dish should take the first opportunity of doing so.

Lang Kail

The morning that we were to have it I went up the garden and picked a large bunch which was washed under the tap and all the flesh stripped off the ribs. It was cooked in a large pot in salted water or a clear light stock such as chicken. Then the cook would put a newspaper and pot stand on the floor and with a potato champer mash the kail to a puree [there were no electric mixers in those days] then return to the stove and with a wooden spoon mix in the siftings of oatmeal to thicken and add a little cream or top of the milk.

When served with oatcakes this made a main course for lunch.

In Orkney and Shetland, a favourite dish dating back at least to the 16th century used to be 'kail and k-nockit corn' (the 'k' prominently pronounced), consisting of dehusked bere boiled with kail and a morsel of pork. Orcadians also sometimes substitute kail for turnip in what amounts to their national dish, 'Clapshot'. Scots rate leeks almost as highly as they do kail.

'The fine qualities of this vegetable,' wrote William Robinson in his 1885 edition of Vilmorin-Andrieux' *The Vegetable Garden*, 'are much better known to the Welsh, Scotch, and French than to the English or Irish.' He went on to describe the *Poireau de Mussel-bourg*, raised near Edinburgh, as an improved form of the Common Long Winter Leek, possessing a longer and thicker stem and broad leaves. Is this the 'Scots Leek' which Patrick Neill praised as superior to all others? The market gardens proliferating round Musselburgh at the beginning of the 19th century may well already have evolved their own, as yet unnamed, strain.

Given the popularity of both vegetables in Scotland in the 18th and 19th centuries, it was probably also Scots who first designated leeks as 'poor man's asparagus', – a surprisingly accurate description of freshly pulled young leeks, gently steamed and served with butter.

Victor McClure's recipe in *Good Appetite my Companion* for leeks the Scots way, can hardly be bettered. Even elderly vegetables respond – young ones emerge superb.

Scots Braised Leeks
(Serves 8)

2 doz. medium-sized leeks, trimmed to the white,
    removing outer skin and roots
2 tablespoons chopped carrot
2 tablespoons chopped onion

2 tablespoons chopped parsley
2 tablespoons chopped green celery tops
2 tablespoons chopped green peppers
salt, pepper, nutmeg, thyme, bayleaf
½ pt (280 ml) bechamel sauce
2 egg yolks
½ cup buttered breadcrumbs

Wash the leeks in lukewarm water, then rinse in several changes of cold water. Drain and wipe dry. Generously butter an earthenware dish with a lid, and lay the leeks out in it. Add the chopped vegetables and seasoning. Pour over enough good bouillon or beef stock to cover. Put a buttered paper over, then the lid, and bake at about 360°F (180°C) gas 4 for 35–40 minutes.

When the liquor has been pretty well absorbed, and the leeks are tender, pour over them a little more than ½ pt of bechamel sauce to which have been added the yolks of two eggs nicely beaten. This custardy sauce should be hot. Return the dish to the oven for 15–20 minutes, or until the sauce is a soft custard. Have ready ½ cup buttered breadcrumbs, not overcrisped, and sprinkle them on top of the dish. Brown under the grill.

Scotland, like the rest of Europe, familiarized itself early with the pea. On one occasion, an entire English army is said to have kept itself fed for two or three weeks on those growing in the Merse region round Berwick. They were certainly not the *petits pois* we enjoy today, being bigger and coarser-flavoured, and largely cultivated to be dried and turned into pease-meal. By 1683, however, the craze for fresh young peas – *piselli novelli* – which had started in Italy and swept through France, was well developed in Scotland; and we find John Reid stressing that peas should be eaten when young, and working out methods of producing an early crop. Their popularity continued during the 18th century, and in 1802 the Reverend Charles Findlater, the Reporter to the *GVA* for Peebles, was making rather remarkable claims:

In hill countries, great heat is often produced in particular spots from reverberation. The reflection from a rocky hill upon the garden of Pirn, in Inverleithan parish, is the reason that, in that garden, two crops of peas, fit for the table, have been often successively raised in one season from the same plot of ground. I do not however imagine the gardeners' boast, in some better climates in Scotland, could there be exhibited, of sowing peas, reaping their produce, and having eatable peas from that sowing, within the season.

Meg Dods, thirty or so years later, was severe on such ambition:

The vanity, and it is no better, which spurs on people to load their tables with flavourless, colourless, immature vegetables is ever punished by the expense and disappointment it occasions.

And serve them right, is the implication.

Lady Clark of Tillypronie, realistic but also a good cook, certainly preferred young peas, but knew how to make the best of old ones. 'Our Tillypronie way' was to boil the fresh-shelled peas in salted water with 2 lumps of sugar (about two teaspoonsful) and butter, then to drain them, and put them on again with 2 oz (50g) butter, a tablespoon of stock and the same of white sugar, and simmer till almost dry. They were served garnished with triangular bits of light puff-paste, or fried croutons.

A more substantial dish, as the name indicates, is Peas, Vegetarian.

Peas, Vegetarian

> 1 pt (600 ml) (1 lb, 250g), shelled green peas
> 2 lettuces cut small
> salt
> 1 teaspoon sugar
> 2 egg yolks
> 4 tablespoons single cream

Put the peas and lettuces in a saucepan with a small teacupful of salted water and cook gently till the peas are quite soft. Beat together the egg yolks, sugar and cream, and add to the pan. Stir the whole well together for a short time, but do not let it boil.

It goes against the grain to be as candid as Lady Clark about the next recipe, which, she says, 'does well for tinned peas or for old garden peas'. Still, old garden peas have to be used from time to time, and with the modification of cooking the sauce and peas separately, young peas too are delicious in the following way:

Peas Stewed

Wash the peas well in cold water and drain, then throw them into boiling water to blanch quickly, with just a pinch of soda (only for old peas). Drain in a sieve, and put into a stewpan, in which you have put 2 oz (50g) cold butter well mixed with a spoonful of flour, also a raw whole onion, a piece of raw ham, a little pepper, salt and sugar, a sprig of fresh mint, or merely the stalk if it is dried mint, and ½ teacupful of stock.

Let all stew, and shake the pan gently that all may mix and melt, and cook till tender from 20–40 minutes according to the age and quality of the peas. Just before serving, take the ham and onion from the pan, and add a tablespoon of glaze to the peas (use the juice from a roast or a little sherry or Madeira if you have no glaze) and a little white sugar; let it mix, and serve the peas very hot.

Entries in the *Ochertyre House Book* (1727–9) suggest that some member of that household must have been inordinately fond of spinach, or perhaps believed in its medicinal properties. Even in January 'spinage and eggs' appeared for supper at least once weekly, and by the summer it was coming to table almost every day. Probably it was in the form described by Meg Dods a century later: the eggs poached, the vegetable boiled, pressed dry, beaten with butter and seasonings, and cut in the form of sippets with an egg on each. It makes as she says, a pretty supper dish.

There occurs in Lady Clark's book a dish with spinach which she describes as a very old Scots recipe. I have not come across it elsewhere, though the combination of spinach and mutton reminds me of some Indian dishes. If lamb's head is unacceptable or unobtainable, other cuts might be substituted – it is a dish worth making for a cold autumn day.

Lamb's Stove

> 1 lamb's head
> 2 pt (1.15 l) stock or water
> parsley
> about 1 lb (450g) spinach
> 1 bunch spring onions
> 2 egg yolks

Wash the spinach well, and reserve about six well-shaped leaves. Cook the rest and set aside. Clean and blanch the lamb's head. If other cuts are used, trim them of fat as much as possible. Cook the meat in broth or stock until tender, add minced parsley, the spring onions and the cooked mashed spinach; thicken with the egg yolks and put large wide leaves of spinach whole into it. Serve the meat and the soup together.

Turnips are the indispensable vegetable with haggis. The gentry have Turnip Purry (Purée), the common folk eat Bashed Neeps. It is the same thing – the vegetable boiled till tender then mashed with seasoning and butter. The *Cook and Housewife's Manual* should have the last word:

Mrs Dods put a little powdered ginger to her mashed turnips, which were studiously chosen of the yellow, sweet, juicy sort, for which Scotland is celebrated – that kind which, in our days of semi-barbarism, were served raw as a delicate whet before dinner, as turnips are in Russia at the present moment ... yellow turnips mashed and eaten with milk, are recommended in scurvy and consumption.

Parsnips which, before turnips became popular, seem to have been fairly widely grown, may of course be cooked the same way. Neill observed that in maritime districts 'hard (*i.e.*, salt) fish and parsnips' was proverbially a favourite dish.

FRUIT

We who live at a time when almost any kind of fruit is obtainable all year round provided someone is willing to import it, with the additional good fortune of having frozen and tinned fruit on sale in every grocer's shop, can scarcely understand the importance which used to be accorded to growing one's own, and preserving some for the winter. Fresh fruit was treated with a respect hardly conceivable nowadays. It was offered to guests, who received it as an honour and a privilege. To grow it, especially the more exotic kinds, was to mark one's status as a person of consequence. Nevertheless peoples' efforts did not always meet with success, and we have seen that Sidney Smith, though he ate the raw peaches he was offered, would have preferred them pickled. There was another way of using up the quantities of unripe fruit which could be the consequence of a bad summer, as Eliza Cleland knew:

Peach Tarts

Take half-ripe Peaches and pare them, and slice them in two, and take out the Stones, put some fine powdered Sugar in the Bottom of a Stew-Pan, place your Peaches in it, put them over the Fire, and stir them often, then put Paste in the Patty-pans; and when the Peaches are cold put them in the Patties with the Syrup they were boiled in, cover them with rich Paste, and bake them in a slow Oven; put the Kernels of the Peaches in the Tarts. You may do Apricocks the same Way.

It is, anyone would admit, wonderful to buy all kinds of fruit all year round; but what we have gained in one respect we have lost in another. There was such pleasure – aesthetic, moral and sensuous – in surveying rows of jars and pots, each richly glowing with the promise of endless pies, tarts, mousses and fools. There was also such satisfaction in being the creator of these beautiful objects, and in knowing that by their means the household would eat well during the dark, bleak winter months.

In memory of those lost delights, here is a recipe from Meg Dods:

To preserve Red Gooseberries

Clip off the top of each berry, and take weight for weight of fine sugar. Clarify the sugar, and put the fruit to it, having made a slit with a needle in each berry, to let the sugar penetrate the fruit. Skim well, and when the skins look very transparent, take up the fruit with a sugar skimmer into glasses or pots. Boil the syrup till it will jelly (if the fruit were boiled so long it would become leathery). Strain it through a fine sieve, and pour it on the berries. This is a cheap and beautiful preserve.

What is Quiddany? *Chambers Dictionary* defines it as a confection of quince-juice and sugar, but Mrs Cleland's two recipes don't include quinces among the ingredients. Her titles are enticing: 'To make Quiddany of Pipins, of an Amber or Ruby Colour'; 'To make Quiddany of all Sorts of Plumbs'. Alas, the recipes are not very enlightening. But the one using apples continues to intrigue me.

To make Quiddany of Pipins, of an Amber or Ruby Colour

Pare the Pipins, and cut them into Quarters, and boil them in as much Water as will cover them, till they are soft, and sink in the Water, then strain the Pulp. Take a Pint of the Liquor, and boil it with half a Pound of Sugar, till it appears a quaking Jelly in the Moulds; When the Quiddany is cold, turn it on a wet Trencher, and slide it into Boxes. If you would have it of a red Colour, let it boil leisurely closs covered, till it is red like Claret.

Another and better-known Scottish confection also takes its name from the quince. Marmelo is the Portuguese word for quince; so quiddany and marmalade are closely related. Waverley Root, the American authority on food, tells us that though a British cookbook of 1669 published several marmalade recipes, most were based on quinces and none used oranges.

Did Janet Keiller call her marmalade of oranges a 'quiddany' in 1770? We shall never know, but hers was the inspiration responsible for the look of millions of breakfast-tables today. If all the recipes for marmalade were put together they would probably fill a whole volume the size of the *Larousse Gastronomique*. Everyone has a favourite elaboration of the basic recipe, adding various ingredients in various permutations. The important point is not to make it too sweet – a fault of which almost all commercial manufacturers are guilty. Here is a basic recipe, to which may be added other citrus fruit, root ginger, even an apple or two, at will:

Marmalade

To each pound of marmalade oranges allow three pints of water. Wash the oranges, peel them, and cut the skin into fine strips. Cut the fruit in half, remove and reserve the pips, and slice the flesh. Place the pips in a small muslin bag and tie the neck, then put the skin, fruit and pips into a large pail and cover with the water. Leave to soak overnight. Next day put all into a preserving pan and boil until the rind is soft. Remove the bag with the pips. Measure the contents of the pan, and to every pint allow one pound (or slightly less) of sugar. Put the sugar and the pulp into the pan, and heat slowly, stirring until the sugar is dissolved. Then boil up fast for about thirty minutes. After twenty minutes it is advisable to test the set by putting a few drops into a cold saucer and leaving for a minute before tilting the saucer to see if the mixture is still runny or is about to set. Pour into warm jars, a little at a time to prevent them cracking, seal with a round of waxed paper, and cover.

The wonderful raspberries grown in Perthshire, Fife and Lothian should be eaten fresh with cream, or in cranachan. But no commercially made jam can approach Meg Dods's raspberry jam, so perhaps it is worth denying oneself a little of the fresh fruit to have a winter supply of jam.

Raspberry Jam

Take 4 parts picked raspberries and 1 of red-currant juice, with an equal weight of sugar. Put on half the sugar in a little water. Heat gently, skim and then add the fruit. Boil for 15 minutes, add the other half of sugar, and boil for another 5 minutes, and when cold pot the jam. This, and all other jams may be made with less sugar if they are longer boiled, but both colour and quality will suffer in the process.

The raspberry brandy which Cockburn thought would be so popular must have been not only easy but cheap to make when smuggled brandy was one of the most common imports from France. All one had to do was to take 4 lb (2 kg) of raspberries and put them in a large crock with 3 quarts (4 l) of brandy. After infusing for a month, the liquid was filtered and sweetened to taste with sugar syrup, and then bottled.

Finally, it is not for reasons of economy, but because modern methods have supplanted the old, that the home-made wines of previous generations have for us only an academic interest. The recipes demonstrate that our ancestors were made of stern stuff. Meg Dods's Best White Gooseberry Champagne must surely have provoked more than one hangover.

Best White Gooseberry Champagne

To every Scotch pint of white gooseberries mashed, add a quart and a half of water, and twelve oz of good loaf-sugar bruised and dissolved. Stir the whole well in the tub or vat, and throw a blanket over the vessel; which is proper in making all wines, unless you wish to slacken the process of fermentation. Stir the ingredients occasionally; and in three days strain off the liquor into a cask. Keep the cask full, and when the spiritous fermentation has ceased, add, for every gallon of wine, a half-pint of brandy, or good whisky, and the same quantity of Sherry or Madeira. Bung up the cask very closely, covering the bung with clay; and when fined, which will be in three to six months, rack it carefully off.

— 6 —

THREE SQUARE MEALS A DAY?

Dinner is the English meal, breakfast the Scotch. An Englishman's certainty of getting a good dinner, seems to make him indifferent about his breakfast, while the substantiality of a Scotchman's breakfast impairs, or at least might be said to impair, his interest in his dinner.

Lord Henry Cockburn, *Circuit Journeys.*

(They) were seated in Mrs Morran's kitchen before a meal which fulfilled their wildest dreams.

John Buchan, *Huntingtower*

'The fate of nations depends on the way they eat,' wrote Brillat-Savarin. Although this book is an attempt to explain Scottish food as we know it today, by discussing not only *what* is eaten but *why*, 'the way they eat' is also of importance in understanding a nation's culinary heritage.

Breakfast, first meal of the day, has some claim to be also first in importance; within living memory it was rated on a par with other nation's dinners. Yet its development to this status was very gradual, and although the 15th-century historian Boece had a propensity for comparing his own times unfavourably with the past, we can believe his statement that his forefathers 'disjunit' sparingly in order to remain alert and active in the day's affairs. In Boece's time, and for at least two centuries after, the lowest rank of the population probably broke its fast with porridge made from bere – a primitive species of barley – or brose made by mixing together oatmeal and water. Further up the social scale a cooked dish – very often of fish – might be added. In the Highlands it was probably fresh-caught grilled trout or salmon; elsewhere, salted herring or, by the coast, fresh herring, whiting, or haddock. The upper classes had still more choice of protein: game (quails, plover or venison), or eggs. Bere bannocks or oatcakes accompanied the meal for most, but the aristocracy might eat manchets – small loaves made of the finest wheat, milled as white as the technology of the day permitted.

We can reconstruct an aristocratic breakfast of the early 17th century from the household papers relating to James Graham, Earl of Montrose – later the famous 1st Marquis of Montrose. For two years, 1628 and 1629, he attended St Andrews University; the housekeeping accounts for the period show that he normally breakfasted frugally on plain bread and milk, although in June 1628, after an illness, there are entries for 'milk-breds dayly to my Lord's breakfast', and for 'quchay' (whey). Occasionally his meal was more substantial, consisting of mutton collops or even soup, and the morning after he had won a trophy at his favourite sport, archery, he ordered a shoulder of mutton to be served, presumably to be offered to the visitors who arrived with congratulations.

Right at the end of Montrose's tragic life, we see him once again breakfasting – a poignant moment recorded by Robert Wodrow from an eye-witness account. At eight o'clock on the morning of 20th May 1650, Montrose, while lying in Edinburgh's Tolbooth under threat of sentence of death, was visited by a group of those Covenanting ministers who had persecuted him since his capture, determined to extract from him confessions of treason, personal vice, and sins against the Kirk. Despite their ranting and bullying behaviour he would not deny the principles he had so long defended, nor confess to fictitious crimes. The Covenanters left. Then, writes Wodrow,

after the ministers had gone away, and he had been a little his alone, my author being in the outer room under Colonel Wallace, he took his breakfast, a little bread dipt in ale.

Within a few hours, he was sentenced to execution, and next day took his last short journey, up what John Buchan has called Edinburgh's 'Via Dolorosa', to the gallows in the High Street.

As part of a hagiography, it is understandable that such a vignette should have been preserved. But most accounts of meals survive only by chance, where among family papers are documents which should have been thrown away but for some reason were not. The Duke of Hamilton's archive is one such collection; and in *The Days of Duchess Anne*, Dr Rosalind Marshall has chronicled the everyday life of the Duchess of Hamilton and her family in the latter years of the 17th century. We learn exactly what the family had for breakfast: rolls, bread, eggs, one or two meat dishes such as mutton collops or roast pigeons, butter, marmalade (of quinces) and milk to drink. The bread for the family was of wheat, but an average of thirty dozen loaves made from oatmeal was baked weekly in the palace ovens for the servants.

Probably this was a typical aristocratic breakfast of the time. A document recently discovered in the Scottish Records Office, however, shows that there could be variations. During the summer of 1671 the Countess of Southesk visited Edinburgh, staying in the house of a vintner who lived just south of the High Street. His bill survives, providing a comprehensive view of the Countess's meals, and it is clear that her breakfast was very much simpler than at Hamilton – indeed, on several mornings she ate nothing at all, though on two of those days she drank a chopin (about 2 English pints) of beer. Twice in the first week a chopin of beer and a roll are itemized. Then, it seems that she was joined by two other people (whether friends or servants is not clear), for on the morning of 29th June three chopins of ale and three rolls were called for: thereafter, though there are no more rolls, 'breaid and Beaire' are listed every day, probably for the same number of people since the cost is only a penny less than for the three chopins of ale and three rolls of 29th June. On one day, wine was ordered, and the cost of breakfast was eleven pence. There was never any kind of cooked dish.

Was the discrepancy between the Southesk breakfast and the Hamilton's merely a matter of personal preference? That daily morning beer hardly suggests that the Countess belonged to the 'my dear, I can't face *anything* at breakfast' brigade. A possible explanation is that she rose later or dined earlier than the Hamiltons, who were running a large and complex estate in addition to their political and social activities, and probably rose early. We know that they dined between two and three in the afternoon. The fashion of an earlier time had been to breakfast at seven and dine at noon, but a later dinner may have put forward the hour of the first meal without altering that at which people left their beds.

Early rising was certainly a feature of the next century. Lord Auchinleck pruned his orchard before breakfast. John Ramsay of Ochtertyre, much of whose *Scotland and Scotsmen of the 18th Century* was based either on personal reminiscence or the recollections of older friends, writes that people generally rose very early, either to business or sport. He adds that lawyers were consulted at four and five in the morning, often in the tavern, where they could get skink (soup) and sweet wine to sustain them.

Not only the lawyers were up betimes. If a gentleman projected a day on the hills, breakfast might be at four in the morning, and was a very substantial meal indeed, as Smollett describes in *Humphrey Clinker:*

The following articles formed our morning's repast: — one kit of boiled eggs; a second, full of butter; a third, full of cream; an entire cheese made of goat's milk; a large earthern pot full of honey; the best part of a ham; a cold venison pasty; a bushel of oatmeal, made in thin cakes and bannocks, with a small wheaten loaf in the middle for the strangers; a large stone bottle full of whisky, another of brandy, and a kilderkin of ale. There was a ladle chained to the cream-kit, with curious wooden bickers, to be filled from this reservoir. The spirits were drank out of a silver quaff, and the ale out of horns; great justice was done to the collation by the guests in general; one of them, in particular, ate above two dozen of hard eggs, with a proportionable quantity of bread, butter and honey; nor was one drop of liquor left upon the board. Finally, a large roll of tobacco was presented by way of dessert, and every individual took a comfortable quid, to prevent the bad effects of the morning air.

After this gargantuan gluttony, the hunters, we are told, had 'a fine chase over the mountains' before returning home in time for tea.

Clearly, the celebrated Scots breakfast was developing. One cause was undoubtedly the increased professional activity created by an improving commercial climate. A new spirit was abroad, a new sense of energy and purpose was driving men from their beds to give the best part of the day to business affairs. In addition, the climate, and the late dinners and early suppers must have contributed to the appetites created by such early rising.

Moreover, agricultural reforms, though taking effect slowly, were gradually producing more and better food. It is true that the only alteration in the diet of the labouring poor was the replacement of bere with oatmeal and of ale with tea. And famines still occurred: in the winter of 1740–1 many people died from starvation, and when the crops failed repeatedly between 1782 and 1788 local communities had to raise money by public subscription to buy imported grain for distribution among the poor. These famines hastened the adoption of potatoes as a basic crop, especially in the west; cotton-weavers in Glasgow and crofters in the Highlands now turned to the new vegetable because it was cheaper than oatmeal. However, in agricultural districts of the Lowlands and the north-east, oats were by now the preferred staple.

In the late 18th century Sir John Sinclair calculated that a ploughman consumed at breakfast '2 lbs of porridge, containing 10 oz of oatmeal, 30 oz of water, and 1 lb of milk'. The results, he claimed (not unreasonably), were flatulence, indigestion, swellings in children, and scrofulous complaints in adults. He had firm ideas about what the poor should eat before starting work:

For the poor, who have strong stomachs, biscuits are much more wholesome than fermented bread, they are not so easily dissolved in the stomach and more nourishment is extracted from them.

By the end of the 18th century breakfast had been set in a pattern which was to remain almost unchanged for the next hundred years. Oatmeal porridge or brose was still the norm for farmers and farm workers, except in the West Highlands, where potatoes were gaining ground. The gentry partook of a hearty, protein-rich meal calculated to sustain them until a late dinner. Tea and coffee were replacing milk and ale among all classes of society.

The French natural scientist Barthelemy Faujas de Saint Fond, who toured Scotland in 1784, sampled breakfast in a variety of places, including peasant hovels and inns, not to mention the Duke of Argyll's castle at Inveraray. The peasants on Mull ate potatoes and milk, though some took oatmeal made into porridge or cakes; for drink, they had pure water and 'some drops of whisky on their festive days give them their greatest happiness'. At the other end of the scale, Faujas de Saint Fond was impressed by breakfast at Inveraray Castle, where he saw family portraits on the walls, bouquets of flowers everywhere, tables laden with tea-kettles, bowls of fresh cream, excellent butter and rolls, and newspapers and books laid out for perusal. The bell announcing the meal rang at ten, but most people had been up well before then, to walk, study, or hunt.

When he visited Maclean of Torluisk, on Mull, he found likewise that at ten,

all repair to the parlour, where they find a fire of peat, mixed with pit-coal, and a table neatly served and covered with the following dishes:
Slices of smoked beef
Cheese of the country and English cheese, in trays of mahogany
Fresh eggs
Hash or salted herring
Butter
Milk and cream
A sort of pap, of oatmeal and water. In eating this thick pap, each spoonful is plunged alternatively into cream, which is always alongside
Milk mingled with the yolks of eggs, sugar and rum. This singular mixture is drunk cold and without having been cooked
Currant jelly
Conserve of myrtle, a wild fruit that grows on the heaths
Tea
Coffee
The three sorts of bread (sea biscuit, oatcakes, barley bannocks) above mentioned
Jamaica rum

But the breakfast which charmed him beyond all – he was a sensitive man – was that at the inn at Tarbet (perhaps the very inn where, twenty years later, William Wordsworth and his sister were to sample and enjoy the local herring for their breakfast):

After a walk of an hour and a half, we returned to our inn, where a breakfast of tea awaited us. It was a kind of coquettishness on the part of our hostess, for she had arranged her china cups on a well-painted and well-varnished tea-table, adorned with every accessory of an elegant breakfast, at least in the country . . . this little set of moveables was the most precious thing in her house, since it had been given her by the Duchess of Argyll . . .

He was never to forget that meal: the lovely morning, the beauty of the landscape, the fragrant tea in pretty cups, the kindness of the landlady, above all the sense of goodness and loving kindness with which he felt the whole experience was imbued.

By the early 19th century others, both in fiction and factual writing, were extolling Scottish breakfasts. The descriptions in the journals of Dorothy Wordsworth and of Southey, the Poet Laureate, reinforced the fictional account to be found in Susan Ferrier's *Marriage*; while Sir Walter Scott might almost have held a retainer from some 19th century tourist board, so frequently and lovingly did he detail in his novels the breakfasts of his characters. Some, like the Antiquary's cold roast beef and mum ('a species of fat ale brewed from wheat and bitter herbs') are painted in muted tones; but Lady Margaret Bellenden in *Old Mortality* presides over a highly coloured meal, more suited, with its 'priestly ham, knightly sirloin, noble baron of beef, and princely venison pasty' to the table of Henry VIII than to that of a lady of the lesser nobility in 17th-century Scotland. Compared to this, Duncan of Knockdunder's hospitality (*Heart of Midlothian*) and Darsie Latimer's 'tea and chocolate, eggs, ham and pastry, not forgetting the broiled fish' in the house of the Quaker, Joshua Geddes, (*Redgauntlet*) were plebeian fare. The two breakfasts in *Waverley*, set a few years earlier than Smollett's *Humphrey Clinker*, are perhaps a little anachronistic and romanticized; nevertheless Rose Bradwardine – presiding over all the delicacies which induced even Dr Johnson to extol the luxury of a Scotch breakfast above that of all other countries – anticipated by only a decade or two what was to become standard in the dining-rooms of the gentry.

As for Scott himself, breakfast was his chief meal. If we can believe James Hogg, it was he who persuaded his friend into the habit, when the latter complained of headaches due to writing or studying late into the night, after fulfilling all the day's professional and social engagements. At Hogg's suggestion, Scott took to rising, like his predecessors in the Law Courts, at five. He lit his own fire, then shaved and dressed, and by six was at his desk. By the time he joined his family round the table between nine and ten, he had, in his own words, 'broken the neck of the day's work' and could do justice to the porridge and cream, the salmon, the home-cured ham and cold sheep's head, the pie, and the bread and oatcakes spread thickly with butter, which he loved so much.

If domestic breakfasts of the period could almost claim the status of gourmet meals, so too, apparently, could those at many inns – rather surprisingly when we take account of the bad press these establishments received from so many travellers for so long. The Wordsworths, it is clear from Dorothy's journal, were easily pleased. But Southey claimed to be something of an epicure, and when we read in his *Journal* that he had eaten 'a good breakfast as usual in Scotland' we can trust his verdict. On that occasion the menu consisted of Findon haddocks, eggs, sweetmeats (including preserved blackcurrants) and honey. Another time he was offered broiled salmon from the Spey, butter (both potted and fresh), honey and preserved gooseberries. A less conventional meal surprised him into expressions of pleasure:

Breakfasted at Auchnault. The want of wheaten bread was so well supplied by good pink potatoes, dug the moment they were wanted, boiled in their skins, and hot enough to melt fine fresh butter, that I was more than ever satisfied how little the want of bread would be felt . . . we had also a cold sheep's head, which, to my surprise, I thought very good, because of the skin, and the flavour which had been given it by singeing.

From the middle of the 19th century, the gentry and middle classes enjoyed continually improving standards of food; but the meals of the poor remained much what they had been in the time of Sir John Sinclair. This is not to say that they lacked nourishment. In general the Scottish rural worker was getting, at less cost, better food than his English counterpart. This was particularly true in areas where a mixed diet was common: a combination of cereal (oats or barley) and peasemeal afforded protein, milk was a source of some vitamins and fats and potatoes provided carbohydrates and vitamin C. Fruit and vegetables from a kitchen garden could bring it all to a very adequate nutritive level. However, the old mode of paying farm labourers at least partly in kind was dying out, to the detriment of family diet. Wages, it was claimed, now went largely on beer, and the remainder was unwisely spent on tea, sugar, white bread, and flour. Less milk, less oatmeal, and fewer vegetables were consumed.

In the towns, the diet of the poor was worse. This was due partly to the inability of local agriculture to keep up with the fast-growing urban population, partly to problems of distribution; there was also the need of industrial workers for cheap and filling, but above all rapidly prepared meals. In terms of breakfast this meant bread, margarine and tea instead of the porridge or brose and milk of former times; even where porridge was still eaten a shortage of milk, especially in Glasgow, led to the substitution of a much less nutritive mixture of treacle and water. Even the food value of the bread deteriorated as new and cheaper methods were found of refining and whitening flour.

Among educated people these circumstances caused concern, and numerous studies were undertaken towards the closing years of the 19th century, both in towns and rural areas. They almost all showed a deteriorating working-class diet, worst in industrial towns and in the western Highlands. One of the very few Highland exceptions was the district of Lochaber where, as late as 1914, a typical breakfast for country folk consisted of porridge and milk, tea, oatcakes, scones and butter, eggs, bacon or fish. Perhaps Marian McNeill had this in mind when, in her *Book of Breakfast* (1932) she describes 'A Scottish Ploughman's Breakfast (old style): Aigar Brose with Milk, or Kail brose, barley bannocks, butter, oatcakes, milk or small beer'. The reality was that bread and strong cheap tea now formed the breakfast of many, and teachers in poor districts, both in towns and the country, complained that their pupils were unable to work properly because they had had such an inadequate meal to start the day.

Like the Borders and the north-east, the Northern Isles escaped this deterioration. A survey in 1871 showed the diet to be in most respects excellent, apart from a marked lack of vitamin C; it consisted largely of milk prepared in various ways, fish, potatoes, beremeal, and oatmeal. Little alcohol was consumed but tea was extremely popular. Few vegetables were grown or eaten.

One report which became famous was put out by the Dundee Social Union in 1905. Its findings were that in most families with young children the usual breakfast was porridge and milk, followed by tea and bread and butter, and generally eggs for the parents. If the family was short of money, only the wage-earner (usually the father) had an egg. However, where both parents worked, breakfast and dinner, for parents as well as children, consisted only of bread and butter or margarine and tea. The children had to grow, work and play with only one proper meal (usually broth) per day.

The First World War probably did more than any reports to bring to people's attention the bad diet of the poor in Britain. With a shock the government realized, when the figures for medical examination of conscripts were published, that only three of every nine men called up to fight could be described as fit. Of the remainder, one was a chronic invalid, three were practically on the point of collapse, and two were simply unfit. Yet efforts to bring the most essential foodstuffs within everybody's reach lapsed as soon as the war was over. Overcrowding in towns (particularly Glasgow), appallingly insanitary housing, and lack of money were aggravated by the Depression to the point where it could almost be claimed that the poor were worse off than they had ever been.

In the meantime, the increasing size and power of the Scottish middle classes brought them, for the first time, into prominence as a group with considerable consumer influence. Improved techniques of refrigeration, canning, milling, commercial baking and all the other modern food processes, allied to better and faster methods of transport, were facilitating the mass production of cheaper standard foods. Bread, butter, cheese, tea, coffee, jam, rolled oats, bacon, ham – even oatcakes – no longer came direct from farm or small home industry, but from large and efficient factories. If standardization was leading to lower average quality, at least it allowed those of even modest income to enjoy the type of meals previously only within reach of the upper classes. And while domestic labour was harder to find and more expensive, the introduction of gas and electric appliances made the cooking of large meals much easier.

Although in Britain generally meals were becoming smaller and lighter, the traditional Scots breakfast was far from obsolete in the 'thirties. Here is Marian McNeill's prescription for 'A Modern Highland Breakfast', where the guests are wakened by 'the skirling of the pipes, as the family piper walks round the house, playing the rouse, "Hey, Johnnie Cope, are ye wauken yet?"'

Porridge and Cream	Baps, Girdle Scones, Oatcakes
Grilled Trout	Heather Honey, Butter,
Fried Bacon and Mushrooms	Marmalade
Findon Haddie with Poached Egg	Toast, brown and white
Potted Venison, Potted Grouse	Tea and Coffee
Smoked Mutton Ham	Fresh Fruit

And – tacitly acknowledging that not everyone had access to piper, hills and heather – it is followed by some 'everyday Scottish breakfasts' for summer and winter. Her proposal for a winter menu is as follows:

> Porridge with milk or cream
> Fried bacon with sliced black pudding, boiled eggs
> Soda scones, oatcakes
> Butter, toast, barberry jam
> Tea or coffee

Meanwhile another Scotswoman, Elizabeth Craig, was writing articles on food in national newspapers and magazines. She was read all over Britain, and her articles show that she was very conscious of regional and economic variations in diet. But she undoubtedly addressed herself chiefly to the middle-class reader, and undoubtedly also emphasized her own Scottish background and its influence on her cooking. Her *Menus for a Year* (c.1938) shows the way meals were changing, but the breakfast menus and those for high tea are distinctly Scottish in tone. For a Monday breakfast in January, she proposed:

> (Porridge or cereal optional)
> Grapefruit

Stewed Finnan haddock
Toast, brown rolls
Tangerine marmalade
Tea or coffee

And for an August morning:

(Porridge or cereal optional)
Stewed prunes
Grilled kidneys and tomatoes
Toast, oatcakes
Lemon marmalade
Tea or coffee

Clearly she was recommending a less substantial meal than Marian McNeill's, with only one cooked dish (except on Sundays) and optional cereal. Yet, though it could be prepared by any housewife, it made no concessions to the servantless career woman.

Recipe books, because they suggest the ideal rather than the real, are not the best guides to social history. For an authentic country breakfast between the wars, we may turn to H. V. Morton's *In Search of Scotland*:

I entered the front parlour and saw on a table a breakfast which I can describe only as perfectly sincere. There were eggs and bacon. There were warm oatcakes. There were warm scones. There were baps. There was toast. There was marmalade. There was jelly. There was honey. In case this was not enough, there was a plate of parkins and a currant loaf.

Of post-war breakfasts, little needs to be said. For some years in the 1950s, after the end of rationing, hotels made an effort to regain the standards of the past. So, in those happy days, did the railways, which used to serve the best breakfast that can be imagined on the West Highland Line from Glasgow to Mallaig. If recollection of one September morning is correct, the train reached the shores of Loch Lomond as day dawned, and at that moment breakfast was announced. It was part of an unforgettable experience: the porridge and cream, the Loch Fyne kippers, the eggs (boiled, fried, or poached), the oatcakes and freshly made toast, the marmalade and honey, and the excellent tea and coffee – all served, with pre-war efficiency and style, as the train travelled from Ardlui to Rannoch Moor, through scenery whose wild loveliness makes this one of the great train journeys of the world.

No longer does British Rail or anyone else serve such a breakfast. It is still possible, in some establishments, to get a cooked meal of quality and even style, but they become harder to find each year. And, if truth be told, there is less and less demand. Their day is past. Dr Johnson, whose dictum was that 'if an epicure could remove by a wish, in quest of sensual gratifications, wherever he had supped, he would breakfast in Scotland', would, if he visited us today, be sadly disappointed.

It is curious how the historian Boece and Lord Henry Cockburn, writing with more than 300 years between them, complement each other's remarks concerning dinner. Boece says that early Scots went without it altogether, preferring not to overcharge their stomachs during the day; and it was Cockburn's opinion that many of his contemporaries, while perhaps not as abstemious as Boece's heroes, cared little enough about the quality of their main meal. It seems that in medieval days as in the 19th century, it was the supper table, with its simple dishes and relaxed, convivial atmosphere, which appealed to Caledonia's hardy sons – and daughters.

Nevertheless there is plenty of evidence that dinners during those 300 years could be as good, or as bad, as in any other country. The well-known meal offered by a Scots knight to Fynes Moryson, who travelled in Scotland in 1598, is often quoted as an example of the frugality, not to say poverty, obtaining in most houses. And yet, if we bear in mind that this was only five years before James VI succeeded to the English Crown, and consequently only a short while after the influence of Mary Stuart and her French court had supposedly introduced new standards of wealth and luxury, it reads oddly enough.

The history books have given us a portrait of the country at this time – at least in the south-east – as fertile, wealthy, and highly civilized and cultured. If money was scarce, provisions were not, and people of moderate social status (provided they were landowners) lived well. The man who entertained Moryson was clearly such a person: he was important enough to have emissaries (of whom

Moryson was one) sent him from the Governor of Berwick concerning Border affairs, and he had many servants in his household. So the much-quoted tale of his hospitality bears examining; Moryson writes:

Myself was at a knight's house, who had many servants to attend him, that brought in his meat with their heads covered with blew caps, the table being more than half furnished with great platters of porridge, each having a little piece of sodden meat. And when the table was served, the servants did sit downe with us, but the upper messe, instead of porridge, had a pullet with some prunes in the broth. And I observed no art of cookery or promotion of household stuffe, but rather rude neglect of both . . .

Really, it does not sound an appetizing meal. But translate it into modern times:

I was in the house of a knight who had many servants. They wore blue caps on their heads when they brought in the food and set on the table great tureens of broth made from barley and vegetables, each with a piece of boiled meat in it. Everyone sat at the same table, but those who sat with the knight and his family were served, not with broth, but with a sort of soup which contained, as well as chicken, vegetables and prunes.

This certainly sounds a great deal more palatable. The translation is quite literal except for the mention of vegetables which, under the name of pot-herbs, were so invariably an ingredient of broth that it is taking no liberty with the text to speak of them.

But what of the phrase 'I observed no art of cookery . . .'? It is fairly evident from other remarks that Moryson did not well understand the customs and economy of the land he was visiting. He expresses surprise, for instance, at the small quantity of fresh meat consumed (had he gone further north than the Firth of Forth he would no doubt have revised his statement), and even greater astonishment that, though mutton and geese were salted, 'they use to eate Beefe without salting'. Now farming practices at this time were hardly more retarded in Scotland than in southern England. In both countries, fresh meat, except game, was virtually unobtainable in winter. In Scotland, however, even in the Borders, pasturage was inferior to that in England, and the grazing season shorter by a month at least. The season for fresh meat was correspondingly shorter, and more meat needed to be laid down against the winter. As regards the statement that beef was not salted, he was incorrect; beasts were killed in November for pickling. But, again, poorer pasturage meant that it was not to the farmer's advantage to graze all his stock to maturity – the land would not tolerate it. Only sufficient animals to provide milk and a calf or two each year could be grazed to adulthood. The surplus were killed when young, and eaten fresh as veal rather than beef.

Fynes Moryson, in short, was making no allowances for the different circumstances of the two countries. He was like a man who, surrounded with good strawberries, raspberries, and currants, complains that the peaches are sour and the oranges bitter.

For comparison it is possible to set his account against a King's Commission decree of 1602 which regulated the diet of masters and students at Glasgow University. The masters' dinner was to consist of white bread and good ale, plus the following: a choice of soups – broth and kail or skink (a clear beef soup); a piece of boiled mutton and another of fresh or salt beef according to the season; and two roasts, one of veal or mutton, the other of chicken, rabbit, or pigeons. The students were to have oat bread, a dish of pease or broth, and one dish of beef, with one quart of ale between four. Diet on meatless days, for both groups, centred on eggs and fish. While the bursars' food might be called plain, neither regimen would qualify as an example of the grinding and primitive poverty which Moryson seems to have been suggesting.

Noon was the dinner hour in the 16th century, though in Boece's day people had eaten at eleven. Mary Stuart dined at noon, but we are told that her husband, Darnley, when alone, preferred to eat at two. Gradually the hour advanced. James VI ate at one, and this remained for long the fashionable time; but by the end of the 17th century, though many still kept to that hour, great people like the Hamiltons dined at some time between two and three.

During this period there had been surprisingly little change in the food. Barley broth with meat and vegetables was still followed by a choice of hot or cold meats. Sauces, however, were beginning to enter the cook's repertoire, with the consequent appearance of ragoûts (the word itself means a sauce) and fricassées.

The Countess of Southesk's dinners were not vastly different from those at Glasgow University more than 60 years earlier. Broth, boiled beef or mutton, and one roast (usually mutton or chicken, very rarely beef), were the usual fare. Vegetables were extending their domain: from a humble position in the stock-pot they had now advanced to the role of accompaniment to the meat. On six occasions during the Countess's six-week stay in Edinburgh she ate 'boylled beiff and kabishe'; twice she was served 'boylled mwtone and caritis'; once (ringing the changes), she had 'boyled beiff and caritis'. Sometimes even vegetables were served separately. On the same table as the boiled beef and cabbage there might be a dish of carrots and another of peas, the Countess being apparently particularly fond of the latter. Artichokes were another favourite, though they figure much more frequently at the evening meal than at dinner.

The account for Tuesday 27th June has a breathless look about it, as if the compiler has been overworked and is trying to remember all that happened. The first entry is 'To denner for broth', and the bread and ale which should have begun the page appear half-way down among the powts (moor-fowls?) and the wine. The habitual phrase 'at night' which prefaces the items served up as supper is missing. The whole day's account seems to be one long gigantic meal and it is not possible to decide whether it was in fact one or two. The Countess, in short, had visitors.

Tuesday the 27:	
To denner for broth	0-00-04
ane Leg of mwtone	0-02-06
ane hen	0-01-08
ane peace of samond	0-01-00
for crabs	0-01-06
ane pair of powts	0-02-08
for braid and aill	0-01-10
a chapine of wyne	0-00-10
for Limones	0-01-06
for ane qwarter of rost mwtone	0-02-06
for pwts & mwre fowlies	0-08-10
ane dishe of peas	0-00-10
ane dishe of artichoes	0-02-00
for lapestires [lobsters]	0-02-06

ane dishe of tairtes	0-08-00
for limones & oringeres	0-03-00
for bread and beaire	0-01-04
fyve pynts of wyne	0-08-04
a chapine of secke	0-01-06

The tarts are worth noting as a new development. (They were not all eaten, for 'ane tairt' appeared at supper next day.) They, and a sorbet on 23rd June, are evidence of the new fashion for sweets. Hamilton Palace, as one might expect, was ahead of the Countess here, for the Duke and Duchess regularly had a sweet dessert such as apple tarts, stewed gooseberries, and baked apple pie with custard.

Before leaving the Southesk account, it is worth looking briefly at the question of supper. If earlier generations saw it as the day's major meal, in the 16th century it was very much on a par with dinner – at Glasgow University, for example, the supper menu closely resembled that at dinner. There were, however, signs that it was becoming a lighter repast, whose hour and contents depended very much on the preceding meal. When dinner was at noon, supper was between five and six. Where the dinner hour was later, supper was served between seven and eight. It now often consisted of eggs, chicken, trout, or mutton collops, and bread and milk. Once when Montrose had spent the day hunting, he asked for 'a henne to his supper', but more frequently he seems to have had only eggs or fish, and bread and milk, which was perhaps prepared as the Duke and Duchess of Hamilton liked it: the bread crumbled and cooked lightly with milk and sugar. They too ate sparingly in the evening, though besides the bread and milk there was always at least one cooked dish, of fish or meat. Sometimes they substituted sowens for bread and milk – convincing proof that these were not exclusively food for the poor.

The Southesk manuscripts suggest that for the Countess, dinner and supper were virtually interchangeable. She did, as a rule, have one main meal daily, and one lighter one, but their position varied. And not infrequently two meals of apparently equal weight are itemized – as on 29th June, when, after a substantial dinner, my lady was able to confront (with help, one hopes) a leg of mutton, three moor fowls, a fricassée, a dish of beef, two lobsters, and five pints (Scots) of beer, nine of wine, and a bowl of punch.

Just as changing social and economic conditions during the 18th century affected breakfast, so they did other meals. Again, it was not the food of the poor which altered: they continued their habits, both in the hours (midday and six o'clock) and the nature of their meals. For dinner, most people had kail or broth, rarely enough with meat in it. On the coast and the islands, fish and brose or oatcakes formed the main meal. Supper consisted of sowens (especially in the north-east) or porridge, or more brose. Buttermilk and whey, when available, were the liquids drunk.

It was natural that the changes in the meals of the gentry should be a great deal more evident, at first, in the towns than in the country. They depended also on education and economic circumstances. There were still to be encountered men of the type of the Laird of Milnwood in *Old Mortality*, in whose house it was the custom that

the domestics, after having placed the dinner on the table, sate down at the lower end of the board, and partook of the share which was assigned to them, in company with their masters ... Old Robin ... placed on the table an immense charger of broth, thickened with oatmeal and cole-wort, in which ocean of liquid were indistinctly discovered, by close observers, two or three short ribs of lean mutton sailing to and fro. Two huge baskets, one of bread made of barley and pease, and one of oat-cakes, flanked this steaming dish ... The large black jack, filled with very small beer of Milnwood's own brewing, was allowed to the company at discretion, as were the bannocks, cakes and broth; but the mutton was reserved for the heads of the family, Mrs Wilson included; and a measure of ale somewhat deserving the name, was set apart in the silver tankard for their exclusive use. A huge kebbock (a cheese, that is, made with ewe-milk mixed with cow's milk) and a jar of salt butter, were in common to the company.

Another old custom observed by some country gentlemen was that of locking the door during meals. In a note to his description of dinner at Milnwood, Scott tells the story (which he got from Ramsay of Ochtertyre) of a wealthy bachelor the terms of whose will were to depend upon the hospitality he received when visiting his kinsmen. His first call was on his own chief, a baronet and, says Scott, representative of one of the oldest families of Scotland. Unfortunately the chief was dining, and refused to open the door to his wealthy relative who, piqued, rode on to another. This man knew full well that his cousin had a will to make, and 'the gates flew open – the table was covered anew – the bachelor and intestate kinsman was received with the utmost attention and respect' – with, eventually, the hoped-for consequences.

Ramsay presents these country gentry as worthy, well-informed people. Like Jane Austen's English squires, their concerns were almost entirely with family, friends, and the management and inheritance of property. Their way of life, however, was less formal and sophisticated than that in England, and though prosperity was beginning to take visible form in the construction of some grand new houses, most lived in homes built by an earlier generation, where the public rooms were cramped, dark and solemn. Except for festivals and ceremonious occasions, dining-room and parlour were seldom used. People lived, says Ramsay, 'mostly in the family bedchamber, where friends and neighbours were received without scruple', and he recollects the 'many easy, comfortable meals I have made long ago in that way through this country'.

Hospitality was a major preoccupation. Like its dispensers it was simple and straightforward, and the quality of meals depended rather on the ingredients than on the skill of the cook.

Few of our gentry kept a full or regular table; and as their guests were for the most part upon an easy footing, broth, a couple of fowls newly killed perhaps, or a joint of meat, was thought no bad dinner . . . In summer there was plenty of lamb or chicken, and towards August excellent little mutton from the hills. Beef was seldom fit for killing in open pastures till October or November, and even then was hardly to be got in the market in small pieces. Salmon, which is now a luxury, was then cheap and plentiful, being in the summer months the chief food of the servants.

Confirmation of this simple, hospitable existence is to be found in another book originating at Ochtertyre, generally known as the *Ochtertyre House Book*. It is a mine of information for food historians, since it gives the daily dinner and supper menus of the family of Sir William Murray of Ochtertyre over a two-year period, 1737–9, and in two different parts of the country, Ochtertyre in Streathearn and Foulls not far from Dundee. Because the *House Book* also makes clear what food was bought and what came in from the estates or was given as presents, it is possible to get a very exact picture of how the Murrays and their friends lived.

Ramsay's account is well substantiated here. When the family dined alone, soup or broth always began the meal, followed by one or two dishes of meat. A typical entry reads:

> Tewsdy 22 November [1737]
> Dinner sheephead broth
> Cold chickens
> Pudding and hagas for servts.

The puddings were savoury dishes of the haggis type. And supper that day was also simple:

> Bufft [pickled] harrings, cold chicken, eggs.

If company arrived, a larger quantity of soup was made, and the number of meat dishes increased – but without the nail-biting problems of today's hostesses, since guests, knowing they would be expected to stay for dinner, took care to arrive in plenty of time for adjustments to be made. An entry for 30th October 1737 suggests such an occasion:

> Dinner skink and tripe
> Fish and puddings
> pidgeons rost
> mutton rost joints
> foulls rost
> The cow's head for the servants

Sometimes there was a house-party. Then the menus for a week or longer are elaborate lists of complicated dishes, at supper no less than at dinner. Vegetables are mentioned as separate dishes or special accompaniments for meat, and sometimes, though not every day, there is a dessert. Some such gathering must have been in process at the beginning of November 1737, for the entry for the

1st of the month is a long one, and both dinner and supper consist of many more dishes than usual:

Dinner rice soope	A mince pye and an omlit
Veall in the soop joints	Pidgeons rost
Beefe rost	Saucagis [sausages] fryed
A fricasie of trippe	Puddings black and white
Fish and a pudding	Beefe for the side board
Geese boyld	Soop for ditto
Ducks rost	Beefe for servants
Pork rost	

For supper, the list is:
Beefe in collops
Mutton with collyflower
Aples and cream
Spinage and eggs
A custard
A pike boyld
Woodcocks rost
For the side board tarts, eggs and a cold duck and collops

Such meals, built around the produce of one's own estates and presents from friends, must at their best have been superb; but their simplicity would have been despised by town sophisticates. For a new approach to cooking was by now influencing the fashionable world, at the centre of which Edinburgh – thanks to a sudden and dramatic flowering of original talent – was rapidly placing itself.

If the historians, philosophers, scientists, artists and poets of the Enlightenment were native Scots, they were not uncompromisingly so. It is pathetically evident that many felt that to be Scots was to be, if not inferior, at least unfashionable and a little unacceptable. To read of the great David Hume's anxiety that the 'Scoticisms' in his work should be 'corrected' is as saddening as it is to plough through Burns' heavy and uninspired poems in the English language. In its extreme form, this attitude was to lead to identity crises which, as in Boswell's case, prevented the full development of considerable ability.

The same uncertainty is evident in the recipe books of the day, which drew heavily on English food, and in which even the French recipes were those which were most popular in England at the time. The old simplicity was being replaced by a predilection for 'made' dishes, and for heavily flavoured, thickened sauces.

Whatever can be said of English cooking of the day, there is little doubt that this approach was unsuited to the Scottish temperament and Scots ingredients. It was surely no accident that the Scots breakfast, which depended on simple dishes and had no French or even English model, was the meal most praised by visitors, and that dinners in fashionable society were less than rapturously received by the same critics.

There were, of course, exceptions. In April 1717 Lady Grisell Baillie, dining with 'the Duck and Duck of Montrose' and Lord and Lady Rothes, had a dinner which despite its obviously Scottish character shows a distinctly sophisticated approach, both in content and form. Here, for example, we see the division of dishes into courses – still an innovation in Scotland, and one which was not to affect the majority of family meals until very much later in the century. Moreover the use of sauces, the way the roast beef is served, and the elegant dessert, demonstrate a refinement beyond anything we have yet observed. (Lady Grisell set out the menu as the dishes were presented on the table.)

Soup   relief cods head with alle [garlic] sauce
fricascy rabits   natle [nettle] cale   3 boyld chickens

boyld hame

Second
a rosted fillet of bief larded with a rague [ragout] of sweat bread
under it

Ptansy   Crawfish   limon puden
rague sweatbreads   sparagass

8 rost ducks

Deseart
ratafia cream and gellies
chestnuts   cheas butter
oranges   confections   aples
cheas   pistoches

sillibubs

By the time Faujas de Saint Fond visited Scotland, this refinement was evident in all the best houses. He was an appreciative visitor, and perhaps wished to flatter his hosts; but it is clear that he enjoyed almost equally dinner at Torluisk, with its broth, black and white puddings, 'roasted mutton of the best quality', excellent beef and game, and milk dishes, and that at Inveraray, where everything was prepared and served after the style of Paris. One custom, though, was unfamiliar to him:

Towards the end of the dessert, the ladies withdrew ... the ceremony of toasts lasts for at least three quarters of an hour ... a great number of healths being drunk with pleasure and good grace ... If the lively champagne should make its diuretic influence felt, the case is foreseen, and in the pretty corners of the room the necessary convenience is to be found. This is applied to with so little ceremony, that the person who has occasion to use it, does not even interrupt his talk during the operation. I suppose this is one of the reasons why the English ladies, who are exceedingly modest and reserved, always leave the company before the toasts begin ...

Informal behaviour of this sort did not prevent grand dinners from being punctilious affairs. The conviviality, the toasts, the free and generous flow of claret, were regulated by a rigid etiquette which, while it encouraged men to get so drunk that they could not leave the table without help (if indeed they had not already fallen under it), limited the topics and mode of conversation. It was chiefly for this reason that supper became the really important meal in the Age of Enlightenment. Edinburgh was the centre of the Enlightenment; and Edinburgh suppers became a byword.

Many were the great supper-givers of the time: David Hume, who 'assembled whoever were among the most knowing and agreeable among either the laity or the clergy'; Lord Monboddo, whose 'learned suppers' took place fortnightly, and whose passion for the Classics extended to strewing the table with roses, as Horace had done, and garlanding his flasks of claret, 'as Anacreon was wont to do at the court of Polycrates'; Adam Smith, who gathered round him all the intellect and talent of both Glasgow and Edinburgh; and, a little later, Lord Cockburn, ensured that these delightful occasions would never entirely slip into oblivion:

Early dinners begat suppers. But suppers are so delightful, that they have survived long after dinners have become late. Indeed this has immemorially been a favourite Edinburgh repast. I have often heard strangers say, that Edinburgh was the only place where the people dined twice every day. It is now fading into paltry wine and water in many houses; but in many it still triumphs in a more substantial form . . . Almost all my set, which is perhaps the merriest, the most intellectual, and not the most severely abstemious, in Edinburgh, are addicted to it. I doubt if from the year 1811, when I married, I have closed above one day in the month, of my town life, at home and alone . . . How many are the reasons, how strong the associations, that inspire the last of the day's friendly meetings! Supper is cheaper than dinner, shorter; less ceremonious; and more poetical.

Frequently all-male affairs, these suppers did not invariably take place in private houses. Taverns were a common venue for men of like tastes and opinions, and thus the clubs came into being – clubs with strange names and stranger customs, like the Right and Wrong Club, whose members (of whom James Hogg was one) bound themselves to agree with any statement, right or wrong, made by anyone in the company; and the Poker Club, which met every Tuesday to 'poke up' resentment against England's treatment of Scotland, particularly in the refusal of Parliament to pass a Scottish Militia Bill in 1762. (The Poker Club survived for many years. Among its founder members were Adam Ferguson and David Hume, and among the last of the ageing members in the 1820s was Sir Walter Scott.)

Whatever the quality of the food at these suppers, whether they took place in taverns or private houses, there is no doubting the conviviality and joyously informal ambience. Years after his sojourn in Edinburgh, the clergyman and polemical writer, Sidney Smith, recalled:

Never shall I forget the happy days I spent there amidst odious smells, barbarous sounds, bad suppers, excellent hearts, and the most enlightened and cultivated understandings.

The menu at supper usually consisted of the lighter dishes one might see at dinner, at least if there were guests, for many families supped very simply if they were on their own. But a host would offer an assortment of dishes – oysters perhaps, and mutton collops;

haggis; roast hens, a partan (crab) pie; broiled bones, Welsh rarebit, or a sheep's head. Nearly always there were excellent claret and punch. It was a meal which varied very much according to the tastes and status of the giver, and some, in their generous endeavour to satisfy their guests, perhaps overdid the quantities. Faujas de Saint Fond found it 'unpleasant to be obliged to take one's seat at table again about 10 o'clock, and remain until midnight over a supper nearly of the same fare as the dinner, and in no less abundance.' The kind of supper he preferred was what he had been given at the inn at Dalmally: two dishes of fine game birds, a cream, fresh butter, local cheese, a pot of preserved blaeberries, and a bottle of port.

As Cockburn's remarks imply, the meal patterns of the gentry were shifting considerably during the 18th and early 19th centuries. 'Early dinners begat suppers', but they had also given birth to the 'four-hours' – that refreshment, initially of light ale, which subsequently turned into afternoon tea. When dinners were held later, the gap between the two meals narrowed; hence arose the custom of serving tea, or coffee, in the withdrawing-room when the gentlemen had finished drinking and joined the ladies.

By the 1820s, fashionable dinner-parties began at five or even six o'clock. Scott dined at five, and so did Francis Jeffrey, one of the founders of the *Edinburgh Review*. Formalities were by now much less of a burden, especially among friends. Elizabeth Grant of Rothiemurchus, young, high-spirited, intelligent, and affectionate, was a welcome visitor at Craigcrook, Jeffrey's house on Corstorphine Hill. Here, wit and argumentative levity replaced the sarcasm for which Jeffrey was famous in his professional life. Here members of the Whig party could relax and freely express their opinion of the ruling Tories. Here

the dinners were delightful, so little form, so much fun, real wit sometimes, and always cheerfulness; the windows open to the garden, the sight and the scent of the flowers heightening the flavour of the repasts unequalled for excellence; wines, all our set were famous for having of the best and in startling variety ... Mrs Jeffrey's home-fed fowl and home-made bread, and fine cream and sweet butter, and juicy vegetables, all so good, served so well, the hot things *hot*, the fruits, cream and butter so cold, gave such a feeling of comfort everyone got good-humoured.

Such informality as this, allied to the ever-advancing dinner-hour, begat, as Cockburn would say, offspring only slightly resembling their parents or predecessors. Once again a need was felt for a midday meal, and luncheon was born, taking on some of the attributes, and fulfilling some of the functions, which had previously belonged to supper. Like the latter, it was the lighter of the two main meals, and similarly it played a social role. Its menu also resembled that of supper. The two chief differences (apart from the time) were that people drank far less at luncheon, and only rarely were guests all of one sex.

One consequence of luncheon was that breakfast moved back an hour, to nine o'clock. A second, more significant effect, was the development of afternoon tea, which bore little relation to the 'four hours' of a previous epoch. It was a meal which became popular throughout Britain, but nowhere did it assume such status and such standards of excellence as in Scotland. Generations of thraldom to those difficult ingredients, oatmeal and barleymeal, and that simple but demanding utensil, the girdle, had conditioned the national subconscious; and early in the 19th century the introduction of coal-fired ranges with ovens, plus a dramatic reduction in the cost of wheat and sugar, enabled every Scotswoman to discover that she possessed a lighter hand and more inventive mind in the production of scones, cakes and pastries than any woman south of the border. Afternoon tea provided the perfect opportunity of displaying these skills, and as supper had been the particular province of men, so the tea-table with its delicacies was recognized as women's territory, to which men were admitted more by privilege than by right.

Supper itself waned by degrees; at the end of the century it had diminished in status so much that it was no longer considered of dietary or social significance by the gentry. Among the ordinary people it survived a little longer. As we have seen, industrial workers, farmers, and children, needed a main midday meal, and supper of sowens, potatoes, or porridge and milk continued to constitute their evening nourishment for a few more years. Even here, however, the habit was being eroded by the development of a somewhat different concept – *high tea*.

Given its popularity during the closing years of the 19th century and the first half of the 20th, the origins and early development of high tea are surprisingly obscure. It has been a somewhat insecure meal, clear enough in its shape yet moving from social class to social class and between different age-groups, without obvious reasons. But it is easy enough to distinguish three different sources which contributed to its development and final place as the repast which, for many, encapsulates the whole ambience of middle-class Scotland in the early 20th century.

The first of these sources was the adoption by the urban poor of bread and tea for their supper. Poverty was the chief, but not the only reason. As a popular drink, tea had long since moved near the top of the league, though it was usually of the lowest quality; and the rise of the Temperance Movement with its emphasis on the evils of drink reinforced the value given it by the labouring classes. Because it was drunk hot and had a mildly stimulating effect it replaced ale more effectively than milk – 'the cup that cheers but not inebriates' was no idle slogan. As for bread, after about 1860 the price of white flour fell below that of brown, and the introduction of roller-milling with its efficient removal of almost all the husk and germ of the wheat, leaving behind only the whitest part, put white bread within reach of all. It could be bought at every cornershop, and was the cheapest way of filling hungry stomachs, besides needing no preparation – the mere addition of butter or margarine and cheap jam made it appetizing enough.

This became the basic, unalterable foundation of the workers' evening meal. When times were good or a family prospered, 'kitchen', or relish, of other foods were added – fish, potatoes, eggs, cheese, even meat, especially in the latter half of the century when cheap tinned goods from Australia became available.

So ubiquitous did tinned food become that even home produce was supplanted by the same item, tinned, from another country. Cost and ease of preparation were the initial factors; but the tragic consequence was that tinned goods came to be preferred, as anyone who observes the sale of tinned carrots in supermarkets cannot fail to notice. Neil Munro has a story in *Para Handy*, set at the turn of the century, which illustrates this enslavement of urban populations to the tin: Dougie, the ship's mate, has tricked a Glasgow woman on holiday into buying a coal-fish from him, under the impression that he was selling her cod.

'I'm only vexed I didna say it wass a salmon,' said Dougie, when he came back to the vessel with his ill-got florin. 'I could have got twice ass much for't.'
'She would ken fine it wasna a salmon when it wasna in a tin,' said the Captain.

Supper, then, was the principal progenitor of high tea. But secondary influences also played their part, notably that essentially middle-class institution, *nursery tea* (at which, paradoxically, milk was the usual beverage although cambric tea, made from hot water, milk, sugar, and a minute quantity of tea, was sometimes given as a treat). Stevenson's *A Child's Garden of Verses* has many references to nursery tea, none explicit enough to quote, but leaving no doubt of its importance in the child's life. Nor was it confined to the very young. Most middle-class schoolchildren went home for a hot meal at midday until free school meals were introduced. In the evening they had their 'tea', until deemed old enough to join their parents at the dinner-table. Perhaps this accounts for the easy adoption by the middle class of what had begun as a working-class custom.

There was also farm tea. This, again, depended on the need of workers for midday dinner with another fairly substantial meal at about five o'clock. In the long days of summer, work continued after tea; in winter it was the signal for retreat to the warm shelter of the farmhouse kitchen. Either way, farm tea was rarely the lavish spread which is sometimes depicted. The good things were there, naturally: new-laid eggs, home-made cheeses, fresh-caught fish from the burn, sizzling rashers of bacon, potato cakes, scones, pancakes, potato scones, oatcakes, bannocks, fresh butter, home-made jam, and heather honey – but not all at the same meal. Rarely could the farmer or his wife afford the time for this kind of repast, unless there were visitors. Then, preparations were elaborate and the table was crowded with good things. Such a meal was the one enjoyed by Dickson McGunn and John Heritage in *Huntingtower*:

They were seated in Mrs Morran's kitchen before a meal which fulfilled their wildest dreams. She had been baking that morning so there were white scones and barley scones, and oaten farles, and russet pancakes. There were three boiled eggs for each of them; there was a segment of an immense currant cake ('a present from my guid brither last Hogmanay'); there was skim-milk cheese; there were several kinds of jam, and there was a pot of dark-gold heather honey. 'Try hinny and aitcake,' said their hostess. 'My man used to say he never fund onything as guid in a' his days.'

Interesting, as proof that supper in the country was still a robust collation at the turn of the century, is the fact that Buchan's heroes, returning the same evening to a late supper, are offered most of the dainties which had appeared at tea, supplemented by 'a noble dish of shimmering "potted-head".'

By the beginning of the present century high tea had attained its position as the evening meal of the rural classes and the industrial working classes, with a kind of optional status among those of the middle class who preferred dinner at midday – a status which rose rapidly after the First World War. From the 1930s to the 1950s high tea was the evening meal of all but the professional and upper classes. For the servantless housewife with children it made sense to have a simple meal which could be enjoyed and shared by the whole family, and saved on the washing-up. If there were visitors it became the most hospitable of occasions.

In the industrial towns, Saturday teas were specially important family events, when married daughters and sons visited or were visited, and old ties with more distant relatives renewed. On Saturdays there was often more than one main course, and an impressive array of baking.

Main courses, frequently borrowed from the great Scottish breakfast, were usually simple – eggs, or finnan haddies, herrings in oatmeal, or kippers. Another favourite was cold meat: corned beef, tongue, or boiled ham. Fish and chips (home-made if the family was 'posh', otherwise bought from the 'Tallie') was a great stand-by. A very popular dish, especially in Glasgow, was the small mutton pies known as 'Twopenny Struggles'. Vegetables were never served, although 'posh' people sometimes ate tomato, cucumber, or cress sandwiches, or used a lettuce leaf and half a tomato to garnish a main dish. Salads were rare indeed. Yet family high tea was, in its way, a splendid meal, making few demands on the palate and conveying all the delightful security of the nursery and the tea-party.

Elizabeth Craig's *Menus for a Year* shows the sort of meal which might have been on a middle-class table; though in the inclusion of salads and fresh fruit her menus are untypical, reflecting her own principles rather than current practices:

A Monday in January:
Stuffed eggs   Watercress
Drop Scones   Bath buns
Almond shortcake
Fruit cake
Spanish melon

A Wednesday in April:
Fish pie
Lettuce salad
Walnut bread   Swiss buns
Treacle Layer cake
Custard cream biscuits

A Sunday in August:
Veal galantine
Lettuce and tomatoes
Brown bread   Toast
Tea cakes   Seed cake
German pound cake
Chocolate wafers
Oranges

Having said so much in praise of high tea, one has to acknowledge that the meal which won fame for Scotland was not the domestic one inspired by people like Mrs Craig, but rather that served in commercial tea-rooms such as those pioneered by Miss Cranston in Glasgow in the 1880s. For over 50 years, from the 1900s to the late 1950s, it was possible to go into any tea-room, anywhere in Scotland and, having asked for tea, to be met with the response 'Plain or High, Madam?' Whether the tea-room belonged to a chain or was a small family-run business, the quality of food and service were almost assured – tea was such a popular meal, and so many establishments were competing for custom. The toast was hot and golden, the butter came in small curls in a little pot, the jam and honey in glass or earthenware dishes, the milk, innocent of plastic and foil, in a proper jug. No microwave oven waited malevolently to heat up cloned frozen scones. The haddock, plump and firm, was served with crisp chips in discreet portions so that one might do justice to the cake or biscuits. And the tea and hot water came in electroplated nickel-silver pots, enabling the customer to mix up the brew he preferred.

A small book, one of a series published in 1935, entitled *Scotland on £10* gave sternly practical reasons for enthusiasm:

A plain tea, which may range in price from 9d to 1s 6d, is a rather tremendous affair in bountiful Scotland. Your table 'groans' with plates of scones, white bread, brown bread, gingerbread, buns of one sort or another, cheeses, jellies and biscuits, and of course a big pot of tea that *is* tea . . .

The high tea of Scotland, which may cost as much as half a crown, includes all the above and much else beside, say ham and eggs or fried fish or cold meats or even (but don't get up your hopes) a portion of grouse. Bannocks also will make their appearance, and all sorts of cakes and 'cakies'. Oh, a bannock? Well, that is a coarse sort of griddle cake and very delectable. The Scotch have made a high art of high tea, and their pastry is an artistic achievement.

A somewhat different view of the Scottish tea-room was presented by the poet Edwin Muir, who saw it as purveying, like Edinburgh's Princes Street, 'floating sexual desire'.

Those whom Princes Street leaves still unsatisfied resort to the tea-rooms and lounges, where they languidly steep themselves until they are quite saturated. Among the tea-rooms in Princes Street, there are places more strange than a dream. Passing through a corridor one enters an enormous room filled with dull and glassy light, and as silent as if it were miles under-sea. Nereids float in the submarine glimmer, bearing trays in their hands, and over glassy tables the drowned sway like seaweeds, the sluggish motion of the tide turning their heads now this way, now that, with an effect of hypnotic ogling. When one gets used to the light one sees that these amphibious sea-plant-like forms are respectable members of the Edinburgh bourgeoisie, that their clothes are quite dry, and that the sea change they have suffered is temporary, having been paid for. They are well-dressed-people, and they are drinking tea and eating scones.

Needless to say, things are no longer what they were in 1935. Both the tourist who seeks high tea with cold grouse and bannocks, and he who desires to experience Edinburgh's submarine life, will be disappointed. The commercial high tea is almost – not quite – as unreal as Muir's nereids. It is still to be found, thankfully, in small establishments in country towns.

Worse news, as retailed in the *Scotsman* of 19 April 1984, comes from a survey showing that high tea has become the least important meal of the day, 'behind breakfast, lunch, evening meal, and even snacks'. Some comfort can be found in the fact that the survey, by Taylor Nelson and Associates, covered Britain as a whole, and that where the meal survives it is bigger and more elaborate than ever before, with 30% more meat and 18% more fish.

There is some comfort, too, perhaps, in reflecting that not one of the meals we have been considering would have looked familiar to an 18th-century housewife, nor would most of us find her meals to our own taste. Meals, like clothes, are evoked as practical responses to a way of life. It is the quality rather than the presentation with which we should all concern ourselves.

— RECIPES —

Although most of the recipes linked with other chapters are for dinner dishes, a number would not be out of place at breakfast or high tea. In this section, however, I am concentrating exclusively on these two very special meals. Almost all the savoury dishes given would be suitable for either – the cakes and pastries, of course, belong to tea, whether plain or high.

Kipper-stuffed Eggs

6 hard-boiled eggs
1 kipper
2 tablespoons cream

1 tablespoon chopped parsley or fresh dill
salt and pepper

Place the kipper upright in a deep jug and fill it with boiling water to cover the fish. Leave to stand for ten minutes. Remove the kipper, bone and skin it, and flake the flesh into a bowl. Cut the eggs in half lengthwise, remove the yolks and add them to the fish with the cream and parsley. Mash thoroughly to get a softish mixture. Taste for seasoning, then pile back into the egg whites and serve cold or heat under a grill for about a minute. This is good with melba toast as an accompaniment.

Scotch Eggs

I have not been able to find the origin of this dish, though it seems to be first mentioned by Meg Dods. It bears an odd similarity, striking though probably coincidental, with an Indian dish called Nargis Kofta, which consists of hard-boiled eggs coated with cooked spiced minced mutton and fried, then cut in half and served in a sauce of curried tomato and onion. It is conceivable that the idea was brought to Scotland from India, just as Kedgeree and curry were, by the nabobs returning with their wealth (see Scott's *St Ronan's Well*) in the early 19th century.

4 hard-boiled eggs
2 small uncooked eggs
¾ lb (375g) pork sausage-meat
fresh breadcrumbs
cooking oil for deep frying

Peel the hard-boiled eggs. Beat the two uncooked eggs, and dip each boiled egg into the mixture, then divide the sausage-meat into four equal portions, and work one portion round each egg, covering it completely and sealing the joints as well as you can. Coat again with the beaten egg, then roll them in the bread-crumbs. Heat the oil until very hot, and fry the Scotch eggs until they are a good brown, about 10 minutes. They are usually served plain but a little leftover gravy may be poured over if you have some.

FISH

The fish dish served more often than any other at breakfast is finnan haddock; at high tea, fried haddock is the favourite. There are many, many others which are equally good, and it has been difficult to make a selection.

Fried Cod Roe

Cod roe is usually bought ready boiled from the fishmonger. If, however, you have bought it raw, it must be boiled before being fried. The usual way is to wrap it carefully in muslin, but greaseproof paper surrounded by a sheet of newspaper does as well. Tie it so that it does not come adrift. Bring water to the boil, add a little salt and a drop or two of vinegar, put in the roe, and boil gently for about half an hour. When it is cold, remove from the pan and take it from its muslin or paper. Then peel off the skin, and cut it into slices about half an inch (less than a centimetre) thick. Dip into beaten egg and toasted breadcrumbs, then fry in butter or oil until light brown. You will need about 1 lb (500g) of roe for 4–6 people.

Roe Cakes

This is a recipe from the Hebrides collected by Catherine Brown.

> 1 lb (500g) cooked roe
> ½ lb (250g) cooked mashed potatoes
> 1 medium onion, finely chopped
> ½ oz (15g) butter
> oil for frying
> salt and pepper
> 1 oz (15g) flour

Melt the butter in a frying pan, and cook the onion until transparent but not brown. Skin the roe. Mix it well with the potatoes, then add onion, butter, salt and pepper. Divide into 8 pieces, and on a floured board shape into rounds about ½ in (1 cm) thick. Leave in a cool place for an hour, then fry in a shallow layer of hot oil.

Ham and Haddie

This is a favourite breakfast or high tea dish. The 'ham' is really bacon, since the Scots refer to any kind of cured pork as ham. (If one is offered ham and eggs, it is bacon and eggs which appear on the plate.)

> 2 finnan haddocks
> ½ lb (250g) Ayrshire bacon
> salt and black pepper
> 1 oz (15g) butter

Lay a piece of well-greased foil in the grill pan, then put in the fish, skin side down. Dot with butter and season very sparingly with salt, but with a good grind of black pepper. Put the grid back into the grill pan over the fish, and lay the bacon on it. Heat the grill and then put the pan under it. Turn the bacon once or twice, and remove it when cooked and keep warm, but put back the fish for a few minutes to finish cooking. Lay the fish on a warm dish, cover with the bacon, and pour over the juices from the pan.

Scotch Scrapple

This recipe from Elizabeth Craig is definitely a high tea dish. It is a slightly stodgy version of ham and haddie, typical of the 'thirties – but it is very comforting on a cold night.

> 1 large finnan haddock
> 1 cup milk
> 6 rashers bacon
> 2 tablespoons flour

3 medium potatoes, boiled and cut in pieces
fresh ground black pepper

Soak the haddock in the milk for an hour, then bring slowly to a
simmer. Cut the rind from the bacon, and cut each rasher into 8
strips crosswise, then fry it. Stir in the flour and the milk from
the fish, avoiding lumps, until boiling. Draw to one side. Skin
and flake the fish, then add it with the potatoes to the bacon
sauce. Grind pepper over, and pile into a hot deep dish.

Salmon Fritters

If you should have some leftover boiled salmon, these fritters
accommodate it very well. Alternatively one could, like the Glasgow woman in *Para Handy*, use tinned fish.

6 oz (150g) boiled salmon
2 oz (50g) mashed potatoes
1 small beaten egg
salt
a pinch of cayenne pepper
browned breadcrumbs
oil for shallow frying

Flake the fish and mix it with the potatoes. Season well, and form
into small flat cakes. Dip them on both sides into the beaten egg.
Heat the oil and cover the fritters with breadcrumbs, then drop
into the frying-pan and fry until crisp but not dry.

Kedgeree

I am well aware that this dish is not confined to Scotland, and the
recipe I am going to give is, indeed, adapted from Eliza Acton's
Modern Cookery, first published in 1845. But it has become so
much a part of Scots breakfast tradition, and is so delicious, that to
omit it would be unthinkable.

½ lb (250g) cooked rice of the best quality
½ lb (250g) cold cooked fish, flaked
　　(salmon or finnan haddock are particularly good)
½ oz (15g) butter
salt and cayenne pepper
2 eggs, beaten

Put the butter in a pan and melt it, then add the rice and the fish, with seasoning to taste. Stir over a medium heat until the mixture is all very hot. Then remove it from the heat and mix in quickly two beaten eggs. As soon as they are set, serve the kedgeree, with chutney if liked.

MEAT

Forfar Bridies

The bridie is something like the Cornish pasty in that it is a meal in itself, though it contains no potatoes and no carrots. Meat wrapped in pastry is a conveniently nourishing parcel which can be eaten on the hoof – an appropriate expression perhaps since Forfar is one of the centres of the Angus cattle trade. Bridies are now sold in bakeries all over Scotland, but it is worth making one's own occasionally, because the quality depends very much on the quality of pastry and beef. The quantity given here makes three rather large ones, which can be shared between six people; but it has been known for folk to come in wet and tired after a day on the hills and eat a whole one each!

　　　　1 lb (500g) rump steak or topside
　　　　salt and pepper
　　　　3 oz (75g) shredded beef suet
　　　　2 tablespoons minced onion
　　　　1 lb (500g) short pastry

Beat the steak with a rolling-pin, then cut into narrow strips and divide each into ½ in (1 cm) pieces. Season with salt and freshly ground black pepper. Divide the pastry into three equal portions, and do the same with the meat. Roll each piece of pastry into an oval about ¼ in (½ cm) thick. Put one portion of meat on half of each oval, keeping it ½ in (1 cm) from the edge of the pastry then sprinkle each with ⅓ of the suet and ⅓ of the onions. Damp the edges of the pastry and fold over, sealing by pinching between finger and thumb. Cut a small hole in the top of each bridie to let steam escape. Place in the fridge while the oven heats to 450°F (230°C) gas 7–8, then bake at that heat for 15 minutes, reducing to 350°F (180°C) gas 3–4 and continuing to bake for about 1 hour. The suet melts and is absorbed by the pastry, turning it into the crispiest of flaky coverings for the delicious filling.

Ayrshire Meat Roll

1 lb (500g) minced Ayrshire bacon
1 lb (500g) minced stewing steak
6 oz (150g) white breadcrumbs
2 eggs
1 medium onion, finely chopped
salt, black pepper, a little fresh nutmeg

Put the bacon, meat, onion, eggs and breadcrumbs into a bowl. Grate in a little nutmeg and grind some black pepper in, then add salt to taste, remembering that the bacon is salty. On a floured board and with floured hands roll the mixture into a long sausage. Take a clean cloth and sprinkle it thickly with flour, then wrap the sausage in it and tie securely at both ends. Put water in a pot large enough to hold the sausage, and place a plate or upturned saucer in the bottom. Then lower in the meat roll and bring gently to the boil. Reduce the heat and simmer gently, covered, for 2 hours. Have ready some dried breadcrumbs and roll the sausage in them before it cools, then serve hot or cold.

Devilled Bones

This dish was most popular at Edinburgh suppers in the 18th century. It survived as a breakfast delicacy into the 19th, but is rarely made now. I include it for comparison with the American method of serving Spare Ribs.

> bones with a little meat on them
> butter
> dry mustard, curry powder, black pepper, cayenne
> Worcester sauce

Work together four ounces of butter, a teaspoonful each of black pepper, mustard and curry powder, half a teaspoonful of cayenne and a tablespoon of Worcester sauce. Keep on ice. Score the meat and then grill the bones. After grilling, coat with the devilled butter and put under the grill for two or three minutes longer. Serve with or without Devil Sauce.

Devilled Kidneys

> 1 sheep's kidney per person
> salt, pepper, cayenne, mustard
> a little butter

Split the kidneys without dividing them, remove the skin and fat, and score them so that the seasoning can reach the meat. Rub in the seasoning, adding curry powder or anchovy essence if you wish. Skewer each kidney across the back so that it lies flat. Brush with melted butter. Heat the grill, then put the kidneys under it for 3 or 4 minutes. Then turn them to cook the other side. They should be well done but will become tough and dry if overcooked. Serve very hot, with toast.

Pig's Liver Tillypronie

My family have always preferred pig's liver to lamb's. It is very tender and has excellent flavour. This recipe from Lady Clark makes the best of it, and is very adaptable – equally suitable for breakfast, lunch, or high tea.

1 lb (450g) pig's liver
1 large onion
2 oz (50g) butter
2 slices ham, cut into strips
2–3 oz (50–60g) mushrooms
1 wineglass good stock
1 wineglass sherry

Cut the liver into ½ inch (1 cm) strips. Slice the onion and fry it in the butter, then add the ham and the sliced mushrooms. Allow these to brown a little, then add the liver. Cook over low heat for about ten minutes, stirring often. Then add the stock, and continue to cook, until there is very little liquid left. At this stage add the sherry. Turn up the heat and stir until the liquid has nearly all gone. This is good on toast, or just as it is. Lady Clark adds 'Pig's liver so dressed, and their pettitoes, previously very slowly and thoroughly boiled and grown quite cold, egged and bread-crumbed and fried, make an excellent dish for luncheon.

Rabbit Brawn

Brawn is similar to potted hough though usually made from an animal's head or feet. The meat is cooked very gently and is then allowed to set either in its own or in manufactured jelly. Rabbit brawn is excellent and decorative, and even children who normally object to brawn often like this version.

1 rabbit, jointed
½ lb (250g) boiled ham, cut into small cubes
1 hard-boiled egg
½ oz (1 sheet) gelatine
1 pt (500 ml) beef stock

Put the rabbit pieces into a pan with water to cover and salt and pepper. Cook very gently for 1½ hours, then remove from the pan and cut into neat pieces about the same size as the ham cubes. Wet a 1½ pt (1 l) mould, then slice the egg and arrange the slices at the bottom and coming a little way up the sides.

Dissolve the gelatine in the beef stock and leave it until it is barely beginning to set. Then pour a very little into the mould, over the egg. Put in the ham as neatly as you can and leave for 15 minutes. Then add the rabbit pieces and pour over the rest of the jelly. When it is set, turn out and serve with salads.

VEGETABLE

The following recipe is the brainchild of a modern Scots cook, Dione Pattullo. It is so delicious it deserves to become part of everyone's repertoire, especially as oatmeal and leeks are so much to the fore in our culinary traditions.

Oatmeal Flan with Creamy Leek Filling

Flan Case

4 oz (125g) flour
4 oz (125g) oatmeal
4 oz (125g) lard
pinch salt
cold water to mix

Mix the flour and meal with the salt, and rub in the fat. Mix to a very stiff dough with the cold water. Knead the paste gently until it is a smooth lump. Roll out and use to line an 8-in (20-cm) fluted flan ring set on a baking-sheet. Line with greaseproof paper and baking beans and bake blind. When half-cooked, remove beans and paper and allow to brown all over. Cool.

Creamy Leek Filling

4 medium leeks
1 pt (500 ml) chicken stock, or a stock cube
1 oz (25g) butter
1 teaspoon curry powder
1 eating apple, peeled and chopped
½ oz (1 sheet) gelatine
¼ pt (150 ml) double cream

Clean the leeks and cut into 1-in (2-cm) lengths. Cook in the stock, or water with a stock cube. Melt the butter, and over a low heat cook the curry powder and the apple. This will take about 15 minutes. Dissolve the gelatine in a little of the stock and put with the leeks, curry and apple into the blender and liquidize. Cool in a bowl, and when just on the point of setting, add the half-whipped cream and correct the seasoning. Pour into the oatmeal flan case and allow to set. Decorate with thin slices of cucumber.

SCONES

It would be pleasant to derive the word 'scone' from the ancient seat of the Scottish kings. *Chambers Dictionary*, however, relates it more prosaically to a Dutch word, *schoon*, meaning fine – which scones certainly are. Every Scotswoman has her own secret which makes her scones better than her neighbour's – be it the lightness of the hand, the coldness of the ingredients, the fineness of the flour, or the quantity and type of liquid used. And there are so many varieties! Plain scones, currant scones, treacle scones, wheaten scones, cream scones, soda scones, cheese scones, sour scones – the list is almost endless. If I were asked to select one above all others, I should choose the plain scone: it goes into the oven a rather unpleasing, small, flat, white object, but when it emerges it is a beautiful sight, its exterior varying in colour from palest gold to deep sienna, just a hint of flour dust still clinging, light and high and not quite dry, the merest breath of steam making its final escape. Inside, the soft golden dough begs to be spread with fresh butter which sinks meltingly into the hot surface. If Proust's aunt had had scones instead of madeleines for tea, *À la Recherche du Temps Perdu* would have been a very different book – for who would ruin a well-made scone by dipping it in tea?

The first scones I ever tasted were made by my piano teacher. They were also part of my first awareness of Scotland, for Helen Thorburn was a most Scottish Scot who just happened to have settled in a small village in South Africa to teach her beloved music to small ignorami like myself. We learnt much more from her than how to play scales, and not a few of her pupils must, like me, have been conditioned by her into early affection for a country we had never seen.

Helen Thorburn's Scones

Pre-heat oven to 450°F (230°C) gas 8

2 cups flour
3½ teaspoons baking powder
2 oz (50g) butter
¾ cup milk
1 egg
salt
1 teaspoon sugar

Sift flour and baking powder with a pinch of salt. Mix in the sugar, then rub in the butter. Beat the egg and add the milk to it, then pour by degrees into the flour to make a soft dough. Turn onto a floured board and very lightly roll out to a thickness of about ¾ in (2 cm). Cut into rounds with a floured cutter, put on a baking-sheet and bake for 8 minutes. The quicker the whole process, the better will be the scones.

Wholemeal Scones

Pre-heat oven to 375°F (190°C) gas 5

6 oz (150g) wholemeal flour
6 oz (150g) white flour
2 teaspoons baking powder (scant)
2 oz (50g) butter
2 teaspoons syrup
¼ pt (140 ml) milk, approx
salt

Put flour and salt and baking powder into a bowl, mix well, then rub in the butter. Warm the syrup very slightly, then add to the flour with the milk, to make a soft dough. Quickly turn out onto a floured board, and roll out to a thickness of ½ in (1 cm). Cut into rounds and bake for 10–15 minutes.

Treacle Scones

½ lb (250g) white flour
1½ oz (45g) butter
½ teaspoon bicarbonate of soda
½ teaspoon cream of tartar
pinch salt
½ teaspoon cinnamon
½ teaspoon ginger
1 teaspoon sugar
1 tablespoon treacle
¼ pt (140 ml) buttermilk

Rub butter into flour, then mix in the other dry ingredients. Warm the treacle and mix it with a little buttermilk, then add gradually to the flour. Add enough buttermilk to get a stiff dough. Roll out on a floured board to ¾ in (2 cm) thick, shape into a round, and cut into 8 segments. Bake on a greased baking-sheet at 400°F (200°C) gas 6 for 10–15 minutes.

Girdle Scones

These have an entirely different texture from the ordinary scone, being closer grained and firmer. Like all their tribe, they are best eaten as soon as cooked.

8 oz (250g) self-raising flour
pinch salt
2 oz (50g) butter
¼ pt (140 ml) milk

Mix the flour and salt before rubbing in the butter. Then add the milk to make a soft dough. Put a girdle on the stove to heat. Knead the dough for a second or two on a floured board, then roll or pat it into a round, ½ in (1 cm) thick. Cut into four wedges. Sprinkle the girdle with flour, and cook the scones for 7–8 minutes on each side, until lightly browned and cooked through.

Another version: 'Dairy Mary's Scones' from Elizabeth Craig.

> ¾ pt (420 ml) buttermilk
> 1 teaspoon bicarbonate of soda
> ½ teaspoon baking powder
> 1½ tablespoons caster sugar
> pinch salt
> ½ cup thick cream
> sifted flour as required

Pour the buttermilk into a large basin. Stir in soda, baking powder, sugar, salt, cream, and as much flour as is required to make a very thick batter, almost a dough. Heat a floured girdle. Lift the batter quickly with a tablespoon onto a floured board, then with floured hands shape nicely into a round without kneading. Place 1½ in (3 cm) apart on a hot girdle and cook over the open fire or hot plate until small bubbles appear on top. Turn carefully with a spatula and brown the other side. Makes 6–7 scones.

SHORTBREAD

'For best shortbread' says Lady Grisell Baillie in her directions to her housekeeper, '8 lb flour 3 lb butter'; 'second shortbread' rated only 2 lb butter to the 8 lb flour. This was *short-bread* – a plain mixture of butter and flour with very little sugar, if any. The traditional shortbread which has become world-famous uses sugar and sometimes other flavouring ingredients such as candied peel and chopped nuts. The proportion of flour to butter is different, and often ground rice replaces part of the flour, giving an agreeable, slightly grainy texture.

Traditional Plain Shortbread

> 8 oz (200g) butter (unsalted)
> 12 oz (300g) plain or self-raising flour
> 3 oz (75g) ground rice
> 2 oz (50g) sugar

Put the butter in a warm place to soften, while you mix the dry ingredients. Then work it into the mixture with the hands, taking care not to overknead it – this would make the dough too difficult to handle. Put into two 8-in (20-cm) sponge tins, well packed down and smoothed flat. Nick the edges with the blunt edge of a knife to decorate, then prick well all over with a fork. Bake at 350°F (180°C) gas 4 for 45 minutes, but check occasionally that it is not becoming too brown – it should be a pale biscuit colour when done.

Rich Shortbread

> 8 oz (250g) plain or self-raising flour
> 1 oz (25g) caster sugar
> 4 oz (125g) fresh butter
> 1 oz (25g) candied peel
> 1 oz (25g) blanched almonds, chopped fine

Mix the fruit and nuts with the flour and sugar. Melt the butter and allow to cool, then pour quickly onto the flour mixture, kneading it well. Form into four circles about 1 in (2 cm) thick, pinching the edges. Prick all over with a fork. Line a baking-sheet with greaseproof paper, and put the rounds on it. Bake at 325°F (160°C) gas 3 for about 1 hour, until light brown.

Parlies

These 'Parliament cakes' – really ginger biscuits – supposedly get their name from the members of the Scottish parliament who, on leaving their place of assembly, bought them from booths and taverns in or near Edinburgh's Parliament Square. At Mrs Flockhart's tavern in the Potterrow, nearby, a plate of Parlies was put each day on a bunker-seat in the window, accompanied by bottles of brandy, rum and whisky.

About noon any one watching the place from an opposite window would have observed an elderly gentleman entering the humble shop, where he saluted the lady with 'Hoo d'ye do, mem?' and then passed into the side space to indulge himself with a glass from one or other of the bottles. After him came another, who went through the same ceremonial; after him another again; and so on. Strange to say, these were men of importance in society – some of them lawyers in good employment, some bankers, and so forth, and all of them inhabitants of good houses in George Square.

Meg Dods claims to have Mrs Flockhart's recipe, in quantities sufficient for the satisfaction of all the elderly gentlemen of Edinburgh. Here is a version more suitable for domestic use:

> 1 lb (500g) flour
> ½ lb (250g) best soft brown sugar
> 4 teaspoons ground ginger
> ½ lb (250g) unsalted butter
> ½ lb (250g) treacle

Put the butter and treacle in a pan and heat slowly. Sift the flour and ginger, and mix in the sugar. When the butter/treacle mixture is boiling, pour it into the flour, stirring vigorously, and as soon as it is cool enough use your hands to knead it well. Roll out very thinly on a slab (Meg Dods says 'a sixth of an inch or less' – 0.3 cm) and mark it into squares with a knife. Bake in a slow oven, 300°F (150°C) gas 2 for about 20 minutes. Separate the squares when soft, but allow to get quite cold and crisp before storing in tins.

A clear relation of Parlies is the following gingerbread, the recipe for which, given by an old friend, makes the best I have yet tasted.

Gingerbread

> 1 lb (500g) plain flour
> 1 level teaspoon bicarbonate of soda
> ¼ teaspoon salt
> 1 rounded tablespoon ginger
> 1 rounded tablespoon mixed spice
> ½ lb (250g) butter
> ½ lb (250g) soft brown sugar
> ½ lb (250g) golden syrup

10 oz (250g) treacle
2 eggs
¼ pt (125 ml) milk

Line a roasting tin with greased greaseproof paper. Sift flour, soda, salt and spices. Put the butter, sugar, treacle and syrup in a thick-bottomed pan, and heat gently until the sugar dissolves, then allow to cool. Beat together the eggs and the milk. Add this alternately with the sugar mixture to the flour, mixing very thoroughly and making sure no lumps remain. Bake in a moderate oven, 325°F (160°C) gas 3, for 1¼–1½ hours. Allow to cool in the tin for 5–10 minutes, then turn out carefully on to a wire rack. Best if not eaten for three days – but I know few who have proved this.

Like gingerbread, seed-cake reminds us how much earlier generations enjoyed the flavour of spices. It is an old-fashioned delicacy, but well worth keeping alive. There are a number of versions, some plain, some fancy.

Seed Cake

6 oz (150g) self-raising flour
1 teaspoon baking powder
1 teaspoon carraway seeds
4 oz (100g) butter
4 oz (100g) sugar
2 large eggs
1 teaspoon brandy or whisky

Mix flour, baking powder, and carraway seeds. Cream the butter and sugar. Whisk together the eggs and the brandy or whisky, then add alternately with the flour to the butter and sugar. Mix well, then pour into an 8-in (20-cm) cake tin, and bake at 350°F (180°C) gas 4 for 45 minutes.

Edinburgh Tart

I first learnt to bake this under a very different title, namely 'Old English custard tart'. But it is not a custard tart – it contains no milk, and it is certainly not English. One can understand, though, the wish to claim credit, for it is very good. This version comes from Catherine Brown's *Scottish Regional Recipes*.

Pre-heat the oven to 450°F (230°C) gas 8

6 oz (150g) puff pastry
2 oz (50g) butter
2 oz (50g) sugar
2 oz (50g) chopped candied peel
1 oz (25g) sultanas
3 eggs

Line an 8-in (20-cm) flan ring with pastry. Melt the butter very gently in a pan and add sugar, candied peel, sultanas and eggs. Beat together and then pour into the pastry case. Bake in a very hot oven for 15–20 minutes and then serve hot or cold with a bowl of cream.

Dundee Cake

This is a fairly inspired fruit cake which keeps well: an agreeable substitute for Christmas cake, if one does not care for the richness of the latter. Do not omit the almond decoration on top – if you do, you have not made a Dundee cake.

½ lb (250g) butter
½ lb (250g) sugar
4 eggs
½ lb (250g) currants
½ lb (250g) raisins
½ lb (250g) sultanas
2 oz (50g) chopped candied peel
½ lb (250g) plain flour
2 oz (50g) blanched almonds

Cream the butter and sugar, and work in the beaten eggs. Fold in half the flour, then all the fruit, then the remaining flour. Grease and line an 8-in (20-cm) cake tin, pour in the mixture, and smooth the top quite level. Make a pattern with the almonds, then bake in a very slow oven, 250°F (140°C) gas 1–2, for 3 hours. If it browns too much on top, cover with foil to finish cooking.

Montrose Cakes

These rather unusual little cakes are quite delicious. You should find rose-water at your local chemist's.

> 4 oz (100g) self-raising flour
> 4 oz (100g) caster sugar
> 4 oz (100g) butter
> 3 oz (75g) currants
> 2 teaspoons brandy
> 2 teaspoons rose-water
> pinch grated nutmeg
> 3 eggs

Cream the butter and sugar, then add the beaten eggs one at a time. Stir in the currants, brandy and rose-water and mix thoroughly. Sieve the flour and nutmeg, then add to the mixture. Grease 20 patty tins, and half fill each with the mixture. Bake at 375°F (190°C) gas 5 for 10–15 minutes.

Selkirk Bannock

This is an enriched yeast bread, first made at Selkirk in the Borders by a local baker. It is quite unlike its Canadian cousin (q.v.).

> 2 lb (900g) strong white flour
> ¾ oz (20g) fresh yeast
> 1 teaspoon sugar
> 4 oz (100g) butter
> 4 oz (100g) lard

8 oz (200g) sugar
½–¾ pt (300–400 ml) tepid milk
¾ lb (300g) sultanas or raisins
4 oz (100g) chopped candied peel (optional)
pinch salt

Cream the yeast in a cup with the teaspoon of sugar and a little tepid water. Melt butter and lard in a pan until soft but not oily. Sift flour with the salt. Add the butter mixture and the yeast to the milk and mix well. Leave for 10 minutes, then pour into the flour and knead well until the dough is smooth and spongy. Cover and set in a warm place until it doubles in bulk – about 1 hour. Then knead in the fruit and remaining sugar. Shape into two rounds on a baking tray, cover and leave to rise again for about half an hour or until they have once more doubled in bulk. Heat the oven to 400°F (200°C) gas 6, and bake the bannocks for 15 minutes, then reduce oven to 350°F (180°C) gas 4 for a further 30 minutes. Take them out, brush with beaten egg white or a syrup of sugar and water, and return to the oven for about 15 minutes to get a good glaze.

Clootie Dumpling

The clootie is the cloth in which the pudding is boiled.

6 oz (150g) margarine
12 oz (340g) flour
6 oz (170g) sugar
1 teaspoon baking soda
1 teaspoon cinnamon
1 teaspoon ginger
½ lb (250g) sultanas
½ lb (250g) currants
1 tablespoon treacle
1 tablespoon golden syrup
2 beaten eggs
a little milk

Mix all dry ingredients in a bowl, and rub in the fat. Make a well in the middle and add the slightly warmed syrup and treacle and the beaten egg. Then add enough milk to make a stiff mixture.

Take a large clean cotton or linen cloth, dip it into boiling water, and sprinkle it thickly with flour. Put the dumpling mixture into the centre of the cloth and draw up the edges and tie firmly with string, allowing room for the pudding to expand during cooking. Lower into a pan of boiling water and boil for 3 hours. Serve with custard.

STRANGERS IN THE KITCHEN

Is there that owre his French ragout
Or olio that wad staw a sow
Or fricassee wad mak her spew
  Wi' perfect sconner
Looks down wi' sneering, scornfu' view
  On sic a dinner?

Burns, 'Address to a Haggis'

Burns was writing in an era when, in Scotland as in England, the influence of French cooking was at its height in fashionable kitchens. Yet it would be wrong to imagine, as some people do, that France is the only nation to have stirred the Scots cooking-pot. Equally false, although widely held, is the view that some specifically French dishes pre-date the 17th century, and that French influence was stronger in Scotland than south of the border. The Scots kitchen was affected by many cultures, but no European country developed its own national gastronomy until the end of the 16th century. Furthermore, English cooking, judging by the earliest printed recipe books which appeared there fully a century before any were published in Scotland, seems to have been as much influenced by developments in France as Scotland itself.

All aspects of the culture of a country develop dynamically when exposed to outside influences. Neighbours, immigrants and invaders enrich the plain fabric of the native garment, creating complex patterns which mingle and intertwine until often their point of origin is lost. This is as true for diet as for art, literature or music. However, in Scotland we find an unusual situation, for with the sea on three sides and a hostile neighbour on the fourth, exposure to foreign elements was both rare and conspicuous. On the one hand, this preserved in astonishing purity the native food and customs of the majority of the population; on the other, it allows us to trace external influences with relative ease – because chronologically and geographically their boundaries are so well defined.

Two main groups of people brought foreign gastronomy to Scotland. First, there were the settlers and traders. Settlers taught not by precept but by example, introducing methods and ingredients which quite naturally entered the culture as integration took place. Traders too made their impact at what might be called the *Cuisine Bourgeoise* level. They came to fetch skins, wool and salt fish, but they brought with them foodstuffs – oil, wine, spices and dried fruits. Often they stayed in the country for several months, either at the port of entry or travelling from town to town. Though their influence was less marked than that of the settlers, the wares they brought quickly became essential ingredients for many traditional dishes. (The last of the breed can still be met today – the 'Onion Johnnies' who make the trip from Brittany each November with hundreds of neatly plaited strings of onions, which they peddle from door to door until the time comes to return to France in February or March to help with the cultivation of the next crop.)

The second group – definable perhaps as courtiers, clerics, and cooks – saw to it that specific dishes and methods were introduced into the repertoire of those who catered for the wealthy. Thus the upper classes continued to enjoy the kind of meals they had experienced when travelling in Europe.

Without doubt the most important settlers, and the first chronologically if we exclude Roman military encampments, were the Scandinavians. By the mid-9th century, colonization of Shetland, Orkney and the Hebrides was well under way, and for the next 500 years some part at least of the Scottish islands was ruled from Norway, though Scandinavian dominance at its fullest extent was of short duration. At the Treaty of Perth in 1266 the Hebrides and the Isle of Man passed to the Scottish crown. Orkney was mortgaged in 1468 as part payment of a dowry. When, three years later, Shetland was added to the mortgage, Norse rule in Scotland came to an end. In many respects, however, the territories retained their Norse character for centuries after. In local law, in systems of land ownership and measurement, in language, and in trade affiliations, the Northern Isles remained more Scandinavian than Scottish until the 19th century. Even today, the voice inflections of islanders make many a Dane or Norwegian feel at home.

From a culinary standpoint, the main Viking contribution, as we have seen, was in teaching the Scots to respond to the great wealth of food in the sea around them. If the origin of the Scots fishing fleet can be ascribed to the Norsemen, so too can the general fondness for fish which becomes evident almost as soon as one crosses the Tweed.

This influence was strongest, naturally enough, in the Northern Isles. There, Nordic elements in the everyday diet survived virtually unchanged until the Second World War. Not only fish dishes, but many made from the two other staple foods, milk and cereals, have names indicating their origin. A few examples will suffice:

Scrae-fish (Old Norse *skreid*): fish dried in the sun
Cuids (Norwegian *kod*, fish-fry): young coalfish stuffed with fish livers
Liver muggies (old Norse *magi*, stomach): cleaned stomachs of fish stuffed with seasoned fish livers and steamed
Vivda (Norwegian dialect *vovde*, leg-muscle): mutton dried without salt in an open stone hut
Bronies (Norwegian *bryne*, a slice): a type of scone, or sometimes a meat patty
Strubba (Norwegian dialect *stroppen*, of a half-brooded egg): coagulated milk whipped until thick

Even when Norway and the Northern Isles parted political company the Scandinavian connection continued. Trade flourished. Norwegian wood for instance provided vital material for ships, houses and furniture in the treeless north until well into the 19th century. As forests elsewhere in Scotland dwindled, demand for foreign timber became more pressing; from the 16th century onward, imports from Sweden, previously insignificant, increased rapidly, bringing in both timber and iron; Scotland exported in return hides and skins, knitted stockings, gloves, wool, mutton, feathers and rabbit skins. Ideas also travelled, and there is an irony (given that the design of Shetland fishing boats had been adapted from the old Viking long-ships) in the interest expressed by Gustaf Vasa, the first king of an independent Sweden, in Scots shipbuilding. When a Scots ship, probably built from Swedish timber tied up in Stockholm harbour in 1550, he wrote to the city governor:

We desire that you cause our shipbuilders minutely to inspect the Scotsmen's ship, and that you have a ship built for us after the same fashion and form as their ship is built.

With the coming of the Reformation a bond of another kind was forged. It was not entirely from mercenary motives that many Scots went to Sweden to fight in the Thirty Years' War. The cause of Protestantism had by that time assumed major importance in both countries, and the similarity of outlook is proved by the fact that many who went to fight stayed and settled, forming a nucleus of Scots-extracted Swedish nobility. Hamiltons, Mastertons, Montgomerys, Murrays, Nisbeths, Setons, Sinclairs and Spens, kept their names unchanged. Clercks, Haijs (Hay), Fersens (MacPherson) had theirs Swedicized.

These constant contacts with northern Europe at many levels introduced the Scots to a very varied culture, though of a limited kind. As Alexander Fenton points out in his book *The Northern Isles: Orkney and Shetland*, culinary influences were seasonal and annually renewed rather than constant. Though Orkney and Shetland were most affected, some gastronomic trends do seem to have spread right through Scotland. One example is the use of mustard with fish, especially with cod. Another is the combination of bacon and fish – particularly interesting since we have here a clear instance of Scandinavian taste over-riding the almost universal taboo by fishermen on the pig and its products.

But Scandinavia was not the only, nor yet even the most important, focus of commercial relations with Northern Europe. From the 15th century onwards, a vigorous trade had existed with the Hanseatic towns, so much so that their merchants came annually to the Northern Isles and Aberdeen, to sell fishing gear, beer, wheat- and rye-flour, barley, tobacco and dried fruit, and to buy salt fish and woollen goods.

Probably the most significant trade of all was with the Netherlands, especially in the 16th and 17th centuries. A few Scots dishes bear Dutch names, or are prepared 'in the Dutch way'; and the availability of cheaper spices and dried fruits brought to Europe by the ships of the Dutch East India Company had a considerable effect on the housewife's baking repertoire. The most important culinary lesson learnt from Holland, as we have seen, was how to pickle herring so that it kept well.

After the Act of Union in 1707, the pattern of trade changed a great deal. Agricultural and economic decline had meant that by 1700 Scotland had little to offer other countries, and could with difficulty buy from them even the most necessary goods. Union with England might, in the opinion of some, be synonymous with exploitation, but at least it afforded a ready and convenient market on the doorstep. The penalty paid was the diminution of European cultural influence, and of Scotland's own cultural independence. Thenceforward a conscious effort was made by the majority of the population to adopt English modes, especially in the area of social life. And for many major enterprises, England was now held to provide the fittest standard of comparison.

An interesting example of this attitude is to be found in an anonymous pamphlet of 1750, designed to educate the agricultural classes and entitled *The Laird and the Farmer*. It takes the form of a dialogue between a traveller and a farmer, and presents a rosy picture of English peasant life:

Trav: You are to consider, that the People in England with their Grass, Hay, Oats and Beans, feeds their Horses, Cattle and Sheep, and with their Oats, Pease, Barley Meal, Milk and other Things proper, feeds Swine, Fowls, Turkeys, Geese and Ducks etc.
Scot: Do not they themselves feed upon Grain as the People in Scotland?
Trav: No, they in general do not, except Bread, and that for the most part is Wheat and Rye.
Scot: What then do they feed upon?
Trav: They feed upon Beef, Mutton, Veal, Pork, all kind of feather'd Fowls, Fish, Fruits commonly baked, Greens, Roots, Butter, Cheese and much Malt Liquor, Cider, Wines and what else is the Produce of the Country . . .

An examination of the *GVA in the Counties of England* (published, like the Scottish volumes, at the end of the century) shows that the difference was less marked than the traveller indicates. At the end of the pamphlet comes a recipe section, consisting for the most part of rather dull dishes, followed by advice on what vegetables to serve with different kinds of meat. Much better, more interesting recipes had already been published in Scotland in Mrs M'Lintock's *Receipts for Cookery and Pastry-Work* (1736), and Elizabeth Cleland just a few years later was also to show that there were plenty of Scots, French and Dutch recipes in circulation. But though Scots cooking did retain some distinctive features in the face of all this pressure, the trend was towards homogeneity with the south.

There were two post-Union trade developments with countries other than England which did make a significant impact on Scottish diet. Both owe their existence to the advantages of Glasgow's geographical position and the fact that by the Treaty of Union Scottish ports were put on the same footing as English ports. In the 18th century Glasgow became the largest sugar importer in Britain, of both raw and refined sugars. The subsequent drop in sugar prices – though the sugar loaf was still locked up in the housewife's press – is the probable origin of the celebrated Scots sweet tooth. Sugar was thought to have medicinal properties, and recipe books of the time show increasing numbers of sweet puddings, cakes, preserves and jams, as well as confectionery.

Tea was the other new commodity which was to transform the habits of the entire population. Tradition has it that it was introduced into the country by Mary of Modena, wife of James II and VII, in 1681 when her husband, as Duke of York, was Lord High Commissioner to the General Assembly of the Church of Scotland. It was an expensive beverage, made more so by taxes and transport costs; in 1705, for example, a shopkeeper in Edinburgh advertised best Bohea at 30s (£1.50) a pound, and green tea at 16s (80p). As a point of comparison, in 1709 a leg of beef cost £3.4s. (£3.20), a stone of butter £3.6s. (£3.30), and Lady Grisell Baillie was paying £1 for six dozen lemons and two dozen oranges.

However, with the founding of the East India Company and the subsequent establishment of British plantations in Assam, prices soon fell sufficiently to allow more widespread distribution. Even so, tea remained something of a luxury in Scotland until the last quarter of the century. The beauty of early tea-caddies, made of finest tin-lined mahogany, each with a lock and key, was proportionate to the value of the treasure they were designed to contain.

Before long the smugglers who contrived to supply Scots with fine claret and cognac at prices which astonished English visitors were adding tea to their wares. An English magazine of 1721, *Applebee's Original Weekly Journal*, wrote of smuggling in the south:

So great a Quantity of Tea is brought up at Ostend, and in Holland, at very low Rates, by our honest Smugglers, and so many new, clever, and successful ways are found of bringing it in Custom-free, that our East India Company need not be at the Trouble to bring any more from China.

and the illicit trade was, if anything, more active north of the border.

Scott, in *Guy Mannering*, put the consumer's point of view:

'Why, Mr Mannering, people must have brandy and tea, and there's none in the country but what comes this way – and then there's short accounts, and maybe a keg or two, or a dozen pounds left at your stable door, instead of a d-d lang account at Christmas from Duncan Robb, the grocer at Kippletringan, who has aye a sum to make up, and either wants ready money or a short-dated bill.'

There was yet another way of looking at the whole affair, as we can read in the *Culloden Papers* of Duncan Forbes, Lord President of the Court of Session in 1742. Deeply concerned at the lack of money in the exchequer ('There is remarkably less coin', he wrote, 'to be met with than ever was at anytime within Memory knowen'), he blamed everything on the popularity of tea.

The Cause of the mischief we complain of is, evidently, the use of Tea; which is now become so common, that the meanest familys, even of labouring people, particularly in Burroughs, make their morning's meal of it, and thereby wholly disuse the ale, which heretofore was their accustomed drink; and the same Drug supplies all the labouring woemen with their afternoon's entertainments, to the exclusion of the Two-penny.

Forbes' proposed solution, had it been implemented, might well have caused severe riots: he wished

by Act of Parliament to prohibit, under sufficient Penaltys . . . the use of Tea amongst that class of Mankind in this Country whose Circumstances do not permit them to come at Tea that pays the duty; and yet whose takeing to run Tea, and deserting the use of Malt Liquor, occasions the Complaint.

In 1784 the offending inequality whereby some tea was taxed and some not, was remedied. All existing tea taxes were repealed, and replaced by a flat rate regardless of price or quality. Far from reducing consumption, this measure increased it, by making tea of reasonable quality accessible to almost all the population. Great ladies, farmers' wives, and village women alike gathered to take their 'four hours' – soon rechristened 'afternoon tea'. Men in general disapproved, probably because they were usually excluded, and there was a veritable storm in a tea-cup over the notion that women, especially working-class women, should drink tea together. Ministers, doctors, teachers, lawyers, moralists, thundered out their criticisms. Tea was said to impair beauty ('the very chambermaids have lost their bloom by supping tea'), cause scurvy, rot teeth, weaken the digestion, and cause paralytic and nervous disorders. Oddly enough, the gentry, who drank tea quite as avidly as their inferiors, were found to be immune from these dreadful consequences.

Even John Galt's minister of the fictitious Ayrshire parish of Dalmailing was uneasy. In *Annals of the Parish*, we find kindly Mr Balwhidder's entry for 1761 reflecting the worries of many a real-life minister:

It was in this year that the great smuggling trade corrupted all the west coast, especially the laigh lands about the Troon and the Loans. The tea was going like the chaff, the brandy like well-water, and the wastrie of all things was terrible. There was nothing minded but the riding of cadgers by day, and excisemen by night – and battles between the smugglers and the king's men, both by sea and land . . .

Before this year, the drinking of tea was little known in the parish, saving among a few of the heritors' houses on a Sabbath evening; but now it became very rife; yet the commoner sort did not like to let it be known that they were taking to the new luxury, especially the elderly women who, for that reason, had their ploys in out-houses and by-places, just as the witches lang syne had their sinful possets and galravitchings; and they made their tea for common in the pint-stoup, and drank it out of caps and luggies, for there were but few among them that had cups and saucers. Well do I remember one night in harvest, in this very year, as I was taking my twilight dauner aneath the hedge along the back side of Thomas Thorl's yard, meditating on the goodness of Providence, and looking at the sheaves of victual on the field, that I heard his wife, and two three other carlins, with their Bohea in the inside of the hedge, and no doubt it had a lacing of the conek [cognac] for they were all cracking like pen-guns. But I gave them a sign, by a loud host, that Providence sees all, and it skailed the bike; for I heard them, like guilty creatures, whispering, and gathering up their truck-pots and trenchers, and cowering away home.

It took several decades for both feminine guilt and male criticism to evaporate. Perhaps the appearance at the tea-table of so many delicious creations to accompany the beverage – scones, tea-breads, cookies, biscuits and cakes – and the gradual admittance of men to the ceremony, helped to change attitudes.

It is now time to leave the traders and return to the settlers. Familiar as we are with the stories of Scots who, having emigrated, congregate to form a Scots community wherever they happen to be, we are apt to forget or ignore that the same thing has happened in Scotland.

Had each group of incomers imposed its diet on the local communities, Scotland could by now claim one of the most varied gastronomies in Western Europe; settlers since the beginning of the 18th century have included glass-makers from Bohemia, weavers from Picardy, miners from Spain and Lithuania, ice-cream vendors from Italy, and pedlars and shopkeepers from India and Pakistan. In effect, of course, all were very much minority groups. Only the two last, because professionally concerned with food, have had a noticeable impact.

Scotland and Italy have been aware of each other's existence since at least 1700, when something like a mania for Italy seized the minds of the educated British. But at the end of the 19th century a rather different relationship between the two countries developed, as scores of Italian peasants left their homeland and travelled to Britain in search of a better life. The Italian population of Scotland rose from 750 in 1890 to 4,500 by 1914. Almost all worked in food shops; and as they realized the need of working-class families (whose members might be out all day, and in whose homes cooking facilities were often limited and primitive) for cheap, filling, ready-cooked food, they made of hot peas, and later, fish and chips, their chief stock-in-trade. Other 'Tallies' introduced ice-cream and the sinful pleasures (in the eyes of the Free Church at least) of the ice-cream parlour. Some shops sold both foods, as the actress Mollie Weir recalls in the first volume of her autobiography, *Shoes were for Sunday*:

In summer-time one of the very nicest ways of trying to fill this space (in our tummies) when we had a ha'penny to spare was at the Tallies. I don't suppose any of us suspected we were abbreviating the word 'Italians' as we raced from school to the Tallies in search of one of the many wonders within its small interior. At that time all the ice-cream in Glasgow seemed to be made by Italians.

In winter we didn't eat ice-cream at all . . . our Tallie went over to hot peas, and no peas cooked at home ever tasted half as good as those bought in that wee shop. A penny bought a cup of 'pea brae' which was actually the thickened water in which the peas had been boiled, liberally seasoned with pepper and a good dash of vinegar. There was always the excitement of maybe finding a few squashed peas at the bottom of the cup, and we would feel about with our spoon, our eyes lighting with joy if we found something solid and knew we had struck gold . . .

The Italian ice-cream parlour and the Italian fish-and-chip shop have become so much a part of Scottish life that it is impossible to exclude either from any survey of the Scottish diet. They made their mark on the fishing industry, on dairy farming, and on potato production. In at least one instance, a sort of gastronomic culture fusion took place: the colours of Clyde football club are represented in that famous Glasgow confection, the MacCallum, consisting of a cone of white ice-cream adorned with a lacing of red raspberry syrup, and named after the club supporter who first thought of it.

The latest of the settlers and traders have been the Asians. By making familiar to the ordinary shopper ingredients which, only twenty years ago, were hardly obtainable, such as aubergines, capsicums, okra, tinned tropical fruit, and the half-forgotten spices beloved by that earlier period of culinary internationalism, the Middle Ages, they have extended the horizon of the Scots cook and consolidated the influence of holidays abroad. In the hands of restaurateurs international cuisine is rarely a joy; but parochialism at the domestic stove is an equal evil. No matter that dishes are sometimes changed beyond recognition. If the diet of future Scots includes curried lamb, aubergine fritters, and okra, so much the better – provided traditional dishes remain in the repertoire. There will be more for culinary historians of the 21st century to write about.

Despite doubts about the nature and extent of the effect of French culinary tradition, there is no question but that France was the most potent influence of them all. Commonly, this influence has been attributed to the effect of the Auld Alliance, that political and cultural relationship between the two nations – expressed in treaties, marriages, ecclesiastical exchanges and trade – which coloured political and court life for several hundred years.

Yet early French intervention in our kitchens, like the Auld Alliance itself, was patchy, intermittent, unevenly distributed, and very much restricted to the upper classes. To understand how it came about, and in which areas it occurred, it is necessary to look for a moment at Scotland's history.

Mythically, the Alliance began in the days of Charlemagne. France enters the chronicles of Scotland in the 11th century, when King Malcolm Canmore took an oath of fealty to William the Conqueror. The immediate effect of this action was negative: the Normans neither over-ran the country nor did they insist on political control, and Norman-French did not (as in England) become the official language. Nevertheless when Malcolm's youngest son David wished to reorganize the country on his accession to the throne in 1124, it was to the Anglo-Norman feudal system that he turned for a model, and the barons whom he invited to settle in south-east Scotland quickly became a powerful force both politically and socially. Among them were men whose names were to become cornerstones of Scottish history: Bruce, Soulis, Murray, Comyn and Lindsay. Furthermore, by persuading French religious houses to establish themselves in Scotland, David secured the supremacy of the Roman rather than the Celtic church. The diocesan network then introduced, and the role of the Church in education, not only helped to stabilize and pacify the diverse elements of the emerging nation, but also weakened the native element in contemporary culture.

David's grandsons continued these policies, when each in his turn became king. They had, after all, a Norman mother, and one, William the Lyon, married a French wife. Both encouraged immigration from France and Flanders to such a degree that an observer commented 'they held only Frenchmen dear and would never love their own people'. By now de Baliols, de Berkelais, de Vescis (Veitch) and de Veres (Weir) had joined the earlier Norman families, and at court the manners, dress and language of the incomers were adopted even by the Scots.

This process of assimilation was brought to a sharp halt by the wars of independence (1286–1371). One consequence was that, though many French words did enter the Scots language before 1286, there was never that thorough penetration which occurred in English. Nor did French influence, confined as it was to the monarch, his immediate entourage, and the Church, permeate society. In the revival of nationalistic feeling which accompanied the struggle for autonomy, much of the recently imported culture was rejected and quickly disappeared.

What remains from that early time? It is difficult to assess, particularly where such humble matters as food and cooking are concerned, for there is very little documentation. Kitchens are conservative places, reluctant to adopt new, foreign, words where a native one is already in use. One looks, therefore, for ingredients and methods which might have been unfamiliar to the Scots; and indeed a few Franco-Scots words seem to be of very ancient origin and may date back to the days of the Canmores. From the early monastery gardens come such words as *syboes*, spring onions (French *ciboulle*); and *groser* or *grosar*, later *grosset*, gooseberry (French *groseille*), both of which are still used today. Two words for cheese appear in the *Fables* of Henryson (c. 1420–90) and it is reasonable to assume that he would not have used them had they not been thoroughly familiar to his readers. *Furmage* (French *fromage*) needs no comment; but *cabok* (which by the 18th century had become *kebbuck*) may well derive, as Francisque Michel has suggested, from *caboche*, a head, since the expression 'heads of cheese' is to be found in the *Rentals and Estate Book of the House of Glenarchy* (1590); on the other hand, it is close to the Gaelic *cabag*. As for words designating methods, the verb to *flamb*, or *flaume*, meaning to baste meat, is also of early date and gives credence to the theory that the Normans introduced the technique of roasting into Scotland. So also does to *broche*, to put on the spit (a word often used, regrettably, when describing what enemies did to each other).

At the end of the 13th century Scotland, already struggling for independence from England, signed the first formal treaty with France. There were to be many more. All were founded on the concept of England as the common enemy. There might be intermittent periods when hostilities ceased – when either France or Scotland thought it expedient to placate the opponent – but in the case of the latter they never lasted long, and from 1295 until the death of Queen Elizabeth I the Auld Alliance was no sentimental conceit but a very real political and military relationship.

Needless to say, it had also cultural elements. A small college established in Paris in 1325 predated the founding of the home universities of St Andrews and Aberdeen, and became a focus for Scots students. For centuries a sojourn in France was considered imperative for those who aspired to real scholarship. Some brought their learning home again, others, like the celebrated Duns Scotus, remained abroad and attracted pupils from many parts of Europe.

Inevitably, too, trading links became increasingly important. When the King 'sat in Dunfermline toun sipping the Blude-red wine' it may well have reached the royal cellars via England or the Netherlands; but by the end of the 13th century Scots merchants were trading direct with French ports, especially Bordeaux, shipping enormous quantities of wine up the Channel and running the gauntlet of the pirates to get it across the North Sea. In 1372 Froissart counted two hundred ships from Scotland, England and Wales lying in Bordeaux harbour waiting to load. By the 17th century, trade with Scotland was sufficiently important to be referred to in a quatrain addressed to a French courtier:

> Tury, vous quittez donc la cour
> Pour vous jeter dans le négoce;
> Ce n'est plus celui de l'amour,
> Mais celui d'Espagne ou d'Écosse.

('Tury, so you're leaving the court to go into business: no longer will you deal in love – your trade henceforward will be with Spain or Scotland.')

However, the connection most important to both countries was undoubtedly military. The French appreciated the excellent fighting qualities of the Scots, who for their part were imbued with such intense antagonism towards the English that they were prepared to fight them anywhere under any circumstances. French accounts of the Hundred Years War constantly record valiant deeds and gifts of land and titles, so that for a time half the French aristocracy was either Scots or of Scots extraction.

Such constant exposure to French ways inevitably resulted in a desire in Scotland for the good life as experienced abroad. We know that James I (1424–37) had a French cook, and many nobles followed his example. But it must be remembered that at the time national and regional differences in cooking were still in their infancy. It was not the cookery of France which was brought back, but that of Europe. Hector Boece, in his *History of Scotland* written at the beginning of the 16th century, hints at this internationalism:

Noch't allanerly ar winis socht in France, bot in Spainy, Italy, and Grece; and sumtime, baith Aphrik and Asia socht for new delicius metis and winis to the samin effect. This is the warld so utterly socht that all manner of droggis and electuaris that may nouris the lust and insolence of pepill are bocht in Scotland with maist sumptuous price, to na less dammage than perdition of the pepill thereof.

In the 15th and 16th centuries, the Alliance was at its most impressive. If the court of France was filled with dukes and counts who on close inspection were discovered to be named Stewart, Hamilton or Douglas, the Scottish kings likewise entertained the French nobility. These latter, however, had not come to stay. They were ambassadors, emissaries, soldiers prepared to fight a few battles and then return home; and – most important of all – often they brought sisters, daughters, or nieces through whose marriages the Franco-Scots connection could be consolidated.

Of all these women, few has had a greater impact on the Scottish imagination than Mary of Guise, the young woman who in 1538 became the second wife of James V. Rosalind Marshall has shown Mary to be a woman of intelligence, firmness of character, and great charm. At the outset she seems to have determined to adopt and be adopted by her husband's country. Accordingly she asked that some Scottish ladies join her household, and set herself to learn Scots. Homesick and missing her young sons (she had recently been widowed), she threw herself nonetheless into the task of adaptation, at the same time introducing much of the French way of life, which appeared to her more civilized than the almost medieval atmosphere of the Scots court.

Her charm and obvious efforts to please captivated Scotswomen, both at court and among the populace. They copied her clothes and imitated the manners of her household. They also took great interest in her food, which, it must be emphasized, was far from the refined and delicate cuisine for which the French later became famous. Indeed, it cannot really be called French food at all. As Barbara Ketcham Wheaton has shown, in *Savouring the Past*, French recipe books of the 16th century reflect without alteration almost all the medieval European traditions. The emphasis was still on the appearance of dishes, designed to be as spectacular and colourful as possible. Few vegetables were eaten, sauces for meat were sweet, thick and spicy, and recipes for showy pies took pride of place.

Visual effects were as important to the medieval diner as flavor – or more so. Relatively few special dishes were served, and their importance derived primarily from their appearance. Vivid colors were highly prized and were often achieved at the expense of flavor . . . The grandest effects were achieved with gold and silver leaf, both still used to garnish festive dishes in India. They are harmless, at least in the quantities people were likely to have eaten, and flavorless . . . The paramount showpieces of the medieval banquet were roast swans and peacocks served sewn back into their skins complete with feathers.

This was banquet food; but lower down the social scale one gets the impression that food was also generously flavoured and spiced, not, as has sometimes been suggested, to disguise a taste of decay, but because spices and sugar, being expensive, acquired value as indicators of social status. Meat was often overcooked, and recooked if not all eaten at one meal. Soups and broths were popular with all classes. Family meals often consisted of one large pot filled with beef, mutton, veal and bacon, cooked with vegetables and herbs. Each member of the family helped himself and what remained was sent back as soup at the next meal, with the meat perhaps served cold.

Nothing here is recognizable as specifically French; on the other hand, it was far removed from the frugal fare of the majority of Scots – and remained so as far as the diet of the peasants was concerned.

For the aristocracy and the merchants, the reign of James V was a prosperous period. James himself, by careful management, had amassed considerable wealth and was prepared to spend it living like a king. His own tastes were frugal, but he kept a full complement of cooks, pastry-cooks, sauciers, carvers, turnspits, and pantrymen. Mary's servants added to the roll, and Mary's preferences and those of her household must have had a significant effect on court diet. Nevertheless, apart from general accounts of lavish and extravagant meals, no documentation allows us to say that this was the period at which French dishes entered the Scottish repertoire. It is all only oral tradition.

The fact is that although France was never so popular, nor so fashionable, as in Mary's early days, this period lasted for only about four years. After James's death following the defeat of the Scots at Solway Moss, Mary's position vis-à-vis both nobles and commoners changed dramatically. As the nobility struggled for control of the Regency, and Mary's advisers plotted to turn the country into a colony of France, the first stirrings of Protestantism and rationalism were making themselves felt. Over the next eighteen years, until Mary's death, admiration of the former ally was replaced by growing hostility. It is most unlikely, under the circumstances, that French cooking should have acquired real and lasting popularity.

In 1561 Mary Stuart arrived in Leith Harbour to claim the Scottish crown. Her story is too well known to need recapitulation, and the period of importance for culinary history comprises only the first few relatively stable and peaceful years of her reign, when the predominantly French character of the court was most marked in manners and the rituals of daily life.

We are still in the 16th century and the dishes have not changed much. Spices are still used but sugar, though very expensive, is becoming an important ingredient. Little cakes and sweet pastries are popular. It has become the fashion in France, as in the whole of Europe, no longer to put all the food on the table at once, but to have several courses, and to finish the meal by moving to another room to eat fresh or preserved fruit and little sweetmeats. While this is done, the tables are cleared, or *desservies*; the word dessert appears in Scots usage as early as the 1590s, a hundred years before it enters the language of the English.

Faced with a turbulent court of ambitious nobles vying for her favours, Mary found herself in a somewhat similar position to that of her mother-in-law across the water, and she may well have tried to imitate Catherine's tactics. The latter's stratagem, intended to distract and dissipate the energies of unruly courtiers, was the creation of great set entertainments which were also meals. Ceremonial pageants and dances of the most elaborate nature were designed, in which the court took part before dining on an ornate collation of rich and beautiful dishes. Mary could not quite do likewise – her Protestant subjects would have been outraged. But she could, and did, encourage an extravagant way of life. Perhaps there was no policy behind the frivolity, perhaps it was merely an attempt to recreate the gaiety and lavish atmosphere in which she had spent her teenage years. At all events, the admonishments she must have expected were not long coming, especially from her mother's arch-enemy John Knox, who had a special interest in how money was spent. Years later he wrote that 'the affairs of the Kytcheing were so gryping, that the mynestris stipendis could nocht be payit'.

Extravagant spending continued even after the queen's departure from Scotland. Shortages of food were always blamed (as in other countries) on the self-indulgence of the aristocracy. In a sense, this was correct; but it was not so much what they ate, as the extortionate rents which they imposed upon their tenants in order to export the produce of their estates, which accounted for the wretched state of the poor. French influence may indeed have been at work here, for the French nobility were accustomed to treat lower classes with scant respect, regarding them simply as suppliers of labour and food. Froissart had written that Frenchmen trying to impound provisions from the Scots peasantry were astonished to encounter not only refusals but retaliation. But now Scots nobles had learnt French habits, and eagerly sought to outdo each other in a sumptuous life-style, by whatever means they could.

Towards the end of the 16th century we find observers complaining as Boece had done, but with more hope of being heard, for the Reformation was creating an ascetic climate which, even in France, was beginning to chill the air. There, a writer in 1574 criticized diners for their wastefulness:

People are not satisfied in an ordinary meal to have three ordinary courses, the first of boiled things, the second of roast, and the third of fruit; it is also necessary for a meat to be served five or six ways, with so many sauces, hashes, pastries, with so many kinds of salmagundis and other varied motley oddities as to make great prodigality.

Jean Bodin, *Discours sur les causes de l'extreme cherte qui est aujourd'huy en France et sur les moyens d'y remedier.* (Quoted in Barbara Ketcham Wheaton, *Savouring the Past.*)

These uneasy stirrings of conscience resulted in a rash of sumptuary laws passed in all the countries affected by the Reformation. In Scotland, the Privy Council of 1550 appointed a Commission whose recommendations included food rationing based on class distinction: archbishops, bishops, and earls were allowed no more than eight dishes at their tables; lords, abbots, priors and deans were limited to six; barons and freeholders might have four, and burgesses three. There was not to be more than one kind of meat at each course. Entertaining foreigners was allowed, but no Scot might invite any other to dine save on his name day or on recognized feast days. How effective these measures were, may be judged from the fact that repeatedly until the end of the century new Acts were passed to try to prevent 'superfluous banqueting'.

The Kirk was working to bring men to a soberer turn of mind, an attitude which suited the temperament of Mary Stuart's son and successor James VI. The powerful but narrow sphere of French influence was being replaced by a more reflective general approach and an intensely nationalistic feeling which affected religion, politics, commerce and education. If there were links abroad they were now chiefly with the Netherlands and with Sweden, although a number of Scots Roman Catholics sought refuge in France, while the Huguenot colleges played host to Scots who lectured in the new theology. However, Catholic and Protestant alike continued to import French wines and to regard France as the arbiter of manners and fashion – and food. 'In the best houses,' wrote a French visitor in 1661, 'they dress their victuals after the French method.'

What this means is none too clear, though French cooking had undergone considerable changes since the previous century. Many new foods had been introduced: turkeys, Jerusalem artichokes, potatoes, tea, coffee and chocolate. There was greater interest in vegetables. Pork was less popular, and creatures such as swans, peacocks, wild geese, whale and wild lampreys virtually vanished from the table. In the great French households the head cook was an increasingly important man. His kitchen, like an efficient factory, produced basic components which could be combined in various ways. Two stocks, one brown, one white; a repertoire of sauces thickened either with almonds and egg yolks or with flour; several kinds of herb-flavoured or spiced stuffings; these were the elements from which a cook could devise dishes of meat, fish, eggs or even vegetables. All was logic and order. But although herbs and spices were less indiscriminately used, subtlety of flavour now being the aim, the food of the rich – *haute cuisine* in embryo – still consisted of expensive ingredients presented in elaborate set pieces.

By contrast, a new attitude was emerging among the French middle class, who were beginning to acquire small properties of their own, where they could cultivate fruit and vegetables, keep a cow for milk and cheese, fatten poultry and pigeons. For them, the pleasure of growing one's own food and eating it, cooked simply but well, was a new experience, and it led to a new kind of cooking, *cuisine bourgeoise*. Nicolas de Bonnefons put it clearly in a passage which no doubt gives devotees of today's *nouvelle cuisine* a strong sense of *déja vu*:

> A cabbage soup should taste entirely of cabbage; a leek soup of leeks; a turnip soup of turnips; and thus for the others, leaving the *compositions* for bisques, hashes, *panades*, and other made dishes . . . (Let us leave to foreigners many of the depraved ragouts; they never enjoy good fare except when they have cooks from France.)

There is a strong similarity here with the outlook expressed in John Reid's *The Scots Gard'ner*, published in 1683 – 30 years after Bonnefons' *Délices de la Campagne* (from which this quotation is taken).

French cooking, in effect, was at last becoming recognizably different from that of other nations. We can see also from the Bonnefons extract that it was not uncommon for French cooks to take the new doctrine abroad.

During the 17th century both England and Scotland had taken France for a cultural model. But it became clear that the latter country still considered hers to be a special relationship. Jacobitism was almost entirely a Scottish movement; and it was based no less on growing anglophobia than on support for the Stuarts. For some time an undercurrent of resentment had existed, against English politicians and merchants who were determined to monopolize the lucrative West Indian trade in tobacco and sugar. Scottish interests were ignored, and the failure of the Darien scheme caused much bitterness. Although many Lowland Scots were in favour of Parliamentary union, believing it to be economically necessary, by the time Defoe toured the country in 1707, most Scots, especially the Highlanders, detested the English. Defoe's party found it convenient, often, to make believe they were French rather than English.

Thus, it was in the late 17th and 18th centuries, and not, as is often claimed, in the 16th, that French cooking really began to influence the Scots kitchen. It was a phenomenon which had its parallel in England, but Jacobite traffic between Scotland and France must have encouraged the adoption of the French techniques and recipes which were now regarded as the height of gastronomic perfection. Wealthy families all over Britain, if they had fashionable pretensions, acquired French cooks, but in Scotland the return of exiles from France introduced the new cuisine at a more domestic level.

There is ample evidence to support this claim for much later French influence than has been supposed. First, we have the slow development of French national cuisine itself, remembering not only the late appearance of any refinements in cooking over an open fire but also the fact that until at least the middle of the 17th century only the very largest households had their own ovens. Ordinary families either took food along to the baker who would set it in his oven, or cooked small pies by placing a pot on a tripod over glowing coals, with more coals on the lid. In Scotland, where most of the fuel consisted of wood or peat, even this would have been difficult. Thus the biscuits and little cakes so often thought to have come into the country in the 16th century simply did not appear in France until almost the 17th, and the first mention of anything similar in Scotland occurs in the 1700s.

Secondly, it is possible to trace the growth of French influence through the recipe books, allowing for a gap of perhaps 20 years between the first appearance of a dish and its inclusion in a book. The first known Scottish collection of recipes, the appendix to *The Scots Gard'ner* nowhere refers to a knowledge of France or French methods – a claim which, if there had been any grounds for it, Reid would surely have been anxious to make. The two next earliest recipe books are Lady Castlehill's manuscript *Receipt Book*, dated 1712, and Mrs M'Lintock's *Receipts for Cookery and Pastry-work* published in 1736.

Manuscript collections and printed cookery books of the same period complement each other in much the same way that a personal diary complements official history books. Manuscript recipes present a narrow and circumscribed view. They deal only with what the writer herself knows, recording dishes in actual use or those which she intends to try because she has tasted them. They reflect fairly closely, therefore, the diet of a very small group of people, and their chief virtue is fidelity to life. Their defect is that they reveal little general truth about the diet of a population or even of a social class.

Printed books represent a wider view. In them we see counsels of perfection, but the ingredients and methods used tell us also much about what was possible, and fashionable, at the time of the book's publication. They are likely to reproduce well-known recipes with popular appeal, but they may also introduce unfamiliar ones. From printed books it is possible to deduce the movement of taste.

What we see when we examine the recipes of Lady Castlehill and Mrs M'Lintock, is a cuisine still in many respects attached to the medieval tradition, lavish with cream, eggs, almonds, spices and wine, and still paying considerable attention to the garnishing of dishes. Though earlier, the Castlehill manuscript, perhaps because of its firmly domestic character, seems slightly more modern in approach than Mrs M'Lintock; the recipes are relatively simple and there are no 'set pieces'. A number of dishes are cooked 'in the French way', and there are the 'friggassys', 'ragoos', and 'compoos' which we associate with 18th-century kitchens. There are some recipes for biscuits and for confectionery, but these show more English than French influence, as can be seen from the names of her sources. Not one of the standard Franco-Scottish dishes is included, and medieval influence is evident in the quantity of candied and preserved fruit recipes, as well as in those for Mead, Metheglin, and Hippocras.

Mrs M'Lintock is distinctly more old-fashioned and insular. She does give a recipe (remarkably accurate, suggesting that it had not been long in the country) for 'Beef Alamode, the French Way', and instructions 'to boil Ducks, the French way'; on the whole, though, her recipes are more elaborate and stylized than Lady Castlehill's. She too is singularly deficient in the Franco-Scottish dishes and in the use of terms which we would expect had there been any marked French influence earlier. Most illustrative of this deficiency is her recipe 'to dress a Leg' (note, not a Gigot) 'of Mutton', which has a strongly medieval character:

Take and skin an Hind-Leg of Mutton, take all the flesh from the Bones, put them on the fire, with a Mutchkin of Water to be Strong Broth for your Collops; save some of the Meat for Collops, shear all the rest very small, season the Meat with black Pepper, Jamaica Pepper, Nutmeg, Salt, then put it in the skin again, you may either bake it or rost it, then fry your collops, force Meat Balls, and take the strong Broth and toss up the Gravy with a little Bread to thicken it, Cucumbers, Capers, Oysters, Mushrooms, Anchovies; lay the leg of Mutton in the Middle of the Dish, and forced Meat Balls round about, and serve it to the Table.

Further evidence of the slow development of the French contribution comes in household accounts, diaries, autobiographies, and memoirs. Lady Grisell Baillie's *Household Book*, covering the period 1692–1733 mentions fricassées (spelt variously friassy, friasy, and friascy), 'ragows' and 'bisket'. She also uses the French 'canelle' instead of English 'cinammon'. The *Ochtertyre House Book* (1737–39) also reveals a cuisine firmly Scots, apart from the tautological entry, occurring several times, of an 'omlit of eggs', and an occasional fricassée of rabbit or tripe. As the century progresses, however, we find David Hume boasting of his ability to make *Soupe à la Reine* (1769); Elizabeth Grant of Rothiemurchus, describing Edinburgh life in the 1790s, mentions the almost universal use in fashionable kitchens of Menon's *La Cuisine Bourgeoise*, 'the best French cookery book then known'. Johnson and Boswell, when they visited Skye, had two meals within three days and only a few miles apart from each other: the first was 'an ill-dressed dinner', without claret or wheat-bread but with a liver-pudding (haggis?), broth, and badly baked bannock; the second was served on a table with cloth, napkins, china and silver, with food which would not have disgraced the politest French society. Lord Cockburn, writing of a slightly later time, asserted that 'the dinners themselves were much the same as at present. Any difference is in a more liberal adoption of the cookery of France.'

Finally, there is the evidence of terminology itself. The two best-known Scots words borrowed from French are 'ashet', meaning a flat or slightly hollow dish for serving meat, and 'gigot', a leg of mutton or lamb. Their derivation is unquestionable. 'Ashet' comes from 'assiette' and 'gigot' of course is unchanged. What has to be examined is the date at which these words entered the Scots language.

Surprisingly, the first Scottish use of 'ashet' seems to be in Lady Grisell Baillie's *Household Book*. On 20th November 1722, describing a dinner at Lord Carlisle's house, she mentions 'Five Ashiets', which comprised the third course: '3 teel, squab pigeons, scolloped oysters, fryd smelts, and buttered scorzonera or something of that kind hartichoes cut in thin slices will do better it was cream bet up with butter was on it'. In 1725 ashets appear again; 'one ashet in each salt tung w^t red cabbage and sausages and boyld Turkie with salary sauce', and at the second course of the same meal, '2 ashets on each side'. Thereafter the word occurs so frequently and on so many occasions that it really seems as though ashets had suddenly become *de rigueur* for every fashionable meal. If we consult Huguet's monumental *Dictionnaire de la langue francaise du 16e siècle*, we find that *assiette* had a number of meanings in the 16th century, none of which corresponds to either the modern French or the traditional Scots usage. *Assiette* could mean:

1. The act of placing, putting in position, or setting down;
2. A place where people stop, or wait;
3. The table at which people sit;
4. A course in a meal;
5. *tenir assiette* meant to serve food and drink.

Like a butterfly emerging from its cocoon, *assiette* is moving before our eyes from its original associations with place to those with meals and food. But not until the 17th century does it arrive at its present form. Nicolas de Bonnefons was one of the first to use it in the modern way:

Les assiettes des conviés seront creuses, afin que l'on puisse se presenter du potage et s'en servir à soi-même, sans prendre cuillerée dans le plat. (*Délices de la Campagne*, 5th edition, 1673)
The diners' plates should be concave, so that they may put soup in them, from which they help themselves without being obliged to eat it spoonful by spoonful from the pot.

So far, so good. These concave *assiettes* bear a tolerable resemblance to the ashet for serving meat.

A puzzling entry in the *OED*, however, lists ashet as a northern dialect word, of which the first known use occurs in a church inventory of 1552, which mentions an 'asset of sylver'. There are two points about this; first, we do not know the precise meaning of the word in this context, and second, although the date given is 1552, it comes from Peacock's *English Church Furniture*, written much later. What is certain, is that nowhere in any household inventory, recipe, or description of meals, does the word appear in Scotland before 1722. Had it been in general use much before that date, surely, somewhere, a written record would have been found?

'Gigot' offers similar surprises. In accounts kept while the first Marquis of Montrose (then the Earl) attended St Andrews University in 1628 and 1629, the word is found once. The usual Scottish phrase well into the 18th century, however, is 'ane leg of mutton', or 'ane quarter of mutton'. Lady Grisell Baillie speaks simply of 'rost mutton', 'leg rost mutton', or 'boyld lame', while at Ochtertyre the household often ate 'mutton boyld joints', or 'mutton rost joints'. Huguet defines *gigot* as the extremities of an animal and its diminutive *gigoteau*, as those meaty extremities which could be eaten. In England, the word was used in the *Household Ordinance* of 1526 (1790 edition): 'giggots of mutton or venison, stopped with cloves'. Gervase Markham's *English Housewife* (1615) has a particularly interesting instruction for roasting 'a Giggot of mutton', which includes a definition: 'is the legge splatted and halfe part of the Loin together'. The suggestion here is clearly that 'gigot' was a special cut which might be unfamiliar to the reader.

Mrs Maciver's *Cookery and Pastry-Making* (Edinburgh 1773) is the first Scots recipe book to use the term, in a recipe where she recommends the cook to 'cut off the loin, and boil the gigot'. If this way of dividing the joint replaced an older cut, we have a valid explanation of how a foreign word came to supplant a native term.

The 19th century saw a gradual merging of Scots and English cookery until they are undifferentiated in the recipe books, for example those of Meg Dods (1826) and Eliza Acton (1845). Both countries continued to borrow from the French and, in both, to have a French chef was the height of sophistication. But the borrowings were always just that. No longer was there the former assimilation of ideas, words, or recipes. It was all at a superficial level. The French language, culture, and style, had become for most people rather remote – to be learnt in the schoolroom, no longer a part of family atmosphere, as once in Scotland (for what was admittedly a very small social class) they had been.

A story told of the Frenchman John Bayle, a celebrated innkeeper and vintner in Edinburgh towards the end of the 18th century, perhaps illustrates the change more tellingly than any further comment:

Previous to setting up in Edinburgh as a vintner and tavern keeper, he had been in private service as chef to General Scott of Balgonie, in Fife . . . having crossed the Forth, he hired a gig at Kinghorn, but the very indifferent roads were almost impassable owing to heavy falls of snow, and further discomfort arose from the fact that he was unable to speak English so as to be understood by his driver. Having proceeded many miles, the horse became knocked up, and could go no further. They were close to the residence of Mr Durham, of Largo, a very hospitable laird, and to this house M. Bayle was conducted to ask shelter for the night. With a good address, and the agreeable manners of a Frenchman, Bayle was introduced to Mr Durham as a gentleman going to Balgonie. Neither the laird nor any of his family spoke, or understood but imperfectly, any French, but after repeated bowings Bayle introduced himself, saying: 'Monsieur, j'ai l'honneur d'être chef de cuisine à M. le General Scott, et je suis en route à son château, mais malheureusement il fait un temps si orageux que je viens d'être arrêté en route.' The honest laird seized upon the expression 'chef de cuisine', which he translated to himself as chief cousin, or first cousin, to General Scott, and shaking M. Bayle warmly by the hand, he expressed himself delighted at the fortunate circumstance which had brought under his roof so near a relative of his good friend and neighbour. Refreshments were produced, and the bewildered Frenchman was introduced to the ladies in the drawing-room as their neighbour's cousin.

Later on he was conducted to a bedroom, from which he descended next morning greatly refreshed, and after indulging in a hearty Scottish breakfast, he rose to continue his journey, but to his further astonishment, he found the laird's own carriage waiting to convey him to his 'cousin's' residence.

P.B. Ainslie, *Reminiscences of a Scottish Gentleman.*

— RECIPES —

Many Scandinavian-based recipes have been cited in the chapter on the sea. Two more fish recipes are so good and so popular that they deserve a place here.

Salt Herring

Off the West Highland coast some people still preserve their own herrings in the old way – though nowadays a plastic tub is more likely to be the container than a wooden barrel.

You need very fresh herring, gutted but with the heads left on, and a quantity of coarse salt.

Into the container shovel a layer of salt, then put in a layer of fish, bellies down, but slightly on their sides. Cover with salt, put in another layer of fish lying in the opposite direction. Fill the container thus, leave for a few days, then take fish as you need them.

Herrings thus preserved may be washed, soaked overnight in cold water, then simmered gently in fresh water and eaten with boiled jacket potatoes. Or you may make herring salad (a Dutch dish):

Herring Salad

5 medium-sized onions
3 herrings
12 peppercorns
1 bay leaf
pepper
vinegar to cover

Wash, skin and bone the herrings by pressing gently all along the backbone until it is loosened, then filleting with a sharp knife. Cut the fish into neat pieces, and put these in a dish alternately with sliced onion. Add the peppercorns and bay leaf, cover with vinegar (you may dissolve a teaspoon of sugar in this if you wish), sprinkle with pepper, and allow to stand overnight. It is then ready for eating.

Cod with mustard sauce is a favourite throughout Scotland. The recipe could be either Scandinavian or Dutch. Scandinavians like a bland sauce made with cream and just a hint of mustard. Scots adapted the dish to their taste, making the sauce stronger and always cooking parsley with the cod.

Cod with Mustard Sauce (Scandinavian style)

1½ lb (750g) cod fillets
⅓ pt (200 ml) water
⅓ pt (200 ml) milk
a good handful of parsley, washed and chopped
1 tablespoon flour
2 tablespoons butter
salt (about ½ tablespoon) and pepper
1 tablespoon cream or top milk
1 teaspoon or more mustard powder

Put the water, milk and parsley into a wide, rather shallow pan, add seasoning and fish. Bring gently to a simmer and poach the cod for about five minutes.

Meanwhile, melt the butter and add the flour in another pan. When the cod is cooked, lay it aside in a warm platter; drain its liquor into a jug and add this slowly to the butter and flour, stirring well. When all the liquid has been added and the sauce is simmering, blend the mustard in a cup with a tablespoon of cream or milk, and add it to the sauce. Check the seasoning, pour the sauce over the dish, and serve immediately.

In all Northern Europe, cabbage was an important item of diet. In Orkney kail and cabbage were grown in *planticrues*, raised beds surrounded by a wall to keep out the cattle. Sometimes the cabbage was preserved, sauerkraut-style, sometimes it was simply boiled and eaten with butter. Orkney Pork and Kale (the word here signifies any type of greens) was made originally with pickled pork. Nevertheless it bears a strong resemblance, both in method and use of seasonings, to the Norwegian *Far I Kal* (Mutton in cabbage). The dish is not found elsewhere in Britain, and I think it quite likely that it is a variant of *Far I Kal*.

Orkney Pork and Kale

1 lb (450g) fresh pork, cut into small cubes
1 small cabbage
1 oz (25g) butter
1 lb (450g) potatoes *or* 1 oz (25g) flour
peppercorns
dill seeds
salt

Slice the cabbage and the potatoes, if used. At the bottom of a
heavy saucepan put butter or pieces of pork fat, then layers of
meat and cabbage with a few slices of potato or a sprinkling of
flour, 2–3 peppercorns, and a few dill seeds between each layer.
Add enough water or stock to come about halfway up, then
season with salt and bring to the boil. Cover and simmer very
gently for about 1½ hours, checking occasionally that the liquid
has not boiled away. Serve very hot.

For a long time I associated Fricadellans with *fricandeau*, a French
word used either of a rump of veal or fillets of tuna fish. In
Switzerland it is also the standard word for Beef Olives. However,
Fricadellans are neither French nor Swiss. They are Danish. *Frikadeller* are a national passion in Denmark, though other Scandinavians like them too. They may be made from different kinds of meat
and seasoned in a number of ways.

Meg Dods's recipe uses veal, with veal suet and stock. I have
adapted the recipe for beef or pork (or a mixture of the two), since
veal is not popular in Britain, as well as being almost impossible to
mince in small quantities.

Fricadellans

1 lb (450g) minced meat
6 oz (150g) suet
2 egg yolks
2 oz (50g) dried breadcrumbs
¼ pt (125 ml) cream

salt and pepper
1 chopped onion
nutmeg
a little grated lemon peel
2 oz (50g) butter
1 oz (25g) flour
about 1 pt (500 ml) good beef stock

Mix together all ingredients except the last three, then with wet hands shape the mixture into round balls.

Poach these in boiling water for four minutes, then lift out and drain. In a large frying pan melt the butter, add the flour, and gradually stir in the stock. Drop the meatballs into this gravy, and simmer for about half an hour. Garnish the dish with slices of lemon. 'The sauce,' says Mrs Dods, 'ought to be very thick.'

Sassermaet Bronies are another type of meatballs popular with the old Vikings. They combined the poorer cuts of meat (which were minced, spiced, and salted for storage in a cool place) with better meat, freshly minced. Margaret Stout, in her *Cookery for Northern Wives* (1925) gave the standard recipe which will interest traditionalists, though it is unlikely nowadays that anyone should want to pickle 12 lb of meat at a time.

Sassermaet (Saucermeat)

A mixture of spices in the following proportion is first made:
¼ oz allspice
¼ oz cloves
¼ oz ginger
¼ oz white pepper
¼ oz black pepper
⅛ oz mace
⅛ oz Jamaica pepper
⅛ oz cinnamon
This along with 6 oz salt, will season 12lb minced meat.

Saucermeat Bronies

1 lb (500g) saucermeat
1 lb (500g) minced steak
1 teacupful breadcrumbs
1 tablespoon chopped onion
pepper and salt
egg or milk to moisten

Mix all thoroughly together with the hand in a basin: form into cakes about ½ in (¾ cm) thick; fry on both sides in smoking hot fat; reduce heat and allow to cook through more slowly for 10–15 minutes; drain and serve hot.

Here are Catherine Brown's adapted quantities in her excellent version, taken from *Scottish Regional Recipes*.

1 lb (500g) minced beef
1 oz (25g) breadcrumbs
1 egg
1 small onion, finely chopped

Seasoning mixture:

1 level dessertspoon salt
a large pinch of the following:
mixed spice, freshly ground black pepper, white pepper,
    ground cloves, and cinnamon
oil or butter for frying

Put the minced beef, breadcrumbs, egg and onions into a large bowl. Make up the seasoning mixture and mix all the other ingredients.

Put some flour onto a board. Divide the mixture into 4 and shape into round patties 1 in (2½ cm) thick, coating with flour to prevent them sticking.

Melt oil or butter in a frying pan and fry them gently for 5–10 minutes on both sides.

Semantically, Bronies and Brunnies may or may not be related. *Bronies* comes from *bryne*, a slice of bread or cake, whereas *brunnie* is supposed to derive from *brun*, brown. Perhaps brunnies should be called Brun Bronies. They are a type of fatless girdle scone, very good when freshly made.

Brunnies

8 oz (250g) wheaten flour
½ teaspoon baking soda
¾ teaspoon cream of tartar
½ teaspoon salt
buttermilk or sour milk to mix

Preheat the girdle. Mix the dry ingredients, then add buttermilk to make a soft dough. Turn onto a floured board, dust with flour, and roll out gently to ½ in (1 cm) thick. Cut in squares or rounds, bake for about 5–10 minutes each side.

We have seen that it was from Holland that the Scots acquired the art of preserving herring so that it kept for a long time. A few other recipes testify to the close links between the two countries. Elizabeth Cleland gives her readers instructions for preserving beef in the Dutch manner, and a recipe for cod with mustard sauce which is rather different from the Scandinavian one above.

To crimp Cod the Dutch Way

1 pt (500 ml) water
2 oz (50g) salt
8 thinly cut cod steaks
parsley

Bring the water and salt to the boil, then put in the fish and simmer for 4 minutes only. Drain the slices, and dish them with raw parsley round them.

'They are eaten with oil, mustard, and vinegar'; a traditional Scandinavian mustard sauce for salt fish fits the bill nicely.

Mustard Sauce

9 tablespoons olive oil
3 tablespoons white vinegar
2½ tablespoons prepared mustard
salt and pepper

Combine the ingredients and blend thoroughly, at least two hours before eating. Just before putting the sauce on the table whisk it again with a fork.

The best-known Dutch recipe in Scots kitchens, though it is now, alas, rarely made, is that for Crulla. It comes from Aberdeenshire, where Dutch influence was once strong. American *crullers* were also taken to the US by Dutch immigrants; however, they are richer and more highly flavoured than the Scotch variety.

Aberdeen Crulla

2 oz (50g) butter
2 oz (50g) sugar
1–2 eggs
7–8 oz (225–250g) self-raising flour
oil, lard or suet for frying.

Cream the butter and sugar, then add the egg. (Use two eggs if you want a richer mixture, but then you will have to increase the amount of flour.) Mix in enough flour to make a dough stiff enough to roll out. Turn onto a floured surface and knead till smooth, then divide into 6 or 7 pieces and roll into thick oblong shapes about 4 in (10 cm) long. Leaving one end intact, cut the rest of each piece into three strips. Wet the edges and plait the strips, then seal the ends with a little water. Have ready a deep pan of hot oil or lard, into which the crulla are dropped. When golden brown all over, lift them out. Sprinkle with sugar, and drain on kitchen paper.

In the 17th and 18th centuries a number of Scots went to Poland, to serve as mercenaries or to trade. What adventurer brought back the following recipe we shall never know, but there it is in Mrs Cleland's book, testifying to one man's curiosity and interest in foreign food. I have not cooked this recipe at the time of writing, but I intend to do so, for it sounds good. (Neat is an old word for a cow, bull or ox; calf or ox tongue would be used.)

A Neat's Tongue the Polish Way

Blanch off the Skin and boil it, cut it in two but not quite off; stick it with slices of preserved Lemon, and Bits of Cinnamon: then put a bit of Sugar, a Glass of white Wine, and a little Gravy: then let the Tongue stew a while, and dish it with the Sauce about it.

Of French recipes, the one which has most claim to be an early import is *Soupe à la Reine*. A French recipe book of the late 16th century contains a version which is said to have been served every Thursday at the court of Marguerite de Valois, who was queen from 1589 to 1610. From this circumstance the soup derived its name; so if it was brought to Scotland by Mary Stuart, it must have been under another title. The first Scottish reference I can find is in a letter from the philosopher David Hume to his friend Sir Gilbert Elliot (the superscription is Edinburgh 16th October, 1769). Hume declares his intention of settling for good in Edinburgh, and of devoting the rest of his life to displaying his 'great talent for cookery': 'I have just now lying on the table before me,' he writes, 'a receipt for making Soupe á la Reine, copied with my own hand.'

Unfortunately he does not describe it; but we have no lack of recipes, among which Meg Dods's, though very much later in date, approximates closely to the 16th-century French version.

The Old Scots White Soup or *Soupe à la Reine*

    1 knuckle veal
    1 boiling fowl, or two chickens
    ¼ lb (100g) bacon
    lemon-thyme
    2 onions
    1 carrot
    1 small head of celery
    1 white turnip
    few white peppercorns
    1 blade of mace
    macaroni or vermicelli or French roll
    water

Take a large knuckle of the whitest veal, well broken and soaked, a white fowl skinned, or two chickens, a quarter-pound of well-coloured lean undressed bacon, lemon-thyme, onions, carrot, celery, and a white turnip, a few white peppercorns, and two blades of mace. Boil for about two hours; skim repeatedly and carefully during that time. When the stock is well tasted, strain it off. It will form a jelly. When to be used, take off the surface fat, clear off the sediment, and put the jelly into a tin saucepan or stewpan well tinned; boil for half an hour, and serve on a couple of rounds of a small French roll; or with macaroni, previously soaked, and stewed in the soup till perfectly soft, or vermicelli.

Lady Clark gives a typically Edwardian version (though she calls it an Old Scotch recipe), as served at the Roxburghe Hotel in Edinburgh. I quote it partly to show how debased Scots cooking had become, but also because provided real chicken stock (not bouillon cubes) is used, it is really very good, though hardly Nouvelle Cuisine.

Chicken Soup No. 1, 'à la Reine' (Roxburghe Hotel 1887)

This is an old Scotch recipe. Two quarts (2½ l) of good strong chicken stock; cut and add 1 carrot, 1 head of celery, 2 onions, 1

sprig marjoram, a blade of mace, and some whole white pepper.
Boil 15 minutes and strain, through a hair sieve.

To thicken it, have butter and flour in a stewpan, and cook
them together, first 10 minutes or more, to take off the raw
flavour of the flour, then add the purée to it, and bring to
the boil.

Warm well a teacupful of sweet cream and put into a well-
heated tureen, pouring in the soup and stirring it gently round.

Friar's chicken is another delightfully named Scots dish ascribed to
French influence. Confusingly, a servant named John MacDonald,
whose *Memoirs of an 18th Century Footman* were edited and
published in 1927, describes the soup in 1725 – he is the first to do
so, but calls it *Queen of Scots Soup*. Boswell, in the *Journal of a
Tour to the Hebrides* (6th September 1773), names the dish but
does not describe it, referring vaguely to 'I believe a dish called
fried chicken or something like it'; this however could not have
been fried chicken as fricassee of fowl was served at the same time.
Usually the 12th-century monks are given the credit for this one,
and it would be pleasant to prove the validity of the claim.
Unfortunately, no trace of any similar French soup exists. The
nearest European equivalent is the classic Roman soup *Stracciatelle*.
Could an Italian, having joined a French monastic order and being
sent, by chance, to Scotland, have brought with him the recipe?
This is being too romantic. If that were the case, surely, Lady
Castlehill (whose manuscript receipt book dates from 1713), or
Lady Grisell Baillie, or Mrs M'Lintock, or Eliza Cleland, would at
the very least mention it. I think it most probable that some of the
many Scots who visited Italy in the late 17th and early 18th
centuries (among them incidentally, the Baillies) lodged, as was
customary, with some monks and were in this way introduced to
the dish.

John MacDonald's book is well worth reading. His recipe, like
himself, is straightforward and uncomplicated, with just sufficient
detail to be clear and interesting. The quantity is vast, but proportions are easily adjusted.

Queen of Scots Soup (Friar's Chicken)

Queen of Scots Soup is made in the manner following. Six chickens are cut in small pieces, with the heart, gizzard, and liver well washed, and then put into a stewpan, and just covered with water and boiled until the chickens are cooked enough. Season it with salt and cayenne pepper, and mince parsley with eight eggs, yolks and whites beat up together. Stir round all together just as you are going to serve it up. Half a minute will boil the eggs.

MacDonald made this soup for his employers in many places, for he travelled a great deal; he tells us that chickens, parsley and eggs were usually easy to find, but that he always travelled with his own supply of cayenne pepper.

Lady Castlehill's Veal Olives are closer to forcemeat balls, or Frikadeller, than to our modern notion of Beef Olives. But her recipe originates in France.

To make Olives the French Way

Take a Piece of the Fillet of Veal according to the quantity yew desire to make, a Marrow bone, or half ane one, a little Beef Suet with as much of Lard or Sweet Bacon; mince these togither with a mincing Knife; season them with white Pepper and Salt, 3 or 4 Cloves, with a little Parsley and Tyme and a little Sprig of Winter Savory; mince them all togither; after they be very small, take one or two yolks of Eggs very weell beaten, and mixe them alltogether, and so Mince them againe for a little while; Then make them up in Balls, or Olives. You may adde to it some Mushrooms, Hartichokes, the tops of Sparagus, and hard yolks of Eggs, Sweet Breads and lambstones. Then afterwards take ane Earthen Pipkine with fresh and good Broth, and let them boile leisurely for your use. You must adde either young onyions or Cibolds, with your Sweet Herbs.

'*Ragoo*': a ragôut is simply a stew, usually of meat. Sometimes it is thickened with flour, sometimes there is no thickening agent. In

Scots cookery flour was always used. This 'ragoo' from Elizabeth Cleland makes a good second vegetable, or light luncheon dish.

A Ragoo of Mushrooms

1 lb (450g) wild mushrooms
salt and pepper
a blade or pinch of mace
½ oz (10g) butter
½ tablespoon flour
2 tablespoons white wine
½ tablespoon vinegar or lemon juice

Wash and dry the mushrooms, put them in a heavy saucepan with the salt, pepper, and mace. Add three tablespoons water and put the pan, covered, on a low fire. Shake it occasionally. Cook for about half an hour. Work the flour into the butter, then add this to the mushrooms and stir over a low heat for several minutes to eliminate the taste of raw flour. Then add the wine and vinegar, and serve hot.

Florys: 'flory' is derived from the word 'florentine'. Once again we have a word which appears for the first time in the 18th century, in Lady Castlehill's receipt book. Italian influence on French cookery was then at its zenith, almost at the level of a craze, but whereas the French invariably use 'florentine' to denote the presence of spinach in a dish, Scots usage signifies that one of the ingredients is pastry. In other words, a flory is a pie; and seems to have by-passed France altogether. Lady Castlehill wrote the word in its full form; and her Rice Florendine is delicious.

To make a Rice Florendine

Take halfe a pound of Rice, boile it. Drain away the water. Mince 3 or 4 Pippins; season it with Rosewater, Sugar, Salt, Cinnamon, Nutemeg, Ginger, 8 yolkes of Eggs and, if you please, some Cream. Mingle all togither, bake it in Puff Paste in a Dish.

A point worth noting in this recipe is that Lady Castlehill uses the English word cinnamon, rather than the French *canelle*, which was quite common in Scotland, and was indeed used by Lady Grisell Baillie.

Finally, a dessert which is still popular in both France and Britain. Frenchmen would never recognize its present English name, Poor Knights of Windsor; had a Frenchman visited Lady Castlehill in the early years of the 18th century, however, he would instantly have been able to identify the Scots name, Pampurdy, as *Pain Perdu*. In France it is usually thought of as an economical dish which uses stale bread and the last egg in the larder, rather in the manner that pancakes finished off the eggs, cream and butter in the house before Lent. Lady Castlehill's recipe is a rather luxurious version, and the quantities would feed about twenty people. I have left it in its original state, for it is one of those recipes whose principle is more important than proportions.

Pampurdy

Take the yolks of 12 eggs 6 Whites a little Nutmeg a little Rosewater; halfe a Pint of Cream, and a little Marrow shred very small; mingle all these well togither, then cut a Manchet or two in toste, i.e., thin slices. Bake them but not too brown, and lay them in Sack then take them out and dype them in the Eggs and Marrow; then frye them in sweet Butter, and Scrape on Sugar, and serve them on a pay [pie?] Plate.

— 8 —

THE BACKWARD GLANCE

As persistently as emigrants anywhere, Scots tried to take food and its habits with them when they left home. It is remarkable how far they succeeded in maintaining culinary continuity, thousands of miles from their own country. A serious analysis of the subject would provide material for an entire book. Here, we can only look at a very few examples and try to determine the varying degrees to which settlers abroad managed both to recall old traditions and to establish a basis for new ones.

There can be few more vivid descriptions of a small Scots community in exile than in the lively little book from which the quotation at the head of this chapter is taken. The setting is London, but a London in which many Scots felt as alien as if they had been in Madrid or New York. The story, of a young man visiting the Metropolis to learn from the great painters of the period (the 1840s), is partly autobiographical and partly founded on the experiences of the author's younger brother, James Burnet. The book's real subject is the artistic theories then current in Britain; the young Scot meets painters such as William Etty and J. M. W. Turner – the latter designated, in a happy phrase, 'the sole patentee of sunshine'. Burnet also has his hero introduced to a thriving colony of Scots artists, among whom (by taking liberties with chronology) he includes Sir David Wilkie, Patrick Nasmyth, and the Reverend John Thomson of Duddingston. It is this portrayal of the Scottish artistic community which interests historians – not least the culinary historian, for it is clear that for many of its members, food played an important role, and one which we have not yet considered.

If the value of food for nostalgic purposes is recognized, it is less often remarked that possibly its more important function for exiles is in proclaiming or reinforcing national identity. In *Progress of a Painter* the familiar dishes are obviously treasured less as reminders of childhood and home as symbols of the difference between Scotland and all other nations. Two extracts may serve to show this. In the first, the young man and his friend are invited to lunch by Wilkie. In the second, they are returning his hospitality and that of other acquaintances, all from Scotland:

you will have nothing but an oatmeal cake and salt butter, and a kebbuck frae the Carse o' Gowrie, but you will get a bottle of Preston Pans beer, which I am sure you both must want after your long walk . . . The cake I can recommend; I have always a barrel of Scots oatmeal sent up by my mother, and the cheese, in the opinion of my friend Allan Cunningham, is superior to Dunlap . . .

Supper being now announced, we adjourned to discuss the merits of some Findhorn speldrins, and some scolloped oysters, in the genuine Meg Dods style. Constable, the bookseller, had sent us a hamper of Johnnie Dowie's ale, from Edinburgh, immortalized by Burns in a poem written in Dowie's tavern, in the lawn market, while the poet was sojourning in Auld Reekie. That, and some small-still Glenlivet, recalled to our Scottish friends 'the post cenam convivialities', as Gibson called them, 'of the land o' cakes.' The evening finished with much hilarity, interspersed with rational conversation.

We shall see that this symbolic significance represents the ultimate rôle of national dishes which have been carried abroad. Before that stage is reached, however, the food usually fulfils several intermediate functions.

Of necessity, the first of these is to provide nourishment on the journey from the old home to the new. In the great emigrations of the 19th century most families travelled steerage on the ships, and took their supplies with them. A would-be emigrant to Canada, contemplating undertaking the journey with three children, was advised by his brother-in-law, who had already made the trip, what he should take for the journey:

1 Boll (about 6 bushels) Oatmeal, ½ cwt fine Ship Biscuit, 2 bushels Potatoes, ½ cwt Beef Ham and Fish, 28 lbs Butter, Cheese and Treacle, some Tea, Sugar, Salt, Pepper. Medicine of some kind (!) some jelly or jam such as cranberries, if they are sour all the better, some cream of tartar or vinegar helps the water a good deal, some bannocks or cakes baked thin and well-fired would keep nicely.

Meals during the crossing, then, were not to be much different from those at home. For breakfast – porridge and tea. For dinner, there might be broth (there were always a few far-sighted individuals who had brought some turnips or kail-stock) or salt meat, and perhaps a pudding made from broken ships' biscuit. Supper usually consisted of oatmeal brose eaten with butter or treacle. Well-organized families, particularly if they came from the north-east, would also have supplied themselves with lumps of dried sowens, to be reconstituted at will with water. If bannocks or oatcakes had not been baked and packed before embarking, they could be made on board. Often two or more families pooled resources and labour during the trip. Through such meals, the break with home was rendered less sudden and less complete; but it is interesting to read, in collections of letters, that because cooking and eating were about the only ways of passing the time, much attention was paid to varying the fare and inventing new dishes.

Once at their destination, the immigrants had, of course, to accommodate to the food of the country. James Thomson, a baker's apprentice who had left Aberdeen in 1844, regularly sent home accounts of Canadian life. At Montreal he went straight into a Scots community, finding work in a bakery run by Scots partners and joining the local Presbyterian church. The cheerfulness of the first letters ('the baking is harder work here than in Aberdeen, but they are better paid and also better fed') soon gave way to a more nostalgic tone the baking is different here from what it is at home ... There are some splendid confectionary stores here but I have seen no gingerbread loaves like what I got from Mr Shanks (his Aberdeen employer) part of which I still have.

Within a few months, even beefsteak for breakfast and supper could not prevent a longing for the products of home:

... the oats that they bring to market are very bad. They would not turn out much meal. They are used only for horses. There is only one mill in Montreal where oatmeal is made. The Scotch people all seem to turn English when they come here and to live on roast beef and white bread ... We will soon have Christmas. It will be a great day here among the Roman Catholics. I do not expect to get any sowens this year but I have a piece of Mr Shanks gingerbread loaf and I guess as a yankee would say I'll finish it on tuesday night. It is as good yet as it was in April. I don't think I'll get any whiskey either as this is a temperate house.

With him, homesickness was long to be a problem, which he often expressed in terms of food. He missed the smoked fish of the East Coast: 'If some Findon Nannie would come here with her creel, I guess she would soon get it empty.' A much later letter, from the California goldfields, described the pleasant winter weather, but he noted that milk cost three times as much as his father paid for whisky in Aboyne. Still, if he could only get some oatmeal he would treat himself to potage and milk despite the high price.

Unluckily for Thomson, though he was often to find himself among compatriots, he always went where they were in a minority. Had he visited Nova Scotia, though he might have experienced a language problem, he would probably have felt reasonably at home with the food. This part of Canada had been colonized from the closing years of the 18th century almost exclusively by Gaelic-speaking Highlanders, whose motive for emigrating was a desperate desire to live unhampered by landlord or government – to possess a piece of land of their very own where they might work and worship in peace. It was for this that families, parishes, even whole clans, turned their backs on all they knew, responding to the glowing picture painted by landlords' agents and shipping companies.

It is touching, today, to read how farmers travelled with their *cas chroms*, the primitive ploughs with which they had ploughed the rigs at home, and housewives with their querns. Little did they understand that before these could be brought into service, the forest must be cleared, a cabin built, and furniture made. Then the fields must be laid out, and drainage and a water-supply established. Only then could life resume according to the accustomed pattern.

In some ways, after the initial back-breaking effort, it was really an easier existence. The land was receptive and fertile – potatoes and grain grew without coaxing; there was abundance of wild fruits, and the forest harboured quantities of game – deer, moose, caribou, and all manner of birds. The sea held even more fish than back home; reading early accounts, one is reminded, indeed, of Sir David Lindsay's description of medieval Scotland:

> The ryche Ryueris, plesand and proffitabyll;
> The lustie loochis, with fysche of sindry kyndis;
> Hountyng, halkyng, for nobyllis convenabyll;
> Forrestis full of Da (doe), Ra (roe), Hartis and Hyndis;
> The fresche fontanis, quhose holesum cristel strandis
> refreschis so the fair fluriste grene medis;
> So laik we no thyng that to nature nedis.

Because of this resemblance, and because Nova Scotian settlers were almost all of them Highlanders, it was possible to maintain very similar patterns of life to those which they already knew. In food, as in everything else, they remained close to their roots until well into our own times. It has been claimed that there was a marked change in their diet, since they had lived in the Old World exclusively on fish and potatoes. While this is true of those who emigrated during and after the Clearances, it was not uniformly the case. Highlanders traditionally had always eaten more meat than Lowlanders owing to the plentiful supply of game. They had kept cattle and sheep for milk, made butter and cheese, and cultivated bere and oats. They had fished the rivers, the lochs, and the sea; so that the colonists were really reverting to the diet of their ancestors.

The difference was mainly in the relative ease with which – barring periods of drought or disease when deprivation could be fully as bad as anything in Scotland – a man could feed his family.

There was therefore much which continued old traditions. Oatmeal and barley were still the staple cereals. Great importance was attached to the production of milk, cream, cheese and butter. Traditional methods of salting down beef, pork, herring and fish, were used as late as the 1950s. And a correspondent who, as a young woman, spent three years in Cape Breton, remembers how people there brewed birch beer, tapping the sap of the trees in spring and fermenting it with the help of sugar or molasses. (Thomas Pennant, travelling in the Highlands in 1772, had commented on the 'quantities of excellent wine extracted from the live tree by tapping'.) Incidentally, the same lady's childhood, spent in British Columbia, also had a Scottish flavour, for she writes 'for our winter evening meal, we often had finnan haddie – I don't know if it came out from Scotland or from Nova Scotia'.

If Nova Scotia was the principal settlement area of the Gael, Lowlanders seem to have preferred other parts of Canada: Prince Edward Island, New Brunswick, Newfoundland, Woodstock (Ontario), Selkirk (Manitoba), and Banff (British Columbia). In these areas, national traditions were also strong; but because the communities were of mixed origin and all sorts of food was readily available, daily diet tended, as Thomson observed, to become more English than Scottish. The old ways and old recipes, therefore, rapidly arrived at their ultimate role – that of asserting identity. A possibly unconscious example is the preference of mainland Canadians for barley rather than rice as a thickener for soup. But the haggis pudding from New Brunswick and the bannock made in Selkirk, Manitoba, are both highly conscious statements about the roots of the makers; so too are the 'good, solid, triangular oatcakes' (the words of my correspondent again) sold by two bakeries in Victoria, British Columbia.

It is, in fact, in baking that Scots culinary expertise has been most firmly kept alive, even though 'traditional' recipes have often been altered quite markedly to conform to the taste of the adopted motherland. Black bun, scones, gingerbread and shortbread, represent for Canadians an essential and very powerful assertion that the history of individual families goes back far beyond the early days of colonization. Even non-Canadians are conscious of this: among the most popular souvenirs for American tourists to take home from British Columbia is shortbread, duly packed in tartan tins and exported to Canada from Scotland.

If North America was the focus for the vast majority of early emigrants, a smaller but nonetheless significant number sought their fortunes elsewhere in the Empire – South Africa, Australia, New Zealand. Here, conditions were so different from those at home that many purely national characteristics and customs were rapidly replaced by a new style of life, accommodating to need and circumstances. It is all the more surprising, therefore, to come across an account of the diet in a New Zealand settlement in the 1850s and '60s:

When domestic animals were introduced, a more varied supply of food became possible without drawing on outside markets. Cheese as well as butter was made from the milk. Another article of diet rarely seen elsewhere was made from sour milk. This was a form of curds. The sour skimmed milk was placed near the fire where it was warmed but not boiled. In a short time, curds were formed. The whey was strained off, the curds were seasoned with salt and were mixed with butter. The result was practically an unpressed cheese. It was highly nutritious.

Another favourite milk product was junket. It was made from fresh milk partly curdled with rennet.

Sheep, cattle and pigs were slaughtered from time to time. Part of the meat was distributed fresh among the near neighbours, who reciprocated when they killed an animal. The remainder was preserved by salting or, in the case of pigs, by curing it in the form of hams and bacon.

No part of the animal was wasted if it was suitable for use. Tripe was obtainable from the stomachs of cattle, while some of the intestines were used as the casing of two kinds of sausage called black and white puddings. The former were black because blood constituted part of their contents. Both kinds were boiled and would keep for months. The fourth stomach also sometimes supplied the rennet required for making junket and cheese.

Fat which was not needed for cooking was used to make tallow candles or soap, and hides were converted into excellent leather by the local tanner or by the settlers themselves.

Every family aimed at fattening a steer or cow to be killed at the beginning of winter.

Wild honey, such as formed part of John the Baptist's means of sustenance, was sometimes procurable.

The passage might have been written of almost any community in the Highlands at any time before potatoes were introduced.

What makes it truly remarkable is that, not only was it written of a group living in New Zealand in the mid-19th century, but that these people had not come from Scotland: they were from Nova Scotia, where they had been living for 30 years.

The full and fascinating story of the Scots settlement at Waipu, in North Island, can be read in *The Gael Fares Forth* by N. R. Mackenzie. Very briefly, the original community, made up of several Highland families led by their minister, the Reverend Norman McLeod, had sailed to Nova Scotia in the 1820s. Their expectations were disappointed for they experienced famine and illness, and found the climate harsher than they had expected, being used to the soft wet weather of the west coast of Scotland. McLeod's uncompromising Calvinism also caused problems; his own son was one of many who rebelled against the rigidly enforced rules of the tiny autocracy. By the time 30 years had passed and a new generation had grown up the group seemed to have lost much of its corporate identity. It was then that McLeod received a conciliatory letter from his son, now in Australia. He acted almost at once. Although well into his seventies, he encouraged his followers to build six ships. Then they and their families (consisting, as 30 years previously, of three and even four generations) embarked on an incredible six-month journey. They reached Australia in remarkably good condition, but the authorities diverted them to North Island, New Zealand, where they established a colony at Waipu.

By the early 1860s, the number of Gaels in the area totalled more than 1000. They lived much as they had done 'at home' in Nova Scotia, though the climate was a distinct improvement. Once again, they cleared land and built houses and a church. Once again they planted crops, raised cattle, fished. They did not, however, grow oats. Like other Scots settlers, they accepted maize as a substitute, though some oatmeal was expensively imported.

One is able to deduce from the quotation how the frugal, rather ascetic Highland outlook was preserved in spite of improved circumstances. Satisfied themselves with a meal of mashed potatoes and milk, or vegetables from the garden plot, they despised those who gave much thought to food. Yet they lived well. Their hens, scratching about in the bush, gave a good supply of eggs, and there was no shortage of game. Only five years after their arrival, a journalist in a local paper was surprised both by the hospitality accorded to visitors and by the comfortable circumstances in which he found the farmers.

The lot of the housewives had not, perhaps, undergone a corresponding amelioration. The old three-legged pot still sat amid the coals; the swee, or metal stand to hold a pot simmering at the side of the fire or boiling above the flames, was still in use; and the lidded pot which accommodated glowing embers on its lid as well as underneath (used since medieval days but now rechristened a 'camp oven') was still the only utensil for baking or roasting. The corn was ground by hand, and the manually operated butter-churn was the only kind known in the settlement for many a long year.

Inevitably, nevertheless, life began to change. The children, growing up secure from the fears which had beset so many generations of Highlanders – fear of starvation, of the cold, of disease, of being dispossessed at the whim of a landlord (a proverb warned, 'A winter's night, a woman's mind, and a laird's purpose, often change') – could relax and seek enjoyment of life rather than mere survival. Their children, in turn, were among the first New Zealanders to receive free, secular, and compulsory education, and were able to overcome the insularity of outlook which for so long had characterized the Gaelic-speaking parts of the country.

This new ease and well-being was reflected in a change of food habits. As agriculture developed, a much more varied and better standard of diet became available to rich and poor alike. Lamb and dairy products of high quality called for subtler recipes; native fish and game, and sub-tropical fruits, required an adventurous, imaginative approach. The self-sufficient family had at its disposal a range of food never before available to any Scot.

This must in part explain the existence of few overtly Scottish recipes (except, as always, for baking) in New Zealand cookery books. There is also the fact that a milder climate not only rendered some ingredients unavailable, but also diminished the need for the high-carbohydrate diet so characteristic of much Scots cooking. Furthermore, in communities like that at Waipu where the strongest survival of traditional food might be expected, poverty had for generations excluded all but the most basic types of dishes, and had, as we have seen, led to a general contempt for those who desired a more sophisticated cuisine.

This said, there remains the hidden evidence of the Scottish presence: the loving expertise of the sheep farmer, and the interest in game, especially venison and trout; the baking skills of every New Zealand housewife, and the fondness for spices in cakes and biscuits. Even the national dish, Colonial Goose (there are various, not entirely convincing, explanations for the name of something which in no way resembles goose) turns out to be a close relative of Lady Castlehill's receipt, dated 1712, 'To Boile or Rost a Legg of Mutton'.

Canada and New Zealand are not, of course, the only countries to which traditional Scottish dishes travelled. The examples above have been chosen partly for their dramatic interest, partly because they seem to typify much that happened wherever Scots made their homes. As a final example, both because it too is characteristic and because the last sentence of the quotation seems to express all that is honest and admirable in the Scots philosophy of food, I quote from a letter sent to me by a lady in Queensland, NSW, Australia, in 1984:

Having Grandmothers with strong ties with Scotland, I felt that I should write.

Mum's mother, whose mother was Grace Sutherland, loved cooking and spent considerable time working with food one way or another. When Grandpa killed a pig, Grandma always made Black Pudding and used every scrap, we had brawn (pig's head pressed) sausages. She dressed her own poultry. Grandma used to make what she called Aberdeen sausage. She steamed chuck or shin beef, with bacon scraps until it was mushy, then finely minced it, with tomato sauce, and depending how she felt, she sometimes set it in a tin or billy-can lined with raspings, or tied it up like a plum pudding with the cloth sprinkled with raspings (dry breadcrumbs). It was served cold and my mother who is in her seventies said, 'Oh, we always had that for New Year and special times'.

Her soups were always very thick and she felt personally hurt if anything was left on the plate.

When anyone came they were always offered food and drink, and when calling on anyone it was usual to take them food; jams, pickles, vegetables, and food was always given to people when they were going home – even if they had just had a huge dinner. Going back late last century there was not a lot of variety of food available.

Dad's mother was Annie Cameron, her grandparents migrated about 1838 and were some of the first settlers in the central west of NSW. Even when I was young that family used a lot of game, hares, rabbits, pigeons, kangaroos, wild ducks. They used a lot of meat . . . it always seemed to me that my people went to more trouble to feed their families well, than a lot of other folk around did, *making the best of what could be got.*

— RECIPES —

CANADA

The following recipes – all traditional in flavour – come from the *Laura Secord Canadian Cook Book*, 1966.

Oatmeal Cookies

Preheat oven to 375°F (190°C) gas 5.

Grease a baking sheet lightly
Sift or blend together
   1¼ cups soft wheat flour
   ½ teaspoon baking soda
Stir in
   1¼ cups rolled oats
Cream together
   1¼ cup butter
   ¼ cup lard
   ½ cup tightly packed brown sugar
Blend in
   ¼ cup warm water

Stir dry ingredients into creamed mixture. Chill for 1 hour. Roll dough out very thinly on lightly floured surface and cut with floured 3 in (7½ cm) biscuit cutter. Place on prepared baking sheet and sprinkle the centre of each cookie with a pinch of coloured sugar, if desired. Bake at 375°F (190°C) gas 5 for 5–8 minutes, or until golden. Makes 6 dozen.

Scotch-Canadian Haggis

Grease a 9 × 5 × 3in (23 × 13 × 7½ cm) loaf pan

Cut in cubes and fry out the fat from
2½ cups pork fat or salt pork

Pour off the liquid grease as it accumulates. When the pieces are golden brown and crisp they are called 'cracklings' in Ontario or 'kips' in the Maritimes. Drain well. Cool.

Wash and place in a large pot
1 pork liver, about 3 lb (1½ kg)

Cover with boiling water and boil for about an hour, or until a fork can easily be inserted. Remove liver and allow to cool. Reserve liquid. Put cooled liver and 2 cups of kips through food grinder. Mix together.

Stir in
1½ cups oatmeal
2 teaspoons salt
½ teaspoon pepper

Add sufficient of the cooking liquid to hold mixture together. Press into prepared pan, cover with wax paper and foil. Steam for 1 hour. Cool. To serve, slice ½ in (1.5 cm) thick and panfry until golden brown on both sides. Serve piping hot.

Scotch Graham Scones

Preheat oven to 450°F (230°C) gas 8

Sift or blend together
1 cup all-purpose flour
2 teaspoons baking powder
½ teaspoon salt
Stir in
1 cup graham flour
⅓ cup granulated sugar

With pastry blender or two knives, cut in till crumbly:
    ½ cup shortening
Break into a measuring cup and beat with a fork
    1 egg

Pour off about 1 tablespoon of egg into a saucer. Fill measuring cup to ⅔ mark with water. With a fork, stir this liquid into flour mixture to make a soft, slightly sticky dough. Turn dough out on a lightly floured surface and knead gently 8 to 10 times. Roll out or pat ½ in (1 cm) thick. Cut into wedges. Brush tops with reserved egg. Bake on ungreased baking sheet in 450°F (230°C) gas 8 oven for 12–15 minutes, or until light golden brown. Serve warm, with butter and home-made jam or jelly. Makes 8 to 10 scones.

Abegweit Oatcakes (Prince Edward Island)

Preheat oven to 375°F (190°C) gas 5

Mix together
    2 cups all-purpose flour
    1½ cups rolled oats
    ⅓ cup granulated sugar *or*
        ½ cup lightly packed brown sugar
    1 teaspoon salt
    ½ teaspoon baking soda
With a pastry blender or two knives, cut in
    ¾ cup shortening or lard
With a fork, stir in
    ½ cup water or milk
(Dough should just cling together.)

Divide in three portions. Roll out each very thin on a lightly floured surface. Cut into 2 in (5 cm) squares with a knife or pastry cutter. Place 1 in (2½ cm) apart on ungreased baking sheet. Bake in 375°F (190°C) gas 5 oven for 10–15 minutes.

Bannock (Selkirk, Manitoba)

Preheat oven to 450°F (230°C) gas 8.

Grease lightly a heavy cast-iron frying pan or baking sheet.
Sift or blend together
  2¾ cups all-purpose flour
  2 teaspoons baking powder
  ½ teaspoon salt
With a pastry blender or two knives, cut in finely
  3 tablespoons lard
Stir in gradually
  ⅔ cup water

Stir with a fork to make a soft slightly sticky dough. Turn dough
out on a lightly floured surface and knead gently 8 to 10 times.
Roll out or pat ½ in (1 cm) thick, or flatten dough to fit frypan.
Cook in frypan on hot ashes over open fire (turn bannock to
brown both sides) or on baking sheet in 450°F (230°C) gas 8 oven
for 12–15 minutes, or until light golden brown. Cut and serve
hot, with butter.

NEW ZEALAND

Barley Mutton

The following recipes are by kind permission of David Burton,
from *Two Hundred Years of New Zealand Food and Cookery*
(Wellington 1982).

        8 mutton neck chops
        2 oz (60g) pearl barley
        4 medium onions, roughly chopped
        6 medium carrots, roughly chopped
        1 large piece lemon peel
        salt and pepper
        1 dessertspoon flour

Trim chops of excess fat and place in a saucepan. Pour 4 cups
water over chops. Add barley, onions, carrots, lemon peel and

season with salt and pepper. Cover, bring to the boil and simmer gently for 2 hours until meat is tender. Thicken with flour and remove lemon peel at end of cooking.

Grilled Mustard Herrings

6 large whole herring, filleted
1 egg, beaten
oatmeal
1 tablespoon butter
1 tablespoon flour
1 dessertspoon dry mustard
1½ cups milk
1 dessertspoon vinegar
salt and pepper to taste

Dip herring in egg, then roll thoroughly in oatmeal. Place under grill to cook at low heat. Meanwhile melt butter in a pan and blend in flour and mustard. Add milk slowly, stirring continuously, and bring to the boil. Add vinegar, season to taste and reheat. Pour sauce over grilled herrings just before serving.

Colonial Goose

1 leg mutton
4 oz (115g) fresh breadcrumbs
2 oz (60g) suet
1 large onion, finely diced
1 tablespoon chopped parsley
½ teaspoon sage
½ teaspoon thyme
salt and pepper
1 egg, beaten
milk

Remove the bone by working around it gradually from each end with a thin-bladed knife, taking care not to break the skin.

Mix together breadcrumbs, suet, onion, parsley, sage and

thyme. Season to taste with salt and pepper. Mix in beaten egg and just enough milk to moisten. Stuff the leg cavity and sew up with string. Tie string tightly around the leg end to form a goose's head.

Roast at 350°F (180°C) gas 4 allowing 40 minutes for each 1 lb (450g)

Compare with the receipt from Lady Castlehill,

To boile or rost a legg of Mutton

Take all sorts of sweet herbs, and the yolks of hard Eggs shred small togither: Then take Marrow (if you have none Beef Suet will serve) let it be in pretty bige pices, then Roll it in your shred herbs and Eggs, and stuff your Mutton with it. Rost or Boile it. For your Sawce take the Gravey, a little Tyme or Sweet marjoram with the Juyce of a lemon and a little sugar. If you please you may add a few Currans plumped in warme water.

Pikelets

1 egg
¼ cup sugar
½–¾ cup milk
1 cup flour
1 teaspoon baking powder
pinch salt
1 oz (30g) butter

Beat egg and sugar until thick and add milk. Add sifted flour, baking powder and salt and mix until smooth. The batter should have the consistency of cream. Leave to stand for 30 minutes if possible.

Drop the batter by the tablespoonful on to a hot buttered frypan and brown lightly on both sides, turning when small bubbles appear on the uncooked upper surface. Serve warm with butter and the traditional accompaniments of jam and whipped cream, if desired.

Kumura (sweet potato) Oatcakes

1 lb (450g) sweet potato
5 oz (140g) oatmeal
½ teaspoon salt
milk to mix

Bake or steam sweet potatoes in their jackets, peel and mash. Mix in oatmeal, salt and enough milk to make a stiff dough.

Form into small cakes and cook quickly on both sides in a buttered pan. Butter while hot and serve immediately.

ENVOI

'And my lords and lieges, let us all to dinner, for the cockie-leekie is a-cooling.'

SELECTED BIBLIOGRAPHY
— FURTHER READING —

Ainslie, P. B., *Reminiscences of a Scottish Gentleman* (London 1861)

Baillie, Lady Grisell, *Lady Grisell Baillie's Household Book, 1692–1733* (Scottish History Society, 2nd series, I. 1911)

Boswell, James, *Journal of a Tour in the Hebrides* (London 1786)

Botsford, T. B., *English Society in the 18th Century as Influenced from Overseas* (New York 1924)

Brown, P. H., *Early Travellers in Scotland* (Edinburgh 1891)

Brown, P. H., *Scotland before 1700* (Edinburgh 1873)

Buchan, John, *Walter Scott* (London 1932)

Burnet, John, *Progress of a Painter in the Nineteenth Century* (London 1854)

Burns, Robert, Letter to his father, December 1781 (quoted, McKenna, J. in *Homes and Haunts of Burns*)

Burt, Captain Edward, *Letters from a Gentleman in the North of Scotland To His Friend in London* (London 1754)

Burton, John Hill, *Life and Letters of David Hume*, (2 vols., Edinburgh 1846)

Burton, John Hill, *The Scot Abroad* (Edinburgh and London 1890)

Cameron, David Kerr, *The Ballad and the Plough* (London 1978)

Cameron, David Kerr, *Willie Gavin, Crofter Man* (London 1980)

Cockburn, John, *Letters to his Gardener* (Scottish History Society, 45, Edinburgh 1904)

Cockburn, Lord Henry, *Memorials of his Time* (Edinburgh 1856)

Darling, J. Fraser, *A Natural History of the Highlands and Islands* (London 1947)

Defoe, Daniel, *Tour through the whole Island of Great Britain* (London 1724–26)

Department of Agriculture and Fisheries for Scotland, *Reports 1960–1982*

Dow, James, Scottish Trade in Sweden, 1512–1580 (*Scottish Historical Review*, Vol. XLVIII, April 1969)

Dunlop, Jean, *The British Fisheries Society 1786–1893* (Edinburgh 1978)

Dunn, Charles W., *Highland Settler, a Portrait of the Scottish Gael in Nova Scotia* (Toronto 1953)

Elder, John R., *The Royal Fishery Companies of the 17th Century* (Glasgow 1912)

Etzel, Eric A., Swedo-Scottish Families (*Scottish Historical Review*, Vol. 9, 1912)

Faujas de Saint Fond, B., *A Journey through England and Scotland to the Hebrides in 1784* (London 1799)

Fenton, Alexander, *The Northern Isles, Orkney and Shetland* (Edinburgh 1978)

Fenton, Alexander, Pork in the Rural Districts of Scotland (*Festschrift fur Robert Wildhaber*, 1972)

Fenton, Alexander, *Scottish Country Life* (Edinburgh 1976)

Fenton, Alexander, Sowens in Scotland (*Folk Life, a Journal of Ethnological Studies*, Vol. 12, 1974)

Ferguson, Thomas, *Scottish Social Welfare 1864–1914* (Edinburgh 1958)

Flinn, M. W., ed., *Scottish Population History* (Cambridge 1977)

Forbes, Duncan, *Culloden Papers* no. CCXXXV pp. 190–191

Foulis, H. N., 'Neil Munro', *Para Handy* (Edinburgh and London 1931)

Gentleman, Tobias, *England's Way to win Wealth* (London 1614)

Gilbert, J. M., *Hunting and Hunting Preserves in Medieval Scotland* (Edinburgh 1970)

Goodlad, C. A., *Shetland Fishing Saga* (Lerwick 1971)

Grant, Elizabeth, of Rothiemurchus, *Memoirs of a Highland Lady* (London 1898)

Gray, Malcolm, *The Fishing Industries of Scotland 1790–1914* (OUP for Aberdeen University 1978)

Handley, J. A., *Scottish Farming in the 18th Century* (Edinburgh 1953)

Hart Davis, D., *Monarchs of the Glen; a History of Deerstalking in the Scottish Highlands* (London 1978)

Hogg, James, *Highland Tours* (ed. Wm Laughlan, Hawick 1981)

Huguet, *Dictionnaire de la langue francaise du 16ᵉ siécle*

Johnson, Samuel, *Journey to the Western Isles of Scotland 1775* (ed. Chapman, London 1924)

Justice, James, *The Scots Gardener's Director* (Edinburgh 1754)

Kames, Henry Home (Lord), *The Gentleman Farmer* (Edinburgh 1776)

Knox, John, *A View of the British Empire, more especially Scotland* (London 1784)

Laird and the Farmer, The (anon. pamphlet, 1750)

Lockhart, G. W., *The Scot and his Oats* (Luath Press 1983)

Lockhart, J. G., *Life of Sir Walter Scott* (abridged edn., Edinburgh 1871)

Lythe, S. G. E. and Butt, E. S., *An Economic History of Scotland 1100–1939* (Glasgow and London 1975)

MacDonald, John, *Memoirs of an 18th Century Footman, 1745–1778* (London 1927)

MacDougall, Hay, J., *Gillespie* (London 1914)

MacIntosh of Borlum, Wm., *An Essay on Ways and means of Inclosing, Fallowing, Planting, &c, Scotland; and that in Sixteen Years at Farthest* (Edinburgh 1729)

McKenzie, N. R., *The Gael Fares Forth; the Romantic story of Waipu and her Sister Settlements* (Wellington, NZ 1945)

Marshall, Rosalind, *The Days of Duchess Anne* (New York 1973)

Marshall, Rosalind, *Mary of Guise* (London 1977)

Marwick, Hugh, *Orkney* (London 1951)

Michel, Francisque, *A Critical Inquiry into the Scottish Language with the view of illustrating the Rise and Progress of Civilization in Scotland* (London and Edinburgh 1892)

Miller, Rev. T. D., *Tales of a Highland Parish* (London 1929)

Morton, H. V., *In Search of Scotland* (London 1929)

Muir, Edwin, *Scottish Journey* (London 1935)

Napier, Mark, *Memoirs of the Marquis of Montrose* (2 vols. Maitland Club, 1845–50)

Napier, Mark, ed., *Memorials of Montrose and his Times* (2 vols. Maitland Club, 1859–62)

Neill, Patrick, *Scottish Gardens and Orchards* (Edinburgh 1813)

Ochtertyre, *The Ochtertyre House Book* (Scottish History Society, ed. James Colville, 1907)

Pullar, Philippa, *Consuming Passions* (London 1970)

Ramsay, John, of Ochtertyre, *Scotland and Scotsmen of the 18th Century* (2 vols., Edinburgh 1888)

Reid, John, *The Scots Gard'ner* (Edinburgh 1683)

Rodgers, Murdoch, Italiani in Scozezia: the Story of the Scots Italians (*Odyssey*, 2nd collection, ed. Billy Kay, Edinburgh 1982)

Scrope, W., *Days and Nights of Salmon Fishing in the Tweed* (London 1843)

Scrope, W., *Days of Deerstalking* (London 1838)

Sinclair, Sir John, *An Account of the Systems of Husbandry adopted in the more Improved Districts of Scotland* (Edinburgh 1812)

Sinclair, Sir John, *General Report of the Agricultural State and Political Circumstances of Scotland* (5 vols., Edinburgh 1814)

Sinclair, Sir John, ed., *General View of Agriculture in the Counties of Scotland* (1792–1814)

Smith, Annette, A Scottish Aristocrat's Diet (*Scottish Historical Review* Vol. LXI 2: No. 172 1982)

Smith, W. McCombie, *The Romance of Poaching* (repr. Stirling 1950)

Southey, Robert, *Journal of a Tour in Scotland 1819* (London 1929)

Symon, J. A., *Scottish Farming Past and Present* (Edinburgh and London 1959)

Thomson, Gordon, *The Other Orkney Book* (Edinburgh 1980)

Thomson, James, *For Friends at Home*, a Scottish Emigrant's letters from Canada, ed. R. A. Preston (Montreal 1974)

Thornton, Col. T., *A Sporting Tour through the Northern parts of England and Great Part of the Highlands of Scotland* (London 1804)

Walker, Rev. J., *Economical History of the Hebrides and Highlands of Scotland* (2 vols., London 1812)

Weir, Mollie, *Shoes were for Sunday* (London 1970)

Wordsworth, Dorothy, *A Tour in Scotland in 1803* (Edinburgh 1874)

Wheaton, Barbara Ketcham, *Savouring the Past* (London 1983)

— COOKERY BOOKS —

Brown, Catherine, *Scottish Regional Recipes* (Glasgow 1981)

Burton, David, *Two Hundred Years of New Zealand Food and Cookery* (Wellington 1982)

Clark, *The Cookery Book of Lady Clark of Tillypronie* (London 1909)

Cleland, Elizabeth, *A New and Easy Method of Cookery* (Edinburgh 1759)

Craig, Elizabeth, *Menus for a Year* (London and Glasgow n.d.)

Fraser, Margaret, *A Highland Cookery Book* (London 1930)

Frazer, Mrs, *Art of Cookery* (Edinburgh 1791)

Johnston, Isobel, 'Meg Dods', *The Cook and Housewife's Manual* (Edinburgh 1826)

The Laura Secord Canadian Cook Book (1966)

Lockhart, Martha, Lady Castlehill, *Lady Castlehill's Receipt Book* (Ms in Mitchell Library Glasgow 1712)

McClure, Victor, *Good Appetite my Companion* (London 1955)

M'Lintock, Mrs., *Receipts for Cookery and Pastry-work* (Glasgow 1736)

McNeill, Marian, *A Book of Breakfasts* (London 1932)

McNeill, Marian, *The Scots Kitchen* (London and Glasgow 1929)

Stout, Margaret, *Cookery for Northern Wives* (Lerwick 1925)

— GLOSSARY —

Aigar: grain well dried – often mixed grains
Athole brose: a drink made from oatmeal, honey and whisky
Bannock: a flat cake of oatmeal, barley, or peasemeal, usually
  baked on a girdle
Bere: a primitive but hardy variety of barley
Brander: a gridiron
Braxy: a disease of sheep, hence *braxy mutton*, meat from a sheep
  dead of disease or accident
Bridie: a meat-filled turnover
Brod: board
Brose: a mixture of raw oatmeal, boiling water, and salt
Brunnies: a type of fatless girdle scone
Bucht: a pen for animals
Caller: fresh
Cabbie-claw: salt cod and horseradish, eaten with egg sauce
Cap: a two-handled wooden bowl
Carlin: an old woman
Clapshot: an Orkney dish of mashed potato and turnip
Clead: to clothe
Clootie dumpling: pudding steamed in a cloth, or clootie
Cock-a-Leekie: a soup made from chicken and leeks
Collop: a slice of meat
Crannachan: a dessert of oatmeal, cream and fruit
Crappit heids: stuffed fish heads
Creesh: to grease
Crimp: to gash, curl, or make crisp
Crowdie: 1. Raw oatmeal with sour milk or buttermilk
            2. A type of cottage cheese
            3. Oatmeal soup
Crulla: a deep-fried pastry
Dauner: a stroll
Drappit eggs: poached eggs
Flory: a tart

Fourareen: a four-manned fishing boat (Shetland)
Fricadellan: meat-balls
Gin: if
Grumphie: a pig
Haaf: a deep-sea fishing ground
Haddie: a haddock
Halesome: healthy
Happit: wrapped
Hatted kit: a milk dish
Host: a cough
Hotch-potch: a vegetable soup with lamb
Howtowdie: a chicken dish
Kailyard: vegetable garden
Kain: rent payment in kind
Kedgeree: a dish of rice, smoked haddock, and eggs
Kumara: sweet-potato (New Zealand)
Lang kail: kail cooked with oatmeal
Liver-muggie: cod stomach stuffed with liver, flour and spices
Luggie: a hooped dish
Pampurdy: a dessert (angl. Poor Knights of Windsor)
Parlies: Parliament cakes (Edinburgh)
Partan bree: crab broth
Potted hough: potted shin of beef
Powsoudie: sheep's head broth
Quiddany: preserve made from quinces or other fruit
Rowies: rolls made from a rich dough (Aberdeen)
Rumbledethumps: a mixture of potatoes, cabbage, and leeks
Runrig: medieval form of Scots land tenure
Rutabaga: a variety of turnip
Sconner: disgust
Scrapple: a dish of smoked haddock, bacon and potato
Seil: to strain
Shirra: sheriff
Sixareen: six-manned fishing boat (Shetland)
Skail the bike: to disperse the swarm
Skirlie: fried oatmeal and onions
Slott: a dish made from fish roe (Shetland)
Smokies: a type of smoked haddock (Aberdeen)

Speldrins: dried haddock
Sodden: boiled
Sowens: a preparation made from oat husks
Stap: a dish made from haddock (Shetland)
Staw: to surfeit
Stovies: potatoes cooked in fat and very little water
Tatties: potatoes
Theek: to thatch; hence, to make snug

— ACKNOWLEDGEMENTS —

The author wishes to thank the following authors and publishers for permission to quote from the works which follow their names:

George Mackay Brown and the Gordon Wright Publishing Co. Ltd (*Under Brinkie's Brae*)

Theodora Fitzgibbon and Pan Books Ltd (*A Taste of Scotland in Food and Pictures*)

Hamish Whyte and the Richard Drew Publishing Co. Ltd (*Lady Castlehill's Receipt Book*)

Catherine Brown and the Richard Drew Publishing Co. Ltd (*Scottish Regional Recipes*)

Dione Pattullo and Johnston & Bacon Books Ltd (*Scottish Cookery in Colour*)

Whitcoulls Publishers, New Zealand (*The Gael Fares Forth*)

G. W. Lockhart and Luath Press Ltd (*The Scot and his Oats*)

Molly Weir and Hutcheson Press Ltd (*Shoes were for Sunday*)

The Editor of the *Scotsman* for the reports of fishing disasters quoted in Chapter Two

Hamlyn Publishing, for the extract from *Larousse Gastronomique*

Alan Davidson and Penguin Books Ltd (*North Atlantic Seafood*)

Laura Secord Inc for the Canadian recipes in Chapter Eight

David Burton and Reed Methuen Ltd New Zealand (*Two Hundred Years of New Zealand Food and Cookery*)

Mrs Valda Grieve (*Lucky Poet*)

Barbara Ketcham Wheaton (*Savouring the Past*)

Blackies Ltd for quotations from Marian McNeill's *The Scots Kitchen*

The author also wishes to state that every effort has been made to contact the following, or their heirs, for permission to quote from work which may still be in copyright:

Victor McClure (*Good Appetite My Companion*)
Sophie Tanner (recipe for Gigot qui Pleure, in *Sunday Times Best British Meat Dishes*, 1976)
R. A. Preston, Montreal (*For Friends at Home*)

INDEX

Words or numbers italicised indicate a recipe or the name of a book.

Books of Scottish interest – in paperback from Grafton Books

Antonia Fraser
Mary Queen of Scots (illustrated)   £3.95 ☐

Margaret Forster
The Rash Adventurer (illustrated)   £3.50 ☐

Eric Linklater
The Prince in the Heather (illustrated)   £4.95 ☐

Moray McLaren
Bonnie Prince Charlie (illustrated)   £2.50 ☐

David Daiches
Edinburgh (illustrated)   £1.95 ☐
Glasgow (illustrated)   £3.95 ☐

Janice Anderson and Edmund Swinglehurst
Scottish Walks and Legends: The Lowlands and
   East Scotland (illustrated)   £1.50 ☐
Scottish Walks and Legends: Western Scotland and
   the Highlands (illustrated)   £1.50 ☐

W Gordon Smith
This is My Country   £1.95 ☐

Tom Weir
Weir's Way (illustrated)   £2.95 ☐

F Marian McNeil
The Scots Kitchen (illustrated)   £2.50 ☐
The Scots Cellar   £1.95 ☐

James Campbell (Editor)
The Grafton Book of Scottish Short Stories   £2.95 ☐

Alasdair Gray
Lanark   £3.50 ☐

J J Bell
Wee MacGreegor   £2.50 ☐

George Mackay Brown
Hawkfall   £1.75 ☐
Andrina and other Stories   £1.95 ☐

<u>To order direct from the publisher just tick the titles you want
and fill in the order form.</u>   **HB981**

All these books are available at your local bookshop or newsagent, or can be ordered direct from the publisher.

To order direct from the publishers just tick the titles you want and fill in the form below.

Name _____

Address _____

_____

Send to:
Grafton Cash Sales
PO Box 11, Falmouth, Cornwall TR10 9EN.

Please enclose remittance to the value of the cover price plus:

UK 60p for the first book, 25p for the second book plus 15p per copy for each additional book ordered to a maximum charge of £1.90.

BFPO 60p for the first book, 25p for the second book plus 15p per copy for the next 7 books, thereafter 9p per book.

Overseas including Eire £1.25 for the first book, 75p for second book and 28p for each additional book.

Grafton Books reserve the right to show new retail prices on covers, which may differ from those previously advertised in the text or elsewhere.